THE EDUCATION OF THE
SECONDARY SCHOOL TEACHER

THEODORE ANDERSSON

REGINALD D. ARCHAMBAULT

GEORGE W. GOETHALS

JURGEN HERBST

GERALDINE MURPHY

W. WARWICK SAWYER

ERNEST STABLER

FLETCHER G. WATSON

THE EDUCATION OF THE

Secondary School Teacher

Edited by **ERNEST STABLER**

WESLEYAN UNIVERSITY PRESS

MIDDLETOWN, CONNECTICUT

Contents

PROFESSIONAL EDUCATION AT HOME AND ABROAD

ERNEST STABLER:

The Current Scene in Teacher Education[1]

SOME years ago Sir John Adams remarked that the function of education essentially is "to teach John X." This cryptic comment raises all manner of questions, one of which is the theme of this book: how to teach John's teacher? Whether above all else he should know his subject, whether he needs to know a good deal about John, and whether he can be taught to teach X to John are all matters of some controversy both in this country and abroad. Behind the debate it is possible to identify two sharply different traditions, two sets of assumptions, that have to do not only with the training of teachers but with the purpose and function of secondary education.

The first of these, which may be labeled the academic, came from Europe and permeated the Latin grammar school of colonial days and the public high school of the nineteenth century. In modified form it is held today and continues to flourish in Europe. The chief function of the secondary school teacher was to train his pupils' minds by seeing to it that they learned a given body of knowledge. Only those students who could develop the necessary skills to master the subject matter were permitted to continue in

1. The early paragraphs of this chapter appeared in an article by the present writer, "The Master of Arts in Teaching Idea," *Educational Record*, XLI, No. 3 (July, 1960), and are reprinted with permission.

secondary education. The curriculum consisted mainly of mathematics, history, and the modern and ancient languages because, in addition to providing the best vehicles for transmitting the cultural heritage, they served as the disciplinary studies whose value lay in strengthening the learner's memory, training his reason, cultivating his powers of concentration, and disciplining his will.

These convictions about the purpose of secondary education determined a teacher's qualifications. Above all, he needed a thorough knowledge of his subject. Teaching itself was not regarded as a particularly complicated art, and the bright young college graduate could pick up ideas from experienced colleagues as he learned on the job. In time, the young teacher found ways of making his pupils behave and of imposing on them high standards of performance. Clearly, the academic tradition demanded no extended period of professional training.

The second tradition [2] had its beginnings in the last two decades of the nineteenth century when the study of pedagogy took root in American universities. By the turn of the century a campaign, sponsored mainly by professors of education, to include professional training as a necessary part of a secondary teacher's education was gaining support. These new notions about the education of teachers were part of a larger movement of educational reform. John Dewey had opened his attack on rigidity and formalism in education and was stressing the concepts of interest and activity. Edward Lee Thorndike, one of the pioneers in educational psychology, was undermining the basic assumptions of the old education by demonstrating that adolescents did not have "faculties" that could be exercised and trained through the disciplinary studies.

As the new education was winning disciples, high school enrollments were growing both in number and diversity, and secondary school men came to regard citizenship and health, social competence and vocational training as valid goals. Both an expanded curriculum and a wide range of pupil ability made the teacher's task more complicated and it was argued that he needed far more than academic preparation and on-the-job training. Professional educators and school superintendents, both loyal to the new philoso-

2. For a more extended discussion, see Chapter III.

phy, succeeded in translating their convictions into state certification laws and in introducing courses in educational psychology, philosophy, and methodology into the collegiate curriculum. This represents the professional tradition in teacher training and is based on a set of beliefs about education, learning, and teaching quite different from those which underlie the academic tradition.

The present curriculum for teachers in most American colleges represents an uneasy compromise between the two traditions. It is now generally agreed that today's teacher needs a broad and liberal education as well as a deep understanding and a firm grasp of the tools of scholarship in at least one of the academic disciplines. There is also a fair measure of agreement that he needs professional training if he is going to deal adequately with the complexities of his task. But as to the nature and extent of that training there is something less than unanimity.

Great diversity resides in the nature of the eleven hundred institutions which educate teachers, to say nothing of their curricula and the quality of their instruction. In 1958 the proportions of high school teachers graduated from five kinds of colleges and universities were as follows:

Teachers Colleges	Private General Colleges	Private Universities	Public Universities	Public General Colleges
17.6%	22.3%	10.3%	27.0%	22.8%

But in spite of the diversity, it is possible to identify the outline of a typical undergraduate program from an analysis [3] of 294 institutions of various types. The four-year curriculum includes both liberal and professional education in the ratio of four to one. Students concentrate on the subjects they will later teach: an English major, for example, takes ten different courses in his field, each a semester in length; his professional training involves the equivalent of eight semester courses, and includes history and philosophy of education, educational psychology, curriculum and methods, and an extended period of half-day student teaching in high school classrooms.

3. *Working Papers for the Kansas Conference* (Washington: The National Commission on Teacher Education and Professional Standards, 1959).

Any attempt to generalize further on the nature and quality of teacher education in this country would be foolhardy. Thus the following sections of this chapter deal rather specifically with an undergraduate program in a particular state college and a cluster of graduate programs. For purposes of comparison, teacher training in England and France is discussed in a following chapter.

State College, U.S.A.

State College is typical, both in its historical development and present status, of many publicly supported teachers colleges. When it opened in 1850 it was the first normal school in the state and it held that name for over three quarters of a century. In the 1930's the state legislature gave it power to confer degrees and changed its name to Teachers College. A quarter of a century later it assumed its present name and was authorized to offer a four-year liberal arts curriculum. The education of elementary and secondary teachers continues, however, to be its primary function. In 1960–1961 enrollment of full-time undergraduates stood just short of two thousand, half of whom were planning to teach in secondary schools.

Admission standards have gone up as the number of applications has doubled; in 1961 the college accepted only half of the candidates who applied. College Entrance Examination Board tests are now required, but this is a recent development and in comparison with private colleges in the state admission is far less competitive. Students come from middle-income homes (fewer than 5 per cent are from other states) and the majority drive to college each day. They pay tuition fees of $100 a year, a figure that is less than one tenth of the tuition costs at leading private colleges in the state. In spite of this relatively low cost nearly half the students have regular outside employment and a visitor meets many students who work twenty-five or more hours a week and yet continue to carry a full academic program. Mortality is relatively high, particularly in the first two years, and only about half the students who enroll stay to graduate. It would appear that by no means all students enter with a clear-cut commitment to teaching, and the number of undecided students will probably increase in future years as the state college concept takes hold. Presently, however, nine in ten of those who graduate become teachers.

The student who intends to become a secondary school teacher is faced with a crowded curriculum. The college feels that it must educate him liberally and professionally, allow him to major in one discipline and minor in another—all in four years. The first two years are devoted mainly to general education which, in effect, becomes a sampling of several disciplines. Thus he is required to study art and music, psychology, English literature and composition, mathematics and science, and history. In the middle of his sophomore year he applies for admission to the Teacher Education Program and acceptance is no mere formality. He must have achieved a credit-point average of C or better and be able to win the confidence of the department in which he intends to major. It is only through this screening process that a student can enter the junior year; in the judgment of the faculty upperclassmen are both capable and well motivated.

The prospective English teacher, for example, now settles into his major field but must carry a minor as well. And it is in the junior and senior years that he gains his professional training. He is obliged to complete a minimum of forty-one semester hours of English on these lines:

	Semester hours
Freshman Course in Language and Literature	6
Freshman Speech	2
Modern American Grammar	3
Developmental Reading in the Secondary School	2
Teaching English in Secondary Schools	2
Teaching Speech in Secondary Schools	2
Five required courses in Literature	15
Three elective courses in Literature or Language	9

The English Department also strongly recommends a course in English history and two years of study in a foreign language. If the student should decide on a minor in history he will complete twenty-two semester hours of study in that field. In his senior year he will teach history as a part of his practice teaching assignment, enroll in a course in the teaching of the social studies, and be certifiable to teach history on graduation.

The professional education components of the program include several courses (fifteen semester hours) in the Department of Education and Psychology and a sustained period of practice teaching. Most of the education and psychology courses fall into the junior year, and the first semester of the senior year is known as the professional semester. For the first and last three weeks of this semester students take intensive methods courses in their major and minor subjects, while in the middle of the term they leave the campus for full-time teaching practice in public high schools. At first they observe experienced teachers but gradually assume responsibility for teaching four classes each day, and otherwise participate in the life of the school. Faculty members follow their students into the schools, observe them in action several times, and give them advice and criticism. Many of these faculty supervisors were at one time secondary teachers themselves.

The student-faculty ratio at State College is about fifteen to one, and the normal teaching load is fifteen hours per week. Half the members of the faculty have doctorate degrees and the administration will try hard to maintain this proportion in spite of increasingly heavy competition from other colleges. Personal qualities, teaching competence, and graduate school performance are the chief criteria used in making new appointments. Previous public school teaching experience is not considered necessary. Salaries are well above the national average for teachers colleges; the present average salary for full professors is $10,325.

State College, like most of its sister institutions, educates both elementary and secondary teachers but it is only the preparation of the latter group that is now under discussion. Both the strength and the weakness of the college in this enterprise need examining because in many respects the nature of teacher education in the United States is State College writ large. The facilities of the college are for the most part adequate and since 1955 six new buildings have risen on the campus. One of these is a library but its 72,000 volumes are scarcely sufficient and the present budget allows less than ten dollars per student to be spent each year for books. The faculty is carefully selected, and with few exceptions, thoroughly competent as teachers, but a far too heavy teaching load gives them little opportunity for research. Faculty members in each academic department take responsibility for teaching the methods courses and supervising student teaching, a policy that is eminently desirable. The screening of students before they are allowed to enter the junior year is thoroughly sound, and the stated aim of the college is to select for the professional program "only those students who plan to teach and have demonstrated scholarly and personal qualities essential for a teacher." One might wish, however, for a higher scholastic standard than a credit-point average of C.

The selection of freshmen puts the college in something of a dilemma. A state institution, so one argument goes, should not be rigidly selective; the close articulation of high school and college is deep within the American tradition and a high school graduate should find the door of a state college or university at least half-way open. Furthermore, during a period of shortage the college feels an obligation to increase the supply of teachers for the public schools. But on the other hand, an influential sector of the public is demanding a higher quality of secondary education through better-trained and more scholarly teachers and, by implication, a more rigorous initial selection of students in teachers colleges. As we have seen, State College has adopted a more stringent admission policy in recent years because of the marked increase in the number of applicants. Nevertheless, in comparative terms, the college is not a highly selective institution nor, apparently, does it intend to be. It prefers to continue the process of selection while students are on course and to raise a set of hurdles at the doorway of the junior year. This policy of a second selection after a trial run of two college years has merit, but it involves a great waste of time, money, and energy. And it forces the question of the rationale of a relatively open-door policy for state colleges. If an institution knows that under present admission policy it will graduate only half the students who enroll as freshmen it should, in the interests of public economy and student welfare, re-examine its selection apparatus. And to argue that a college whose function is the education of teachers should have relaxed admission standards, simply because it is a state institution, is to pervert the meaning of democracy. A democracy cannot thrive if its public school teachers have only mediocre intellectual stature.

The faculty of State College agree that their students are attempting to do too much in too little time. General education in several disciplines, concentration in a major and minor teaching subject, and professional training cannot all be accomplished satisfactorily in four undergraduate years. A prescribed program of general education in art, music, science, mathematics, social science, health, and physical education is an open invitation to superficiality. Less prescription, more student choice, and greater depth would make the prospective teacher less of a dilettante. The study of a major and minor subject can be defended, particularly if the two fields are so related that the exploration of one illumines the other. If, however, a minor must be selected simply because a school superintendent may later insist on a two-subject teaching assignment, the educational rationale for concentrated work in two subjects disappears. Moreover, when a teacher enters the classroom the distinction between a major and minor has no further relevance. Whatever he is teaching at any given moment *is* his "major," and the practice of preparing him well to teach one subject and barely adequately to teach another is indefensible.

Professional education at State College accounts for 20 per cent of a student's total number of credit hours. An introductory course in psychology is followed by two others: Adolescent Psychology and Learning Theory. Courses in education include Principles of Secondary Education, Evaluation in the Secondary School, and Philosophy of Education. (The courses in teaching method are included in the student's major and minor departmental requirements.) There is ample evidence that the professional courses overlap and need to be vigorously pruned. The "Principles" and the philosophy course could be merged, and "Evaluation" might appropriately find its way into a course in educational psychology. Educational theory is largely derived from other disciplines, and courses in education should be taught by faculty members who are trained in one of the parent disciplines. There is, however, no faculty member at State College with a doctorate in either philosophy or psychology.

Under reform and simplification of the kind suggested it is still doubtful whether the collegiate education of secondary teachers should be attempted in four years. In this country we cannot claim, as European countries may, that a secondary school graduate has largely completed his general education. Thus we must address ourselves to the breadth and depth problem, and give professional training as well. It can, of course, be argued that four years are sufficient to get a student started in teaching, and a fifth year of training through part-time and summer school courses is preferable after he begins to teach. This is a persuasive position but it fails to recognize the importance of initial preparation and its relationship to a teacher's later growth. Public high school teaching is a difficult and demanding task and the quality of a teacher's performance in his early years often determines whether or not he will stay in the profession. If he has deeply grounded himself in the humane studies, acquired a particularly strong grasp of his subject matter, and known something of the excitement and rigors of scholarship he will probably be successful in awakening the intellectual life of his pupils. If, furthermore, he has plunged deeply into philosophic questions which relate to education and mastered relevant psychological theory he will better understand his role as a teacher and his relationship with adolescents. And if he has had continuous teaching practice under competent supervision he will enter his first position with some measure of confidence. It is of course true that he will learn a very great deal about his subject and about adolescents after he enters the classroom, but the nature of that growth may in large part be determined by the quality of his initial preparation. Sound, thorough, and stimulating early training can open the way for continued growth and a teacher who has been well nourished to begin with will not likely wither on the vine.

If the collegiate phase of a teacher's education is crucial, four years of preparation may be too few. A five-year program at State College would permit several significant changes: a reduction in the number of courses a student now carries each semester and, hopefully, greater depth in each course; deeper concentration in both the major and minor subjects; the elimination of a "once over lightly" pattern of general education; and the continued use of a full semester for teaching practice and courses in methodology, but not at the expense of other equally important components of a teacher's education.

State College is familiar with the pains of growth and change. It is too early to tell whether its new name will significantly change its present function but there can be no doubt at all about its growth. In the last five years its enrollment has increased by 50 per cent. In the world scene it is a unique institution: a four-year college that offers liberal education and professional training to both elementary and secondary teachers, and grants each group the same degree. Through state support, relatively low admission barriers, and minimal fees it is closely articulated with the public school system. Its students come from the public schools of the state and return to them as teachers. It is, therefore, a college with a deep and pervasive influence and for that reason should be so supported, reformed, and strengthened that it may fulfill its high purpose.

The M.A.T. Programs

Although the four-year undergraduate curriculum still dominates the field, various graduate programs are emerging, among which is the Master of Arts in Teaching. The M.A.T. is a new degree in the academic hierarchy and different in its demands from the older master's degrees. It does not require the specialization in one subject of the M.A., nor the heavy emphasis on professional education of the M. Ed. For students of liberal arts colleges and universities who intend to become teachers but prefer not to get involved in professional education during their undergraduate years, and for those who make a late decision toward teaching, the M.A.T. is a welcome development. The programs have successfully tapped a new source of teacher supply—the liberal arts colleges in the East which offer little, if any, professional training. The idea was born at Harvard in 1936 with the active support of President Conant, who saw the need for a new kind of training for secondary teachers that would appeal to both academic scholars and professional educators and attract able students. Very little was heard of it, however, for nearly fifteen years, but in 1951–1952 fifty students were enrolled, and the program had the active support of the Fund for the Advancement of Education. Yale opened its program the same year, Wesleyan followed a year later, and there are now thirty such programs, and at least as many others that award different degrees but are quite similar.

Behind the M.A.T. program lies the assumption that the academic subjects should be taught to all high school pupils and the person who can most effectively do that job is the scholar-teacher. Hence, an undergraduate education in the arts and sciences should be supplemented by graduate work in the subject a student intends to teach. But a scholarly penetration of his subject is not enough. The nature of the adolescent and the process of learning, the meaning of education and the role of the school, are necessary and valuable areas of study for the prospective teacher, and educational psychology and philosophy of education, *taught appropriately for graduate students,* should find their way into the program. Professional knowledge must, in turn, be supplemented by teaching practice under competent supervision and the more "real" that practice is, the more aptly will the novice sharpen his skills. And finally, each student should be challenged to synthesize and integrate the several components of his program. He should, in short, know his subject, know to what end he is teaching it, and know how to teach it effectively to adolescents.

These are ambitious objectives for one graduate year of study and teaching and not every program measures up to its stated aims. The balance between professional training and graduate study is difficult to maintain, particularly if students are involved, as many are, in a full semester of teaching. Unless the traditional estrangement between liberal arts professors and the professors of education is reconciled and the program has support from all corners of the campus it will probably languish and die. The small college with no graduate school is frequently unable to offer a sufficient number of graduate courses, and the highly specialized graduate seminars of the large university are often more appropriate for the Ph.D. than the M.A.T. candidate. And it is not uncommon for a student to be burdened with too heavy a course load, to have all his doubts about education courses confirmed, or to suffer from inadequate or incompetent supervision.

The Harvard M.A.T. has the largest enrollment, 230 students in 1961–1962, a third of whom are involved in the Internship Plan. Interns enjoy their first taste of teaching in a summer high school organized jointly by Harvard and ten school systems of suburban Boston. Classes are scheduled only in the morning and interns teach under the critical guidance of experienced secondary teachers and Harvard School of Education faculty. Courses in curriculum and methods and a series of lectures in principles of teaching follow in the afternoon. In the following school year two interns are employed as a pair by a co-operating school system and each is paid a salary of $1900. One intern teaches the first half year while his partner studies at Harvard. At mid-year they exchange places. During his study term an intern takes two or three "middle-group" courses (open to both undergraduate and graduate students) in his major field and one or two in education. In June, one calendar year after the program began, both interns are awarded the M.A.T. degree and have decided which of several teaching offers to accept.

The internship scheme, pioneered by Harvard and now gaining acceptance on many a campus, has several strong features. Salaried teaching allows the intern to pay a share of the costs of his graduate program. The intern enters into a contractual arrangement with the school system, becomes a member of its staff, and is guided by its experienced teachers. Thus the university and the schools have formed a genuine partnership in the education of teachers. In contrast with the conventional student teacher, the intern is regarded by his pupils as the "real" teacher and, although he is teaching four-fifths time and is supervised, he has both the freedom and the responsibility of a full-time teacher. He is rather rigorously tested under realistic classroom conditions and at the end of the semester both he and his supervisors can make an informed judgment of his potential as a teacher. The rigors of the plan have appealed to able students, and Harvard has managed to attract candidates with academic records comparable to students entering other graduate and professional schools.

Strong in many respects as the program may be it is not without its flaws. A summer session and one semester altogether devoted to professional training leave only limited time for graduate study. The majority of interns enroll for three semester courses (two are considered the minimum) in the Faculty of Arts and Sciences but these scarcely serve to maintain the M.A.T. ideal of a balance between scholarly work and professional training. During the teaching term, when an intern needs time to reflect on his experience and prepare his classes with care, he is required to attend a course in educational psychology and a seminar which deals with his teaching problems. The summer session based in a high school is an admirable setting to achieve what the director of the Harvard program refers to as "a closely-knit and well-integrated alliance" of theory and practice. Four interns work closely with one "master teacher," plan their work co-operatively, and observe and criticize each other. But the limitations of the situation allow for only a modest amount of actual teaching. Few interns teach more than fifteen class periods over the seven-week session and none has the advantage of teaching a unit of work continuously. Thus, in spite of the values of a team enterprise and competent supervision, the summer term gives only a taste of real teaching and is not a fully satisfactory preparation for the demands of the internship.

Successful performance during the internship depends, in some measure certainly, on the quality of supervision each school provides. At the inception of the plan Harvard failed to realize the importance of defining in rather precise terms the conditions under which experienced teachers would serve as supervisors. The brief teaching experience of the summer session left the intern with a good many anxieties and uncertainties as he faced his classes and the need for competent supervision, particularly in the early weeks of the term, quickly became apparent. Harvard and the co-operating schools have now developed a policy of appointing able supervisors, giving them a sufficient amount of released time from their own classes to visit an intern four times a week, and recognizing their services by awarding tuition vouchers and honoraria. School of Education supervisors are also on the scene to offer an intern criticism and advice, but in spite of all these arrangements the director of the internship plan believes that the quality of supervision is not entirely satisfactory and has said that the systematic analysis of classroom teaching is "on a relatively low level."

A second problem arose when parents and school officials expressed legitimate concern over the change of intern teachers midway through the school year. In order to eliminate, or at least minimize, the dangers of transition, Harvard requires each pair of interns to work together closely as a team. Both interns attend the orientation period for new teachers arranged by the school at the beginning of the school year, and both are introduced to their classes in September. Together they work with their supervisor in developing the design and scope of the year's work, and the second-term intern regularly visits his partner's classes. Through these procedures the transition can be effectively made.

The performance of the interns since the plan began in 1955 has been remarkably good. School officials have been impressed with both their competence and their dedication, and each year fewer than 5 per cent have been obliged to withdraw. The process of selection may in good part account for their success. They achieved a B average or better in their undergraduate years and majored in the subject they wish to teach. Through detailed application forms and interviews they were asked to reveal their background and their commitment to teaching. They were also interviewed and screened by superintendents of the co-operating schools before receiving appointments. Another phase of the selection process lies in the close relationship now existing between Harvard and each of thirty eastern liberal arts colleges. These colleges have appointed faculty committees to advise students, evaluate applicants, and make careful recommendations to Harvard's admissions board. In these thirty colleges more and better students are seriously considering secondary teaching as a career, and in the past ten years the number of graduates seeking M.A.T. admission has increased threefold.

The internship plan has taken root in other colleges but in varied forms. Johns Hopkins and Oberlin students enroll for a summer session of professional course work but gain no teaching experience in a summer high school. During the academic year they teach as salaried interns and spend the alternate semester in study. At the University of California (Berkeley) and Stanford the interns teach throughout the school year, return each week for seminars at the university, and attend two summer sessions. As a means of providing adequate time for graduate study, the necessary professional courses, and a teaching internship Chicago and Wesleyan offer two-year programs. Chicago students spend their first year in residence at the university concentrating on graduate study and beginning their teacher training through an interdisciplinary seminar on educational theory. They also visit high schools to observe experienced teachers in action. In the second year they serve as interns on three-fifths time, continue the education seminar, and make "an extended investigation into some aspect of the teaching of their special field." The program ends with an intensive summer institute of five weeks designed "to assist candidates in analyzing their experience to date and to strengthen themselves as needed, with the assistance of University scholars."

At Wesleyan both one- and two-year programs are in operation, each allowing the option of a teaching internship or an apprenticeship in practice teaching. Wesleyan makes a strong case for two graduate years of preparation if a candidate has undertaken no professional training as an undergraduate. In the two-year program a student takes no more than four courses each semester and thus has time to penetrate the content of each in some depth. During the first year he takes one seminar in the philosophy of education, another in curriculum and methods, several courses in his teaching field, and a trial run of practice teaching. One semester of the second year is given over to the teaching internship and an accompanying tutorial on teaching problems, the alternate semester to further major-field courses and educational psychology. Under this pattern students supplement their undergraduate education with at least seven semester-length courses in the subject they will later teach; they have adequate time to examine philosophical and psychological contributions to educational theory, and they gain firsthand experience with a sampling of high school students through continuous teaching in two schools. Chicago and Wesleyan are convinced that a two-year program is desirable if the image of the scholar-teacher is to be taken seriously.

By no means all M.A.T. and fifth-year programs offer the internship plan. Harvard's alternate plan requires an apprenticeship in teaching and does not include a summer session. Yale gives its students a resident year of graduate study followed by practice teaching in a summer high school. The purpose of the summer session is to provide an intensive experience in teaching and observation under close supervision. A team of three interns and an experienced teacher is responsible for teaching two or three classes during the four-period school day. In contrast to the Harvard plan in which summer session teaching is an introduction to the internship, the Yale program ends with the summer term. Yale's purpose is "to provide a pattern of teacher training which will infuse the liberal arts tradition into the American high school," but its program gives little opportunity for the prospective teacher to gain the skills necessary for this ambitious task.

The fact that the programs have flourished in widely different institutions illustrates the administrative flexibility of the M.A.T. idea. At Yale, Brown, and Notre Dame the programs operate under the control of the graduate school, at Johns Hopkins and Smith they are based within the department of education, at Wesleyan under the guidance of a faculty committee, and at Harvard under the sponsorship of an administrative board appointed jointly by the School of Education and the Faculty of Arts and Sciences. Whether the institution is large or small, public or private, it can initiate an M.A.T. program if it has the resources to offer a good graduate program, a desire to work closely with the schools, and a staff that can make education courses intellectually demanding. But a program will succeed only through the co-operation of two groups who have for many years glared suspiciously at each other: professors of education and liberal arts faculty. Both should share about equal portions of the student's time and both should contribute to his liberal and professional education. Indeed, the more blurred the boundaries of these two concepts become the more successful the program will be.

Perhaps the major problem facing all the programs lies in staffing the education courses. The well-trained philosopher, historian, or psychologist is seldom interested in the education of teachers and far too many professors of education are inadequately nurtured in a parent discipline. The teacher of teachers should, preferably, be a former secondary school teacher who makes the transition from the high school to the college classroom via rigorous and scholarly graduate work. But this will be possible only if wider opportunities for graduate study are made available. At present, the able and ambitious high school teachers who aspire to leadership normally look toward careers in school administration and in vacation time pursue graduate work in that field. If, however, generous fellowships sufficient to support teachers and their families allowed them to enroll as full-time students in graduate schools they might well consider careers in teacher education. If, furthermore, their graduate training were provided jointly by graduate schools of arts and sciences and schools of education, and if their first college teaching appointments were made jointly by an academic department and an M.A.T. program, then the quality of teaching in education courses would improve. The term professor of education should disappear and be replaced by professor of education *and* philosophy or history or psychology. Such a teacher, with a firm grasp of his discipline and earlier experience in high school classrooms, would be prepared to teach at a level appropriate to M.A.T. students.

Only high salaries and a secure place in the academic hierarchy will attract teachers of the quality and experience just described. They will certainly not be satisfied with an instructor's rank or salary. For this and several other reasons the M.A.T. program needs a generous budget. Prospective high school teachers, even those on salaried internships, need scholarships or fellowships as they usually come from middle-income homes and their parents are either unable or reluctant to support them in graduate work after the heavy expenses of four undergraduate years. Instructional costs are inevitably high for graduate-level seminars and administrative costs are heavy for recruitment, interviewing, supervision of student teaching, and the placement of graduates. Two major sources of revenue have appeared. School systems are now prepared to pay interns, and the foundations have been generous. Between 1951 and 1957 the Fund for the Advancement of Education granted an average of four million dollars a year to teacher education, a good share of which was channeled to five M.A.T. programs. In 1959 the Fund directed eleven million dollars toward achieving a "major breakthrough" in the education of teachers, and again the M.A.T. and similar programs were on the grant lists. But the stated policy of the Ford Foundation is to support experimental programs, and now that the M.A.T. has proved itself the grants will not be made indefinitely. Unless the colleges and universities are themselves ready to budget generously the future of the programs is cloudy.

In the past decade some three thousand M.A.T. graduates have gone into the nation's classrooms, certainly not enough to have any marked effect on the teacher shortage. But they tend to stay in teaching. Fewer than 25 per cent of Wesleyan graduates in the past eight years have left the classroom and fewer than 10 per cent have turned to careers outside the field of education. A recent survey of Harvard alumni who graduated between 1947 and 1957 reveals that 71 per cent of the men and 57 per cent of the women have stayed in teaching. A high proportion of the married women reported they intended to return to teaching at a later date. In comparison with national figures of teacher "mortality" these percentages are remarkably high. The schools of suburbia, not those of the big city or small town, have attracted the M.A.T. alumnus. It is there he finds higher salaries, better working conditions, and brighter pupils. The pressures from parents to prepare their children for "good" colleges, the difficulty of finding a home in expensive surroundings, and the warped values (to him) of suburban culture frequently depress him, but he likes the intellectual climate and community attitude toward education. A graduate now teaching in suburban Chicago has said, "One thing that impresses me here is that the profession has the prestige and dignity it deserves. The community regards both teachers and education with respect." In making their way to well-financed school systems the M.A.T. graduates are reinforcing an unhappy fact of American life: the communities that most need to strengthen their schools cannot attract the better-trained teachers. To him that hath shall be given. . . .

To sum up, Master of Arts in Teaching and similar programs are filled with promise. If they can set high standards of faculty competence, provide an adequate number of graduate-level courses, and preserve a balance between liberal and professional training, they will enrich and invigorate teacher education in America. Their virtues as seen by Francis Keppel, Dean of the School of Education at Harvard, are these: [4]

First, they provide a sensible way of recruiting our ablest college graduates into teaching and giving them an academic and professional preparation appropriate to their abilities. Second, they bring about closer relations between "educators" and "scholars" by enlisting the resources of school, college, and university in the task of teacher preparation. Third, and most important in the long run—they encourage high standards of scholarly achievement, professional competence, and long-term career commitment in the teaching profession as a whole.

4. *Saturday Review,* XLIV (June 17, 1961), 65.

CHAPTER II

ERNEST STABLER:

Teacher Training in England and France

The English Secondary School Teacher

The training college and the university department of education form the two major strands in the pattern of teacher training in England. The training college had its origin in the nineteenth century when it was believed that elementary teachers for the new state-supported schools needed a brief training of a strictly useful and practical kind in an institution where the Master of Method was an important figure. The present training colleges which educate the great majority of primary and secondary modern school teachers have greatly increased their scope and now offer both academic and professional work in a three-year course. The secondary grammar school teacher, on the other hand, is a university graduate who may or may not have the benefit of a year of professional training. That the Ministry of Education officially approves such training is indicated in its policy of graduate student grants, but a graduate is under no legal compulsion to enroll in a university department of education before entering the classroom. Currently, the number of trained and untrained graduates who are securing posts in the various types of secondary grammar school is, roughly, the same.

Several contrasts immediately strike the American visitor. The graduate who enters a department of education is the product of a long and thorough secondary education and a highly specialized university course. At the age of sixteen in the fifth form of his grammar school he wrote the Ordinary Level General Certificate Examinations in six or eight subjects. He then spent two years in the sixth form preparing for the Advanced Level exams and devoted the bulk of his time to three subjects on either the arts or science "side." In the upper sixth he attained a level of work comparable, in the three subjects studied, to the sophomore year of a good American college. As a grammar school student and a university undergraduate, he was one of a carefully screened group. Grammar schools of all types enroll some 20 per cent of the twelve-year-old population and the universities take only the top cream of the grammar schools. At the university he studied one or two subjects for three years and continued his general education through reading and attending lectures outside his field, and through membership in university clubs, associations, and societies. The English hold rather strongly to the belief that it is possible to learn something without taking a course in it. The able honors undergraduate has both the inclination and the energy to move outside the boundaries of his subject, but many of his less able fellows who have to fight hard to stay in the honors course graduate as victims of a specialization which began at the age of seventeen. When they arrive at the doors of the department of education they are highly competent in their subject, but may have limited breadth. The chemist may have done next to nothing on the arts side since the fifth form, and the historian may not have studied, at least in a formal sense, any science.

The days when an honors degree was almost a guarantee of a place in the one-year training course appear to be over. Competition for admission is keen and students usually apply to several universities. Each department of education calls in its most promising applicants for interview and judges a candidate not only on academic performance, but also on interview impressions and the statements of two references.

The national government has decided that financial need should bar no one from becoming a teacher. Ministry of Education grants are scaled according to assessed parental income and only a small proportion of students, fewer than 10 per cent, pay total tuition and maintenance costs. Some 35 per cent of the students at the Institute of Education at the University of London are on full grants which include tuition, maintenance, and a modest vacation and travel allowance. Grant recipients are not permitted to take on part-time work during term time. In contrast with American practice, student loan funds are almost nonexistent. In accepting a grant a student assumes a moral obligation to enter teaching and, as with so many matters in England that are understood rather than legalized, the grant system works very well.

The course of study leading to the Certificate or, in the case of Oxford and Durham, the Diploma of Education, is entirely professional. That is, it includes lectures and tutorials on educational theory and methodology, and practice teaching. It does not allow a student to continue the study of the subject he will later teach. There is a firm and widely held belief that university graduates are adequately grounded in subject matter and therefore the certificate year of rather less than thirty weeks of term time should be given over to professional training only. The unit course which allows a student to earn a given number of credits is unknown in an English university. In its place is a series of lectures given by one or several staff members and extending over several weeks or months depending on the nature of the subject and its relative importance in the certificate program. Students attend these lectures at their discretion and select their reading from extensive bibliographies. At the end of the year they write examinations in which separate papers are set on principles of education, educational psychology, the English system of education, and teaching method.

Lectures in the main fields of theory, optional courses, and, perhaps of greater importance to the student, the group tutorial, constitute the major aspects of the certificate year. The tutorial group seldom includes more than a dozen students and may number, as at Oxford, as few as three. Students are normally divided into tutorials on the basis of their teaching subject although Bristol is convinced that more is to be gained by mixing than by isolating the disciplines. The group meets once a week or oftener, and each tutor, who holds the post of lecturer in the department, is entirely free to decide the topics for study and discussion. He may relate the work of the tutorial to the lectures in philosophy or psychology, he may deal with methods of teaching, or he may select topics quite apart from those covered in the lecture courses. The tutor also supervises the teaching practice of his group and serves as an advisor and counselor on personal matters. In a large and impersonal setting the tutorial gives the student a friendly and informal base.

There is a tacit understanding among the universities that students in the graduate year should spend sixty days in classroom teaching but there is somewhat less than unanimity on the way those sixty days should be spent. Oxford students scatter to schools throughout England and Scotland for a sustained period of twelve weeks of teaching, and the staff of the department follows its flock into the field. Supervision normally does not constitute more than a one-day visit. London, on the other hand, places its students within the metropolitan area for three distinct blocks of teaching practice. As the English are fond of saying, what you gain on the swings you lose on the roundabouts. Oxford students lose touch with their department but have the advantage of a full term of continuous teaching. London students keep in close touch with their tutors and, by attending classes every Friday, enjoy a continuous exposure to theory. But their three short sessions of teaching give them little in the way of continuity.

In a department of education most staff members assume the combined role of lecturer, tutor, and supervisor. The typical staff includes one professor, perhaps one or two readers, and a group of lecturers. Before his first appointment, which usually is for three years but carries an underlying assumption of permanency, a lecturer frequently will have taught for five years or more in a grammar school. His teaching load is not heavy, nine hours a week or less, but he is busy in other ways. He maintains a close relationship with his tutorial group, he may teach an evening or late afternoon course to in-service teachers, and he frequently serves as an examiner for the Ordinary and Advanced Level examinations. The lecturer is a teacher first and a scholar second; he seldom has either the time or the inclination for sustained research. He does not forget that he was once a schoolman, and he has few of the superior attitudes toward teachers that frequently mark his colleagues in other university departments who have never darkened the door of a masters' common room. The lecturer does, indeed, find ways of keeping his bridges to the schools in good repair and it is not uncommon for him to teach an occasional demonstration lesson.

In his own subject and the methods of teaching it, he is an expert. The rub comes in a small department when he is asked to lecture in educational philosophy, psychology, or sociology with only a limited training in these fields. The department might prefer to have a professional psychologist or philosopher on its staff, but where does it find one who has several years of secondary school experience and is interested in teacher training? The easier solution is to ask one of the lecturers to "get up" a series of lectures as best he can; the result is frequently the curse that falls on small education departments everywhere—superficiality.

For quite different reasons there is a further danger of superficiality. Students in the majority of departments are exposed to at least three, often four, lecture courses on education theory; they attend two courses on teaching method, and one or more optional courses; and they meet regularly with their tutorial group. It is, of course, quite true that these courses are of varying length and intensity but a student usually attends a large number of lecture courses in any one term. In the autumn term at Birmingham, for example, there are six different courses which, the catalogue states, are attended by all students. Methods and optional courses are not included in this list. Why, one is forced to ask, is it necessary to give so much "breadth" in so short a time? The answer appears to lie partly in the increasing amount of professional knowledge it is assumed a teacher should possess, partly in the competing demands of practicality, and lastly in the belief that the graduate year should be something of a humanizing and liberalizing restorative after the specialization of the undergraduate years.

Two developments, evident in both England and America in the past half century, have complicated the issue of the extent and kind of professional knowledge a teacher needs. Studies in educational philosophy, history, psychology, and sociology have expanded enormously and, while they have not yet become disciplines in their own right, they are now important branches of the parent disciplines. Further, the role of the secondary teacher has changed and he is now expected to be more than a subject-matter specialist. He is, for example, expected to know a good deal about child development and the nature of contemporary society. He should, in short, be far more than an instructor, a classroom manager, or an examination coach. Departments of education, are, of course, involved in both these developments. Their staff members have developed and deepened the study of education and, as leaders of educational thought, they have helped to create the new notions of what a teacher ought to be. But the departments are presently faced with a thorny problem. Granted the new concept of a teacher's role and the extent of professional knowledge he should possess, how is it possible to train him adequately in one academic year, sixty days of which are reserved for practice? Different universities have reached different solutions. Birmingham, as we have seen, offers a wide variety of courses; Bristol has established one Foundations Course which meets six times a week and provides lectures on topics drawn from philosophy, psychology, sociology, and history; and Oxford limits the number of its lecture courses and requires of its students a good deal of individual study and essay writing. But the dilemma persists and an observer is left with the impression that the time available is too short to allow a student to gain a firm grasp of the professional knowledge which each department believes is essential.

Theory and practice, instead of feeding and supplementing each other in professional education, all too frequently make rival demands for a student's time. The student himself feels the need to learn the schoolmaster's craft before taking his first appointment and his anxiety convinces him that his graduate year should be practical and down-to-earth. His conviction is often bolstered by the experienced teachers with whom he works during teaching practice who smile at the theorists in the university and tell him that his chief assets will be common sense and a firm hand. Of course the student and his mentors are not alone in voicing the demands of practice. All departments of education recognize that some measure of practicality must permeate teacher training. Over a period of one year the intent appears to be to expose the student to many aspects of professional knowledge and at the same time allow him to serve an apprenticeship in teaching. Theory and practice tend to compete with each other, and the situation is further complicated by the desire to ameliorate the student's earlier specialization.[1]

> For a long time now degree courses have been growing more and more specialist. The separation between Science people and Arts people is wide, not merely in the language and vocabulary they use, but in the things they take for granted. . . . One hardly expects the young philosopher to be understood easily by the young economist (or for that matter anyone else) or the young physicist by the young historian. . . .
> Now one of the jobs of the Training Year is to get men and women fresh from the study of their different specialisms to do some thinking about big questions. The year must be a humanizing one. Its function is partly restorative, bringing them back from being specialists to being everyday human beings.

The prospect of humanizing, professionalizing, and apprenticing the student all in twenty-eight weeks ought to make even professors of education blanch but a visitor can detect no widespread discussion at the moment toward reducing present requirements or lengthening the period of training.

There is, however, at the University College of North Staffordshire at Keele a radically different program. Keele, a residential college for both students and staff founded ten years ago, has broken with English tradition by instituting a four-year undergraduate program. The first, or Foundation, year is based on a broad but carefully designed series of some two hundred lectures in which all departments participate. In the words of the college prospectus the lectures are designed as a single course "to give an understanding of the heritage of Western civilization, of modern society, and of the nature, methods and influence of the experimental sciences." Discussion groups and tutorials supplement the lectures. Following the Foundation Year each student studies two Principal subjects

1. W. R. Niblett, "Teacher Training and the Graduate Today," *Journal of Education*, LXXXVI, No. 1014 (January, 1954), 10.

for three years and two Subsidiary subjects for one year each. The four subjects must include one from the experimental sciences and one from the humanities and social sciences. Narrow specialization is therefore impossible, as is dilettantism. Keele has attempted to find a middle way and to allow for both breadth and depth.

The Keele student who intends to become a teacher begins the study of education in the second year and also carries two Principal and one Subsidiary subject. He continues the study of education in the third and fourth years and is then eligible both for a degree and the Diploma in Education. During these years he takes courses in the English educational system, child development, theory of education, principles of teaching method, and educational psychology and sociology. Teaching practice is rather ingeniously scheduled from the beginning of the school term in September to the beginning of the Keele term in October in each of the three years. Thus students teach for a month each year in three different types of schools: primary, secondary modern, and grammar.

For the student who can make an early decision to prepare for a career in teaching, the Keele program has much to commend it. Liberal and professional education are not sharply separated and a student is able to relate the theory and practice of education to his other studies. There is, furthermore, much to be gained by spreading the study of education and teaching practice over a three-year period rather than concentrating them into one year. Spaced intervals of teaching allow for a highly desirable aspect of training: time to reflect and analyze successes and mistakes, time to recollect the experience in tranquillity and to plan the next campaign with deeper insight. The program also allows a student a trial run before he makes a final career choice; after an introduction to practice and theory he can make a more informed decision about his aptitude for teaching. Moreover, for the intending teacher there are many advantages in an undergraduate course which stresses both breadth and depth.

At the moment the Keele program is unique in England and there are no signs that it will be imitated in the near future. The graduate year of professional training has become a tradition and will probably continue to be the means by which grammar school teachers are trained. A two-year course is not considered either feasible or desirable, but several departments would like to gain more teaching time by shortening the month-long vacations at Christmas and Easter. A few departments are concerned over the number of courses which have found their way into the curriculum but have yet to face the internal turmoil and dissension which a reduction of courses would almost certainly create. There is no apparent dissatisfaction with the provision of sixty days of practical teaching but several teachers' associations have attempted to persuade the universities to place their students continuously in one school for the total period.

But the real issues in educating and training a teacher lie much deeper. What kind of professional knowledge should the beginning teacher possess, how can theory and practice be more effectively integrated, and how can the evils of overspecialization be modified? These are questions which departments of education are wrestling with, but they also, in characteristic English fashion, do not dismiss the importance of tradition and the pressure of practical considerations. We can expect, therefore, that any reform in the training of teachers will be based, not entirely on theoretical grounds, but on a compromise between procedures of the past and the realities of the present.

The French Lycée Teacher

The day is long and the work is hard for the child in a French school. A circular dated July 27, 1882, which discusses elementary education is no less appropriate today: "The primary school's ideal is not to teach a great deal, but to teach it well. Children leave school with a limited knowledge, but what they have been taught they know thoroughly; their learning is restricted, but not superficial. They do not possess half-knowledge." The French child is rather severely "put to school," and, in comparison with English and American children, to speak of his "limited knowledge" is sheer understatement.

At the age of eleven secondary education begins and for the

first two years, the *cycle d'observation,* all children are under observation and guidance. On the basis of performance, aptitude test results, and parental request they may be transferred from one to another of the several types of secondary school training. Some 15 to 20 per cent of French children are selected for an academic secondary education in a *lycée* or *collège.* The others continue their education to the age of fourteen or beyond (the minimum school leaving age has been raised from fourteen to sixteen, effective in 1964) in general secondary or vocational schools. The course of study in a *lycée* extends over seven years (ages eleven to eighteen) and terminates with the *baccalauréat.* The first four years stress general education, and each student takes eight or nine subjects which, typically, include French, Latin, history, geography, mathematics, science, art, and a modern language. The final three years are given over to specialization in three or four subjects, for example, Latin, two sciences and a modern language, and the *baccalauréat* examinations are written over a two-year period. The intensity and thoroughness of this study can hardly be overstated. The course of study and the examination in English, for example, would prove difficult and demanding for American and English students at the end of their secondary schooling. The *baccalauréat* examinations, both written and oral, are the same in each subject for students in all parts of France, and of the 200,000 or more who sit for them each year fewer than 60 per cent pass. The French attitude toward competitive examinations is revealed in this comment: [2]

> Any . . . competitive examination is an act of *intellectual selection.* One does not pass judgment on intentions, not even on the effort made, nor on the experience supposedly acquired after a certain number of hours of work and attendance, but on the actual results which a student is capable of attaining, in terms of an ideal of knowledge and intellectual aptitude. . . .

> This attitude is not based on our individualism, but on a *demand for intellectual universality.* However, the multiplication of technical careers where the part of routine is more important than that of theory and general culture, as well as the increase in population which is not

2. Edouard Morot-Sir, *Education in France* (New York: French Cultural Services, No. 8, December, 1959).

necessarily accompanied by a proportionate increase in intellectual aptitude, pose new problems for the pedagogy of examinations. It is probable that new examination tactics will be perfected, following the current concern with results. But one must hope that the demands of the intellectual ideal will not give way to the concern of immediate utility or the pressure of a multitude in search of easy success.

The *lycée* and *collège,* in the words of a recent Minister of Education, have "the responsibility for training our national elites before they receive the specialized training in accordance with their several aptitudes and the needs of the country." In spite of criticism, old and new, that they are too bookish, put too much stress on memorization, or bear too little relationship to the contemporary world, these schools are the pride of France as they continue to impart *culture générale* and "without preparing them for anything specific, make their students apt for everything." Their importance in the national life may explain the very high qualifications demanded of their teachers.

Two pathways to a teaching appointment are open to the young man or woman who has survived the rigors of the *baccalauréat:* the university or the *école normale supérieure.* If he chooses one of the seventeen universities his first year will be preparatory and probationary, *l'année propédeutique,* a general foundation for later specialization but also a further process of screening. He then spends two or three years specializing in the subject he intends to teach and writes the state examinations for a teaching license, *la licence d'enseignement.* At this point he may begin to teach or go on for advanced degrees. If he decides to teach he will start as an assistant teacher and his duties are, by a detailed set of regulations, carefully defined. Unlike the *professeur,* who is well above him in the teaching hierarchy, he has responsibility for correcting papers, supervising study halls, and assisting with administrative tasks. There are, indeed, several ranks of assistants all of whom have clearly stated functions, and it is this group who make it possible for the *professeur* to devote himself entirely to teaching and escape from extracurricular activities, corridor and cafeteria supervision, record-keeping, and chaperoning.

Rather than join the ranks of the assistants a prospective teacher who has completed his *licence* may proceed directly toward the C.A.P.E.S., *Certificate d'aptitude au professorat de l'enseignement public du second degré,* a competitive certificate which first appeared in 1950. Examinations, both oral and written, are set in the subjects a student intends to teach and 30 per cent of the candidates are, as the French say, admitted each year. A successful candidate then spends one year on a stipend of about $110 per month in professional training in a *Centre Pédagogique Regional,* located in one of the university towns, where he is initiated into teaching. Groups of three probationers, *stagiaires,* are attached to experienced *lycée* teachers for nine-week periods and over the academic year they observe, assist, and teach in three types of schools. In addition, they attend conferences on general educational topics and teaching methods and become familiar with the French system of education and its intricate patterns of legislation. At the end of the year they demonstrate their teaching ability before ministry officials, but at this stage the screening process is not as severe; fewer than 3 per cent fail the practical test. On winning the *C.A.P.E.S.* the young teacher enters a *lycée* or *collège* as a *professeur certifié,* enjoys all the rights, privileges, and status of a civil servant, and assumes a teaching load of eighteen hours a week. He has contracted to teach for a period of five years and his first post will be in a school chosen for him by the Ministry. If he has been on stipend throughout his university education and *C.P.R.* year under a national recruiting scheme for teachers, *Institut de préparation aux enseignements du second degré,* he is obliged to teach for a period of ten years.

At the top of the hierarchy is the *professeur agrégé* or registered specialist teacher. He, too, has secured his degree, which is fully equivalent to an American Ph.D. and far more difficult to win, through continuous study after the *licence,* or by taking a position as an assistant teacher and, in his spare time, preparing for the *agrégation.* The fastest and most desirable route is by way of the *école normale supérieure* which is a part of the network of *grandes écoles,* highly specialized institutions offering rigorous training for the professions. Competition for entry is sufficiently keen that a student spends two years beyond the *baccalauréat* preparing for the entrance examinations. Only one candidate in five is successful. Life in a *grande école* is at once both pleasant and exacting: all students are on scholarship and, in contrast to less fortunate university students, they eat well, live comfortably, and enjoy the social life of college residences. The *École Normale Supérieure de la rue d'Ulm* in Paris has a library of 600,000 volumes, and all the schools have a vigorous and exciting intellectual climate. The first two years of the four-year course prepare students for the *licence,* the third year is given over to writing a thesis for the *diplôme d'études supérieures,* and at the close of the fourth year the students write the *agrégation* in their teaching field. Candidates in history, for example, suffer through four full-day examinations in ancient, medieval, and modern history, a similar test in geography, and in addition, several oral exams. These are, of course, external examinations set by juries of examiners for candidates in all parts of France.

Professional training is minimal in the preparation of the *agrégé.* At some point in his third or fourth year he spends a month or six weeks in a *lycée,* first as an observer, later as a student teacher. He may also attend a series of lectures on educational topics and read a little pedagogy on his own. But the chief function of the *E.N.S.* is to give its students deep, thorough, and specialized training in the academic disciplines. When asked about the rather desultory attention given to professional training in his institution, the Secretary-General of the *E.N.S.* at St. Cloud replied, "We think it is more important for our students to learn *what* they are going to teach. Besides, they will teach bright young people in the upper forms of a *lycée.*"

Perhaps a quarter of the secondary teachers of France are *agrégés* and the proportion is not likely to increase. Fewer than 20 per cent of the several thousand who try the examinations each year are successful and many of the others try again year after year. The students trained in the *E.N.S.* are, of course, more successful than practicing teachers who are reaching for the top rung of the career ladder and are able to study only part time. The *agrégation* is, however, a prize worth struggling for. With it goes the guarantee of a well-paid position, high status, and the possibility of a career later on in university teaching or research. More immediately, there is the likelihood of a post in a Paris *lycée* with a teaching load of fifteen hours a week and the freedom to continue scholarly work.

Teacher training in France must, of course, be seen within the context of the nature and function of French schools, the highly centralized system of education, and, more generally, the characteristics of national culture. Because French education is designed to transmit the cultural heritage and to develop the powers of the mind it is not surprising that French teachers, particularly those at the secondary level, are expected to be highly trained scholars and to serve as priests of the intellect. It is no less surprising that in a country where legend has it a ministry official can tell what is being taught in the schools of his country by glancing at his watch, the teaching cadre should be educated in state institutions and admission to the profession controlled by state examinations. Highly competitive examinations are not peculiar to the teaching profession but are essential for many aspects of public employment and entry into the professional elite. But given this context there are still several features of French education at large and teacher preparation in particular that are not beyond criticism.

The relatively new two-year period of trial and observation with similar courses of study in the different kinds of secondary schools is, in theory, a great advance over the old system which insisted on an almost irrevocable decision at the age of eleven. But, in fact, the children in the "classical sections" of the cycle of observation have only a three-month period of instruction similar to that of other children and immediately thereafter begin the study of Latin. Whether the system will provide methods of identifying the pupils who should be transferred from one stream to another, and sufficient flexibility to allow these pupils to begin receiving instruction in new subjects at the age of twelve or thirteen, it is too early to predict. It is also too soon to tell whether recent reforms will tap the reservoir of talent in the children of the lower socioeconomic classes. In past years fewer than 15 per cent of children in rural districts have attended school beyond the age of fourteen, and a recent study made by the National Institute of Demographic Studies reveals that very few working-class children make their way into higher education. For those who succeed in gaining entry to a *lycée* or *collège* the seven-year course all too frequently places so heavy a stress on academic subjects and preparation for the *baccalauréat* that there is little chance for creative experience in music, art, and games.

(That a process of *bourrage*, cramming, is not necessary for success in the *baccalauréat* has been demonstrated by the pilot *lycée* at Sèvres where arts, crafts, and music are stressed and "active methods" employed. The performance of its students on the *baccalauréat* is well above the national average.)

A highly competitive examination system with its emphasis on a detailed knowledge of a special field has its merits, but as the sole device for teacher selection it is open to question. Scholarly attainment is a crucially important qualification for secondary teaching but success in the classroom also demands qualities of sympathy, understanding, and dedication. Without these a teacher never really communicates with, never "reaches," the adolescent. Although teaching practice is offered in the *C.P.R.* the majority of French teachers are selected on scholarly criteria and do not experience a sustained period of practice during which their pedagogical aptitude, or the lack of it, can be discovered. Furthermore, the French system assumes that professional knowledge, systematically imparted, discussed, and acquired, need form no part of a teacher's preparation. In spite of all the sins that have been committed in the name of education courses the disciplines of philosophy and psychology have, in their present state of development, much of value for the teacher both for his work in the classroom and for his wider role in making educational decisions.

A hierarchical structure in teaching similarly has much to commend it, particularly as it frees highly qualified instructors from less important tasks and allows them to concentrate on the main business of teaching. It attracts gifted young people to the profession and endows them with dignity and recognition. But again, important as scholarship may be, too high a premium may be placed on it. In assessing the merits of a practicing teacher there are several criteria by which to judge him, and surely one of these should be his ability to teach. French teachers are divided into several cadres and there is, certainly, opportunity for advancement on the bases of merit and seniority within a particular rank. But a teacher's journey from one cadre to another is determined almost entirely by the degrees he can win. As a result, the top ranks of the profession may number too many able scholars and too few inspiring teachers.

CHAPTER III

ERNEST STABLER:

The Professional Education Movement

Origins

THE professional tradition in the education of American teachers is well over a hundred years old. It began in the 1830's with the normal schools of Massachusetts and expanded by way of the normal departments in the state universities of the Midwest. In both institutions the intent was to prepare teachers for the common schools and the work offered was well below college or university level. After the Civil War the universities recognized the need to educate teachers for the growing number of high schools, and in 1873 the State University of Iowa abandoned its normal department and created a chair of didactics which the president insisted would be on "the same footing with other professorships in the collegiate department." Courses were offered to seniors and were taught by men trained in philosophy. The catalogue of that year was careful to explain that "Didactics, in the higher sense is a liberal study. It includes the philosophy of mind, the laws of mental development, and all those branches of study and methods of instruction that are employed in general education." This was the beginning of a new movement in American education: the training of secondary school teachers through the study of the history, theory, and practice of education.

Six years later the University of Michigan appointed a professor of the science and arts of teaching who quickly organized a department and within a decade was offering professional education to high school teachers, principals, and superintendents. "Why not teach in the University," he said, "the cardinal doctrines of education, so that the entire public system of the State may be affected through a process of downward diffusion?" By the turn of the century the department offered ten courses, and a graduate of the university who had completed three of these was eligible to teach in any of the schools of the state. Professor W. H. Payne at Michigan was but one of several able and aggressive leaders who pioneered the cause of professional education.

Nicholas Murray Butler, soon after completing his Ph.D. at Columbia, spent a year in Europe where he fell under the influence of Frederick Paulsen, professor of philosophy at Berlin. In his lectures on educational theory Paulsen opened up for Butler a new and unknown field of inquiry: "The notion that the great activity and human interest called education might be subjected to scientific examination and analysis and might be shown to rest upon definite principles was nothing short of a revelation. In America education had always seemed to be—well, just education." On his return to Columbia as assistant in philosophy Butler played an important part during the late 1880's in founding Teachers College. The first charter described the college as a purely professional school whose object would be to give instruction in the history, philosophy, and science of education, psychology, and the science and art of teaching. When the college officially opened its new building, Main Hall, on Morningside Heights in November, 1894, Presidents Eliot of Harvard and Gilman of Johns Hopkins were on the platform, and in his address Gilman referred to the college as a unique institution which "breathed the spirit of the times."

James Earl Russell, one of the early deans, saw Teachers College as a West Point of the teaching profession in which competent leaders could be systematically trained and where theory and methods could be investigated and invented. Russell, too, had been influenced by Germany. During two years abroad he studied at Jena, Berlin, and Leipzig and visited Prussian secondary schools. He was particularly impressed by the requirements imposed on secondary school teachers in Prussia: four years of university, another to prepare for a state examination, and two more of on-the-job training.

By the turn of the century Russell was probably the most influential spokesman for the new philosophy of teacher education. In addressing conventions of teachers and superintendents he pressed for four goals: general culture, special scholarship, professional knowledge, and technical skill. The secondary teacher should be a college graduate and his general cultural background must be "liberal enough to inspire respect for knowledge, broad enough to justify independent knowledge, and accurate enough to beget a love of truth." Russell was unimpressed both with the typical college and the normal graduate of his day. He believed that neither liberal culture nor technical skill could substitute for that "solid substratum of genuine scholarship on which all true secondary education rests. . . . Now as never before do we need to emphasize the possession of special knowledge as a prerequisite to secondary teaching." The teacher also needed professional knowledge; he must understand the nature of the mind and the process of learning; he should know the history of educational theory, the characteristics of school systems both at home and abroad, and the philosophic foundations on which sound practice could be based. Finally, Russell stressed the need for technical skill which, he insisted, is not necessarily the natural equipment of every educated person. He regarded teaching as an art but he believed that the artist in any field must develop consummate skill in the use of his tools and techniques. "The art of teaching . . . is founded on the science of teaching which takes account of the ends and means of education and the nature of the material to be taught."

If the new collegiate departments of education would accept their responsibility, Russell was convinced his objectives could be realized. Specifically, this would mean that colleges and universities should grant teaching diplomas only to candidates who, in addition to securing a degree, had completed these requirements: at least three years of collegiate study in the subject to be taught; courses in the history and philosophy of education, educational psychology, and methods of teaching; observation and practice teaching in secondary school classrooms. All of these requirements could be met in Teachers College, which by 1900 had a faculty of 15 professors and 55 instructors, and an enrollment of 1470.

Such, then, were the beginnings of professional education for secondary teachers in Iowa, Michigan, and New York. The origins of the movement may be found in part in the pioneer efforts of the normal schools and university normal departments, the model provided by Prussia, and the vigorous leadership of professors of pedagogy. But behind all these influences were the swelling enrollments of the public high schools which by 1890 exceeded 200,000, a sevenfold increase in twenty years. But competent teachers of the kind Russell wanted were in short supply. By 1898 only 32 per cent of secondary teachers in New York State were college graduates. Some normal schools were preparing their students for high school teaching but frequently the normal school graduate himself had less than a secondary education. The scarcity of qualified teachers was the weakest point in the mounting offensive for the extension of secondary schools, and it was not long before the professors of education, school superintendents, and, more cautiously, college presidents, marched into the breach.

When the Department of Superintendence of the National Education Association met in Cleveland in 1895 the Superintendent of Providence, Rhode Island, submitted a report on the training of teachers which reflected the opinion of his colleagues in the major cities of the country. For "the very difficult and responsible positions" which they fill, secondary school teachers need "ripe scholarship, more than ordinary ability, and an intimate knowledge of adolescence." The report also made the point that professional training was a necessity. In the discussion which followed one superintendent remarked, "I do not believe in the born teacher. The truly born teacher must receive a second birth, either through professional training or an extended uphill experience." This view corresponded with that of professors of education and, indeed, the alliance between the two groups was forged early in the history of the professional education movement. It grew stronger in later years as graduate schools of education assumed the task of training school administrators. By the end of the nineteenth century a fourth of all institutions of higher learning were offering professional work in education and twenty-four colleges and universities had established departments of pedagogy.

Pedagogy 1890–1905

The typical department of pedagogy in 1900 offered juniors and seniors elective courses which were both theoretical and practical. The emphasis, however, was on theory, and courses in history, philosophy, and psychology outnumbered those in classroom management, methods, and student teaching. Only five departments made any provision for classroom observation and practice teaching. Courses in supervision were available for experienced teachers, particularly those who were ambitious to become principals and superintendents. A department normally offered six courses from which undergraduates chose three or four to qualify for the teachers' diploma issued by the university. Students at Cornell were required to complete the two-semester course in the science and art of teaching, a course in the history of education, and attain "marked proficiency" in the subjects they intended to teach. At California (Berkeley) the requirement was twelve semester hours of "professional knowledge," eight of which could be secured in the department of pedagogy and the other four in an academic department through a course in methods of teaching. This gesture of co-operation from the older departments was not uncommon and "teachers' courses" in methodology were available at Cornell, Harvard, and Michigan.

A member of the philosophy department frequently taught the courses in philosophy of education and many of the first occupants of pedagogical chairs were former philosophy professors. It was not unusual for a chair in pedagogy to remain for several years as a sub-department of philosophy. These relationships did not last long, however, and a rather bitter comment made by Charles DeGarmo several years earlier was prophetic.[1]

1. Quoted in Charles A. Harper, *A Century of Public Teacher Education* (Washington: American Association of Teachers Colleges, 1939), pp. 113–114.

Our chairs of pedagogy in American universities are fatally defective in that they are component but not organic units of university life. They are mechanically but not organically connected with their own allied subjects . . . the professor of pedagogy is neatly glued on the university as a whole, but he has no group of men with whom he can organize an education department.

When William Payne began his work at Michigan one of the older professors gently inquired as to what literature there was for a professor of pedagogy to teach. Payne recognized the problem and within a few years he had written a short history of education and translated Gabriel Compayre's *History of Pedagogy*. During the 1890's E. E. Brown of California, Paul Monroe of Columbia, and Ellwood Cubberley of Stanford were beginning to open up the field of educational history. William James published his *Principles of Psychology* in 1890 and gave his twelve lectures, "Talks to Teachers on Psychology," at Harvard in 1892. William T. Harris, the U.S. Commissioner of Education from 1889 to 1906, was giving an Hegelian flavor to educational theory and Charles DeGarmo and the McMurry brothers were writing monographs in support of Herbartian methodology. The educational thought of Rousseau, Pestalozzi, Froebel, and Herbert Spencer was made available to American students and the departments of pedagogy offered courses in educational classics and discussed recent educational developments in foreign countries. G. Stanley Hall was laying the foundations for the study of child growth and preparing the way for the doctrine that no education could be efficient if it persisted in ignoring the nature, needs, and development of the child. In his doctoral thesis, *Animal Intelligence,* Edward L. Thorndike established his doctrine of connectionism and vigorously argued that it had a contribution to make to pedagogical science. And John Dewey entered the educational scene by challenging several of the basic concepts of Herbartian pedagogy and founding in the same year, 1896, the Laboratory School at the University of Chicago. It was in three lectures to parents and patrons of the school, later published as *The School and Society*, that Dewey condemned the "old school" for its rigid curriculum and passive pupils where "the educational center of gravity" for too long had been "in the teacher, the text-book, anywhere and everywhere you please except in the immediate instincts and activities of the child himself." It was a decade of scholarly production and active debate out of which came valuable new content for the discussion of educational theory in the university departments of pedagogy.

Several of the evils which later were to beset professional education may be traced to these years. When a department of pedagogy was founded it was usually staffed by one professor who was obliged to teach courses in several disciplines. When DeGarmo left the presidency of Swarthmore to become professor of pedagogy at Cornell he gave courses in history and psychology, and a seminar in the science and art of teaching. Hanus at Harvard, Butler at Columbia, and Barnes at Stanford all taught philosophy, history, and psychology. It is small wonder that the members of older departments viewed the new professor of pedagogy with suspicion. They felt that he was not only teaching without adequate training but was trespassing on their preserve. As pedagogy departments expanded new courses were added and frequently these were proliferations of existing courses. By 1900 Michigan offered three courses in the history of education, one in the history of educational thought, and one in comparative education. Within eight years of its founding in 1892 the department at California (Berkeley) had a faculty of four and was offering, in addition to the standard courses, school hygiene, ethology, and the development of character. Clark had a course in the motor education of children and New York University offered physiological pedagogics.

When a research worker from Teachers College asked fifty college teachers of pedagogy what subjects they considered essential in professional education, the history of education and educational psychology headed the list. But there was a singular lack of agreement on other subjects. There was uncertainty on another score. Some professors had rather vague notions as to the limitations of their particular subject. One course proposed "to lay the basis for a scientific theory of education considered as a human institution. The process of education is explained from the standpoint of evolution, and the fundamental principles thus arrived at are applied from the threefold standpoint of the history of civilization, the developing powers of the child, and the cultivation of individual and social efficiency." Another examined the aims, principles, and methods of education "from the standpoint of the physical, intellectual and moral nature of man." Courses so grandiosely conceived were justifiably criticized by other departments. The dilemma was deep. As professors of pedagogy tended to expand and proliferate their courses, they failed to win the support of men in the older disciplines of history and philosophy, and the newer fields of psychology and sociology. And yet such support was a necessity if a new discipline or set of disciplines were to be created in education.

A further source of tension lay in the trend away from theoretical study toward greater practicality. As we have seen, when the universities made their first excursions in the field of pedagogy the basic studies were in history, philosophy, and psychology. There was, indeed, a belief that the study of didactics would form a part of a liberal education if its subject matter were drawn from the parent disciplines. By 1900, however, classroom management and school hygiene, general and special methods, school law and administration had all found their way into the departments of pedagogy. Harvard was sending its students out to the schools of suburban Boston, and student teachers from Brown were serving as teaching interns on salary. The Horace Mann School, an affiliate of Teachers College, served both as a training and observation center. There was general agreement that practice work was a necessary part of a teacher's training but the extent and purpose of student teaching and the relative merits of theory and practice were under controversy.

At the annual meeting in 1904 of the National Society for the Scientific Study of Education John Dewey entered the debate by presenting a paper, "The Relation of Theory to Practice in Education." He makes the initial assumption that the professional instruction of teachers should not be exclusively theoretical but should include a certain amount of practical work. Practice may, however, be approached from two sharply different points of view. One is that of an apprenticeship under which teachers in training are expected to gain command of the tools of their profession, control of the technique of instruction and classroom management, and proficiency in the work of teaching. In contrast is the laboratory point of view which uses practice as an instrument for making knowledge of subject matter and educational theory real and vital, and supplying "the intellectual method and material of good workmanship, instead of making on the spot, as it were, an efficient workman." Under the laboratory approach the student teacher will, incidentally, develop some proficiency in the instruction and management of a class but the primary objective is a deeper understanding of principles rather than the acquisition of skill.

Dewey saw the problem of educating teachers as "one species of a more generic affair—that of training for professions." He believed it was both incredible and shameful that the vocation of teaching was practically the last to recognize the need for specific professional preparation, but now that the need was conceded teachers would do well to follow the lead of other vocations. He pointed to the place of chemistry and physiology in medical training and compared the growing emphasis on the arts and sciences with the chairs of "practice" and *materia medica* of a generation earlier. The schools of medicine, law, architecture, and engineering were now demanding high scholastic attainment as a condition for admission and the practical work of the professional schools was becoming typical and intensive rather than extensive and detailed. The function of practice in this new approach was to vitalize and illuminate theory and principle and postpone the acquisition of technical skill until the student actively entered his career. One very cogent reason for this trend was the inability of the professional school to furnish realistic conditions under which skill could be acquired and used. Schools of law and medicine could provide only simulated copies of the actual conditions under which these professions were practiced. A similar limitation was true in education: practice teaching with its carefully prepared lesson plans, close supervision, and lack of responsibility for discipline was far removed from the realities of the day-to-day life of the classroom.

The teacher-in-training is faced with two problems, the mastery of subject matter from the standpoint of its educational value and use, and the mastery of the technique of classroom management. These problems are related rather than isolated but the student who fixes his attention on the second will develop a technique which has, in Dewey's terms, an empirical rather than a scientific sanction. He will be guided not by the principles derived from philosophy, psychology, and history of education but by a blind kind of trial and error, the advice of experienced teachers, and precepts which are more or less arbitrary and mechanical. For Dewey, the more desirable procedure is to involve the student in an apprenticeship of teaching after he has gone through a training in educational theory and history, in subject matter, and observation and practice work of the laboratory type. Only then is he ready to develop a technique of teaching and classroom management.[2]

Ultimately there are two bases upon which the habits of a teacher as a teacher may be built up. They may be formed under the inspiration and constant criticism of intelligence, applying the best that is available. This is possible only where the would-be teacher has become fairly saturated with his subject-matter and with his psychological and ethical philosophy of education. Only when such things have become incorporated in mental habit, have become part of the working tendencies of observation, insight and reflection, will these principles work automatically unconsciously and hence promptly and effectively. And this means that practical work should be pursued primarily with reference to its reaction upon the professional pupil in making him a thoughtful and alert student of education, rather than to help him get immediate proficiency.

For immediate skill may be got at the cost of power to go on growing. The teacher who leaves the professional school with power in managing a class of children may appear to superior advantage the first day, the first week, the first month, or even the first year, as compared with some other teacher who has a much more vital command of the psychology, logic, and ethics of development. But later "progress" may with such consist only in perfecting and refining skill already possessed. Such persons seem to know how to teach, but they are not students of teaching. Even though they go on studying books of pedagogy, reading teachers' journals, attending teachers' institutes, etc., yet the root of the matter is not in them, unless they continue to be students of subject-matter, and students of mind-activity. Unless a teacher is such a student, he may continue to improve in the

2. John Dewey, "The Relation of Theory to Practice in Education," *The Third Yearbook of the National Society for the Scientific Study of Education* (Chicago: University of Chicago Press, 1904), p. 15.

mechanics of school management, but he can not grow as a teacher, an inspirer and director of soul-life.

American educators embraced many of the ideas of John Dewey, but for nearly half a century they chose to ignore his philosophy of teacher education. The new departments and schools of education and the normal schools which became teachers colleges did not adopt the Deweyan image of the "student of teaching."

The Movement Accelerates: 1905–1930

In 1905 the N.E.A. appointed a committee "to consider the subject of securing proper professional preparation of high school teachers." This was the Committee of Seventeen which included nine professors of education, four public school administrators, and one professor of psychology. There was no representative from the older academic disciplines, and no college or university president. Two years later, at the N.E.A. annual meeting in Los Angeles, the Committee submitted its recommendations. Academic preparation should include both a detailed and specialized study of the subjects to be taught and work in other subjects "sufficient to give some insight into the different fields of knowledge." Professional education should require a study of the history of education, educational psychology, principles of education, special methods, organization and management of school systems, and school hygiene, and all students should be involved in observation and practice teaching. These subjects should be offered in the junior and senior years and should form an "irreducible minimum" of one eighth of the college course. All secondary teachers should be graduates of four-year colleges.

The Report was influential in establishing two concepts: a proportion of undergraduate work should be devoted to professional training, and such training ought to include study in six different fields. Practical subjects were henceforth to be regarded as fully respectable. The Committee implied that these subjects were of equal value to the more theoretical subjects and worthy of equal time and attention. Nowhere does the Report carry a statement of the relation of theory to practice. The approach is, rather, that the education of a teacher should include certain components and within the professional component certain subjects are desirable. The relationships among these subjects receive no attention, nor does the timing of them within the junior and senior years. By placing the stress on separate subjects, rather than on an integrated pattern of professional study of the kind Dewey wanted, the Committee left the way open for all manner of subdivisions of existing subjects. The result was proliferation, overlap, and confusion in the years ahead. Sixty different areas of study in education were listed in the catalogues of twenty-eight universities in 1913–1914. One institution offered eighty-seven different courses, including eleven in the hygiene of education and twenty-six in supervision. Courses as closely similar as "The High School Curriculum" and "Principles of Secondary Education" made their appearance, and "The Question as a Measure of Efficiency of the Recitation" was offered as a course.

Members of the Committee of Seventeen added individual comments to the Report. The Superintendent of Boston argued that professional training could not be carried on successfully under "the direct domination and control of the regular college or university faculty." He conceded there were advantages to be gained by affiliation with a university but his final judgment was that "professional training in its best form is possible only when the department of education is large enough to attain the dignity and organization of a separate college, to have its own professors, and to dictate its own policy." It was a prophetic remark. By 1915 twenty-three universities had created schools or colleges of education in which students combined liberal and professional education in the undergraduate years. At Chicago, Pittsburgh, Ohio, and Pennsylvania professional work began in the freshman year and one zealous professor of education explained why: "This makes it possible to baptize the student with the professional spirit much more successfully." The creation of separate schools and colleges gave to professional education an autonomy it was scarcely ready for and denied it the sustenance of other disciplines it so badly needed.

The acceleration of the professional education movement after World War I is closely related to the "new education" reforms of the period. In the final decade of the nineteenth century the N.E.A.'s

Committee of Ten on Secondary School Studies, chaired by President Eliot and including five college presidents, had submitted a report which was to influence secondary education for a generation. In the eyes of the Committee the chief function of the secondary school was to provide four years of strong and effective mental training in which the powers of observation, memory, and reasoning would be developed. College preparation was not the chief aim of a high school education, and the Committee recognized that only "an insignificant percentage" of graduates would ever enroll in a college. The essential task of the high school was "to prepare for the duties of life that small proportion of all the children in the country—a proportion small in number, but very important to the welfare of the nation—who show themselves able to profit by an education prolonged to the eighteenth year." The Committee accepted five groups of subjects as proper for secondary schools— languages, mathematics, history, natural philosophy, physics, and chemistry—and drew up several courses in which different amounts of time would be assigned to the various subjects. In all programs each subject should be studied thoroughly and consecutively because, if it is "to provide a substantial mental training, it must have a time allotment sufficient to produce that fruit."

This curriculum composed mainly of academic subjects remained dominant throughout the first two decades of the twentieth century. But a large majority of the two million pupils enrolled in the high schools by 1920 had neither the intention of going to college nor the ability to profit from a Committee of Ten curriculum. Educational leaders were beginning to search for ways of "relating the high school to life" and of adopting programs to meet "the varying needs of students." The change can be seen in the aims expressed by the Commission on Reorganization of Secondary Education in its *Seven Cardinal Principles* of 1918: health, command of fundamental processes, worthy home membership, vocational efficiency, worthy use of leisure time, and ethical character. As the high schools increasingly enrolled ever-larger segments of the youth population nonacademic studies (industrial arts, home economics, business subjects) became more popular, new courses were offered in the traditional subjects (business English and practical mathematics), and experiments were launched in "core," "broad fields," and "experience" curricula. New services such as guidance and psychological testing were introduced and work experience and extracurricular activities were greatly expanded.

The adoption of a new philosophy, the modification of the curriculum, and the expansion of services reflects the influence on the high schools of the progressive education movement. As Lawrence Cremin [3] has demonstrated, progressive education grew out of social and political reform movements following the Civil War and reached its peak of influence in the twenties and thirties. It had a profound effect not only on elementary and secondary education but on professional education as well. Under the leadership of John Dewey, William Heard Kilpatrick, Harold Rugg, and George Counts, all of whom wrote extensively and taught influentially at Teachers College, the tenets of progressivism spread to teacher training programs throughout the country. The belief that education should be made more scientific led to the development of courses in psychological testing and educational measurement. Interpretations of the "project method" and the "activity program" found their way into courses in method and curriculum. The concepts of child-centered education stemming from the doctrine of expressionism ("the creative impulse is within the child himself") led to a greater emphasis on the study of child growth and development. And the philosophic bases of progressivism found their way into many a philosophy of education course. Although Dewey was chief among the founding fathers of the movement it was his disciple, Kilpatrick, who was its most influential interpreter. During his twenty-nine years at Columbia Kilpatrick taught some 35,000 students, a good number of whom were later to become leaders of American education. By 1930 nearly one fifth of the faculty and administration of all normal schools and teachers colleges had taken at least a part of their training on Morningside Heights.

As new concepts took root concerning the nature of the child, the function of subject matter, and the design of the curriculum, the leaders of the movement realized that the subject-matter specialist with no professional training could no longer qualify for the role of

3. *The Transformation of the School* (New York: Alfred A. Knopf, 1961).

teacher. As a "director of learning activities" in a school which offered a flexible curriculum and a wealth of services to adolescents from all kinds of home backgrounds and of differing abilities and motivations the teacher needed a sustained period of preparation. By 1930 professional training had won almost total acceptance as a necessary phase of a teacher's education. More than one thousand colleges and universities were offering education courses, and the *National Survey* [4] could report that the typical secondary teacher had devoted about one fifth of his college work, or twenty-four semester hours, to professional training. Two companion developments help to explain the astonishing success of the professional movement: the growth of teachers colleges out of the normal schools, and the changes in certification requirements.

Normal Schools to Teachers Colleges

The state normal schools began in the 1830's as a means of supplying teachers for the common schools but only eleven had appeared by 1860. Steady growth came after the Civil War and 167 normal schools had appeared by 1900. Massachusetts was then admitting only high school graduates but elsewhere the usual requirement was two years of high school work. The nineteenth-century normal school was an integral part of the state school system. Its students came from the public schools and went back to them to teach. In the words of one state normal school president, "The normal must go down to the common school and lift it up." The normal school staff did not forget their graduates, and teachers had all kinds of opportunity for in-service training through institutes, summer schools, and extension courses. It was the normal schools that originated "professionalized subject matter" or that knowledge selected from the academic disciplines which a teacher would find most useful. In contrast to the emphasis on theory of the early departments of pedagogy in the universities, the normal schools stressed practical training. Their students observed experienced teachers and engaged in practice teaching either in model or ex-

4. *National Survey of the Education of Teachers.* Bulletin 1933, No. 10 (Washington: U.S. Government Printing Office, 1935).

perimental schools on campus or in co-operating public schools in the vicinity. Within the normal school the atmosphere was professional, or more accurately, vocational. The schools had one primary aim: to train teachers. The test of whether this aim was accomplished was entirely pragmatic; if the graduates became competent teachers (as judged by the normal school faculty), their training had been effective.

The rapid growth of high schools gave to normal schools a new challenge: Where should high school teachers be trained? To ambitious and dedicated normal school presidents the answer was clear. Historically, the normals had been formed to train teachers for the common schools, and was not the high school essentially an extension of the common school, a part of the public school system? But the majority of normals were scarcely more than secondary schools themselves and in no position to meet the demands of the newly formed regional accrediting associations. The North Central Association, for example, in developing a set of standards for evaluating high schools recommended, in 1902, that high school teachers should have a college degree. The normal schools could hardly fail to see the signal and a transition to teachers colleges began. At its meetings in 1908 the Normal Department of the N.E.A. drew up a statement of policy in which it urged normal schools to accept only high school graduates, to prepare them for elementary teaching in two years, secondary teaching in four, and to change their name. "Good as the word 'normal' is, it should be dropped from the name of these schools and they should be called Teachers Colleges."

The normal schools had served the nation well in supplying technically competent teachers for the common schools, but they were singularly ill-equipped to offer collegiate instruction and educate teachers for the public high schools. Their development into teachers colleges was a hard struggle. State legislatures were reluctant to award adequate grants and active opposition came from colleges and universities. Low salaries and heavy teaching loads made it difficult to recruit faculty. In 1915 average salaries in teachers colleges and normal schools were a third less than those of private liberal arts colleges and universities but teaching loads were nearly twice as heavy.

During the period 1920–1930, 108 teachers colleges were established and although many were legally able to prepare secondary teachers their main function was elementary teacher training. High school graduation was becoming a standard requirement of admission but academic standards improved slowly. In 1938 the Regents Inquiry into the preparation of teachers in New York State found that the faculties of the normal schools and teachers colleges were providing mediocre teaching, were burdened with heavy teaching loads, and were not engaged in productive scholarship and research.

From its parents the teachers college inherited a pragmatic approach to teacher training. Neither the liberal disciplines nor educational theory were, in the early years, as important as the study of contemporary civilization and the analysis of teaching procedures. When the American Association of Teachers Colleges celebrated, in 1939, the centennial of public teacher education its official historian made this statement: [5]

> The teachers colleges are just beginning to emerge from the paralyzing effects of the old classical, traditional, medieval, liberal-arts curriculum pattern. There is a definite striving for a new curriculum, new relations to the public schools, and new technics of teaching. A firsthand study of society and its problems and a close scrutiny of the American schools is leading to the creation of new materials which will prepare teachers for the great task of leadership in a twentieth-century democracy. No thought of growing respectable by becoming arts colleges can deter the modern teachers college from its historic path of pragmatism and its obligation to point out the road of progress for public education. . . .
>
> After all, the success of the teachers college depends not on its ability to build up courses with imposing names, nor load its catalog with decorative Doctors' degrees, nor spend annually enough money for books and equipment; but on its ability to turn out teachers who can do the job. If it is possible to measure in some way the effectiveness of the results of the whole teacher-education process in terms of what the student can do in teaching children in the public schools, then the teachers colleges can do what they have always liked to do— they can attack directly and immediately the task at hand.

The teachers colleges have had a marked influence in emphasizing the importance of professional training and, in former years at

5. Harper, *op. cit.*, pp. 154–159.

least, in directing it toward practical ends. In more recent years as they have become state colleges they have changed markedly. State legislatures have given more adequate appropriations and admission standards have risen. With its greater emphasis on liberal education, and a more scholarly faculty, the present state college is far different from the teachers college of the thirties and a totally different institution from the old normal school.

Certification

When Ellwood Cubberley investigated certification procedures in 1906 he found that only a few states issued a separate certificate for high school teachers. California insisted on a bachelor's degree plus one year of further training, Indiana required all teachers to take an examination in the high school subjects they expected to teach, and New York prescribed college graduation including fourteen semester hours of professional courses. A small number of other states recognized, but did not require, the diplomas of state universities as the equivalent of a teaching certificate. But otherwise, in almost all the states, the lowest grade of town or county certificate gave a teacher the legal right to teach in any part of the school system.

Certification was acquired through examinations administered by local school committees (Massachusetts and Connecticut), by county boards (Maryland and Wisconsin), and by state systems (Arizona and Alabama). In more than half the states it was possible to become a teacher simply by revealing a knowledge of the common school subjects and passing an examination in the theory and practice of teaching. Local autonomy did, of course, have its advantages, and some New England school committees were able to secure well-educated teachers. In 1906–1907 nearly 80 percent of high school teachers in Massachusetts were college graduates.

By 1910 new trends in teacher certification were beginning to emerge. State authority was replacing town and county autonomy and by 1911 fifteen state boards were issuing all certificates. Special certificates for high school teachers were becoming more common and an increasing number of states waived all examinations for candidates holding college degrees. And the practice of requiring a given number of courses in professional education was growing. As early as 1905 California insisted on twelve semester hours of education and by 1915 five other states had a similar or more demanding requirement. In the decade 1920–1930 earlier certification trends continued. Some forty states modified or abolished local autonomy and assumed authority for issuing all certificates. The granting of special certificates to high school teachers became firmly established, and the requirement of both a college degree and a given amount of professional education replaced the old examination system. By 1930, thirty-three states insisted on a college degree and all but one (Rhode Island) required professional training. The median number of semester hours of such training was fifteen. California was the only state which asked its high school teachers to undertake a year of graduate study.

Certification laws appear to have been somewhat less concerned with the academic preparation of secondary teachers in the subjects they would later teach. Nearly half the states issued blanket certificates which allowed a college graduate to teach any subject. But these minimum standards of certification do not accurately reflect the academic or professional preparation of secondary teachers. The typical high school teacher of 1930 as revealed by the *National Survey* had taken over thirty semester hours of credit in the principal subject he was teaching and over twenty hours in his second subject. Similarly, his professional training (twenty-four semester hours) was well above the certification standards of most states. Thus it is evident that it was the colleges and universities, not the certification authorities, that were deciding both the nature and extent of academic and professional preparation. It is also evident that it was the private colleges and state universities, and not the teachers colleges, that were preparing the majority of high school teachers. More than three quarters of the senior high school teachers included in the *National Survey* were graduates of state universities, land grant and private colleges; only one eighth came from state teachers colleges.

In recent years many states have raised their certification requirements although it was not until 1960 that all states insisted on a bachelor's degree for secondary teachers. The trend toward required units of credit in professional courses has continued and by 1961 the median for all states was eighteen semester hours of which five to six hours were normally earned in practice teaching. The improvement in standards of academic preparation has been slow in coming. As late as 1959 in some states the requirements in a teaching field such as English were lower than those in education; but more recently academic standards have been stiffened. In 1960 New York doubled the requirements for provisional certificates in foreign languages, mathematics, and science, and substantially increased them in English and the social studies. The following table reveals the minimum preparation necessary for initial certification in four states that are among the leaders of this new movement.

Semester Hours of Credit Required in the Teaching Field

	English	Social Studies	Science	Foreign Languages	Mathematics
New York	36	36	42	24	18
Pennsylvania	30	36	40	24	24
Connecticut	30	30	21	24	18
Ohio	24	45	45	20	18

In the past seventy-five years the education of secondary teachers has moved through three phases. In the early years of the university departments of pedagogy the emphasis was on scholarly preparation in the academic subjects and theoretical study in the history and philosophy of education and educational psychology. Professors of pedagogy during this period were not divorced from their colleagues in the academic disciplines. As professional preparation achieved acceptance, and as departments and schools of education grew and normal schools became teachers colleges, the professional educator fell into greater isolation both in his training and his career. This was also the period when teacher-education programs placed relatively less stress on academic preparation and more on professional training. And to the theoretical studies were added courses of greater practicality. A third phase, as we have seen in Chapter One and in the recent reform of certification requirements, is emerging and is marked by a greater stress on scholarly preparation, a reduction and consolidation of professional courses, a growing rapprochement of liberal arts professors and professional educators, and a search for meaningful relationships between educational theory and classroom practice. No one would have more heartily applauded these recent developments than John Dewey.

USING THE PARENT DISCIPLINES

CHAPTER IV

REGINALD D. ARCHAMBAULT:

The Role of Philosophy in the Education of a Teacher

> Philosophy may be defined *as the general theory of education.*
>
> —JOHN DEWEY

Philosophy and Education

PHILOSOPHICAL reflection arises from the need to make judgments concerning problems which have practical bearings. In the final analysis, philosophy is related, albeit often indirectly, to the practical concerns of men. Education is a vital, purposive activity, complex in its functions and its problems. For these reasons it serves as an ideal source of issues for philosophical analysis. Yet, although philosophical speculation often begins with practical concerns, it quickly leads to an investigation of more basic problems in the fields of logic, ethics, epistemology, and metaphysics. Even a casual discussion of everyday educational issues leads to considerations that are philosophical in nature—the relation between church and state, the teaching of moral principles, the balance between authority and freedom. Educational theorists are soon led to an investigation of those root problems. Conversely, professional philosophers, in analyzing abstract issues in ethics and epistemology, constantly use educational problems as a starting point.

The feasibility of using educational problems as a focal point for exploring philosophical issues in politics, epistemology, and ethics has been demonstrated by philosophers from Plato to Dewey. The relation between philosophical analysis and educational problems is aptly demonstrated in the *Republic,* where it is difficult to determine whether Plato's major concern is the solution of a practical problem of education, or the use of an educational problem to provide a means for building a system of abstract philosophical principles.

For the philosopher, then, the field of education offers a source of practical problems that lend themselves to philosophical analysis. And problems in education lead quickly to the root problems of philosophy. But what has philosophy to offer to the field of education in general and to teachers in particular? There is considerable controversy in the field of philosophy of education concerning this issue. The failure to establish an identity for the philosophy of education has led to confusion regarding what a course in the field should be expected to accomplish. This confusion is a reflection of the difficulty in defining philosophy's function when compared with that of the other disciplines. Students of education expect definite theories from the educational psychologist based on sound evidence. They expect the historian to present them with an accurate reconstruction of past events. From both they expect information which will bear on their practical educational decisions. Philosophy does not provide that kind of information. Nor should it serve, as it has so often in the past, as a means of introducing a belief system for acceptance by students, or by the public at large. It is not the proper function of philosophy to provide directives or imperatives for educational practice, or to inculcate a system of beliefs concerning knowledge, value, and method. Its function is much more modest: to make clear the relations between the diverse factors that are involved in educational decisions. To recognize this would be a major step in eliminating the confusion and misapprehension on the part of students concerning its utility in treating practical problems. It is *ultimately* practical. Its function is to organize, clarify, and justify rather than to inform or to preach. Its proper aim is to make students independent and intellectually self-sufficient.

There are many who would maintain that the scope of philosophy of education is either broader or narrower than that which is outlined here. Some would claim that it is the nature and function of philosophy not only to analyze and clarify, but also to provide direction for activity by arriving at synthetic statements or theoretical positions which are logically justifiable. I am not maintaining that philosophy cannot function in this fashion, or that it is undesirable for it to do so. Nor am I suggesting that philosophical analysis cannot be concerned with the immediately practical. I am, however, suggesting that philosophy can function most fruitfully in education by concentrating on the clarification of theoretical factors that impinge on important educational decisions. To insist that it be immediately practical would be to narrow its scope and lessen its value. To maintain that each exercise in philosophical study in education must be clearly related to some ultimate metaphysical and ethical system would place similar burdens on such study. And to maintain that philosophy of education should serve as a means of conveying a series of previously decided beliefs to the student or the public at large would be to engage in propaganda rather than philosophy. The analytic function of philosophy has been central to the discipline since its use in Plato's dialogues.

The field of education is broad. It includes a wide variety of activities ranging from acculturation to conditioning, from mass communication to tutoring, from formal lecturing to parental training in etiquette. The concepts underlying theories of education are complex and varied. These include poorly defined "common sense" principles, as well as clearly stated theoretical propositions. Often concepts of differing degrees of clarity are interwoven into an educational theory. It is in the clarification of these concepts and of the logical relations between them that philosophical analysis can be most helpful. Insuring consistency, clarity, and adequate justification of principles is the proper function of the philosopher.

Because the field of education is so broad, and the modes of philosophical inquiry so diverse, a major task facing the philosopher of education is that of delimiting the function of his discipline in studying educational issues. There is a great range of philosophical opinion on this question. Recognizing this, a general definition can be attempted. The philosophy of education is a disciplined mode of inquiry that employs the techniques and principles of philosophy in order to explore problems in education and to arrive at justifiable conclusions concerning them. The application of philosophical techniques to educational problems is analogous to its application to the fields of art, science, or history. The philosopher uses his techniques in analyzing problems inherent in these fields. These problems are often specialized, but nevertheless relate to root problems in the basic branches of philosophy—metaphysics, epistemology, logic, and ethics. Thus there is a basic relation between the philosophy of art, of science, of history. Similarly, the philosophy of education treats problems that are fundamentally related to those which are examined in other specialized branches of philosophy. It is the *focus* of the study, that is, the concentration on educational issues, which gives identity to the philosophy of education. And, just as other areas of study in philosophy can be treated narrowly or broadly, the same is true of philosophy of education. The discipline deals with a very wide range of problems which relate to basic philosophical issues.

Psychology, History, and Philosophy of Education

Perhaps the distinctive nature of philosophy of education can best be made clear by comparing it with its two counterparts—educational psychology and history of education. Educational psychology is a disciplined mode of study which employs scientific techniques in order to explain and predict significant phases of human behavior. The scope of educational psychology is determined by the problems of education with which it deals. Thus a great deal of attention is given to such areas as learning theory, transfer of learning, heredity and environment as factors in human development, and other problems central to educational theory. Although the philosophy of education treats many of these same issues, and often uses theories and principles developed in educational psychology as a source of problems for philosophical investigation, the aims and methods of the two disciplines are different. The psychologist collects data and orders them into principles and theories which will explain or predict certain aspects of behavior. The philosopher has a different concern. His aim is not to experiment, classify, and organize data in order to explain or predict, but rather to investigate the adequacy of such data and principles and their relevance to crucial educational decisions. It is for this reason that philosophers are concerned with the assumptions both explicit and tacit underlying certain principles in psychology (and the other sciences), the bases of selecting the problems which are investigated in that science, the conclusions which can be validly drawn from limited evidence, and the sufficient conditions for establishing general theories.

Modern philosophical analysis concerns itself with two types of investigation: the analysis of root problems—definitions, assumptions, and basic principles on the one hand, and the implications and relevance of the principles derived from them on the other. The psychologist *qua* psychologist is not concerned with these considerations, although as a practical decision-maker he might be. To be sure, the psychologist is interested in definitions, principles, and assumptions to the extent that they are helpful in explaining and predicting phenomena. These factors are essential to theory-building, yet the investigation of the logical adequacy of these factors is usually left to the philosopher. And conversely, the philosopher is not concerned with experimentation, explanation, or prediction, but with the clarification of the grounds and criteria for success in these attempts. Hence the roles of the philosopher and the psychologist in dealing with educational issues are distinct in several respects. It is the function of the psychologist to gather and organize data in order to determine what is the case, to explain, in terms of scientific laws, the causes of phenomena, and possibly to predict the occurrence of future behavior given a certain set of conditions. The philosopher's concern is with the justification, relevancy, and implications of such principles through the use of logical analysis. There is another major respect in which these two roles differ. The psychologist is not concerned with the relation between his researches and other considerations (for example, priority, relevancy) in the broader context of educational decision. He is not concerned with the broader implications involved in the application of discovered principles. However, these are major concerns of the philosopher—to clarify the relations which exist between principles, and to show the relevance of and implications of these principles for problems of value. In this respect the philosopher's role is unique.

Perhaps a simple example will illustrate the point. When the psychologist investigates the transfer of learning from one area of study or situation to another, he approaches the problem experimentally. He sets up as many controls as possible, collects data, and presents evidence to support or deny that learning in one "subject" facilitates learning in another. His conclusions are generalized from the specific data that his experiments yield. When the philosopher is confronted with the problem of transfer his approach is quite different. He is interested in the definition of "transfer," in the clarification of the *meaning* of the concept. He may approach the problem without considering any experimental evidence, but with only the conventions of ordinary language usage as a guide. Or he may use the evidence provided by psychological experiment to examine the extent to which general and justifiable theoretical principles can be drawn from this evidence. The example is a pointed one, for there has been a history of confusion in transfer theory due not to shoddy experimental techniques, but rather to inadequate analysis of the meaning and relevance of the evidence derived from them. After the philosopher has established the adequacy of principles thus derived he may proceed to relate them to other factors in judging their importance. For example, evidence might suggest that the most effective method of insuring transfer of training is by a system of constant repetition and drill. In deciding whether or not such a method is *desirable* the philosopher would consider its total consequences as compared with those of a less efficient alternative technique. Here the philosopher moves from the philosophical analysis of a psychological issue to the investigation of a wider educational issue beyond the scope of psychology itself. The philosopher can fruitfully function in both ways. His investigation is not in opposition to that of the psychologist, but rather complementary to it.

So we see that although philosophy may employ the method of science and the logic of science, it is different from science insofar as it explores value considerations as a definite objective, and insofar as total contextual analysis is a major aim. It is for this reason that philosophy of education as a discipline differs from educational psychology (and indeed sociology and anthropology). The implications of this distinction for the teaching of the two subjects should be clear. They have a different function, a different mode of investigation, a different scope, and employ different kinds of evidence. Consequently, the knowledge resulting from the study of the disciplines would differ accordingly.

A brief word can now be said concerning the history of education in order to illustrate how philosophy is distinct. History is concerned primarily with the accurate description of past events, and of their causes.

The results of historical investigation can be used in drawing relations between sets of events in one time and those in another, including the present, and possibly in the prediction of future events on the basis of the application of historical "laws" to present conditions. The last two functions, however, are not essential to the study of history. They are possible by-products.

The study of history is analogous to the study of psychology in that it employs its own methods of investigation and research in accordance with established rules of procedure in order to explain those factors which cause specific effects in specific instances. The historian provides us with knowledge of the past. Yet it is not the function of the historian to derive principles from his study which will directly inform future practice, or indeed to establish the relation between such principles and current practice. To be sure, principles derived from historical investigation can be used to inform current decisions, but it is not the historian's function to provide or apply them.

The educational historian's function is, of course, limited by his subject matter. He establishes those causal factors and conditions which have led to the establishment of institutions, policies, and principles in the past, and explains the way in which these were effected. The historian of education functions, then, with a different scope and different methodology from that of the philosopher of education. Similarly, the course in the history of education aims at the development of different knowledge and skill from that of the course in philosophy of education. The former aims at the acquisition of the knowledge of past events and their precedents, and skill in the interpretation of causal relations in history. The latter may use these principles as source material but attempts to investigate their relevance to questions of broader scope.

This analysis, then, suggests that philosophy of education often deals with problems similar to those treated by other disciplines; that the study of philosophy, psychology, and history of education are distinct but related through the focus of their study; and that although the philosophy of education draws on the principles and data derived from other disciplines, its subject matter is distinct because of the selection of and treatment of the problems which are investigated. It is fundamentally concerned with philosophical issues *per se* as they relate to education: the relation between fact and value, between means and ends, the justification of ends or objectives.

We have maintained that philosophical inquiry arises as a result of the need to make judgments concerning issues which have practical bearings. Education offers a rich source of such issues. Specific examples are many. The postulation and justification of educational aims is a prime example of a problem which leads to more abstract theoretical issues in the field of ethics. A typical problem is to establish a desirable balance between discipline and freedom which can and should be maintained in a given social order. The definition and classification of knowledge and the judgment of what knowledge is of most worth are basic philosophic issues. The selection and justification of curriculum is a key educational issue that raises questions of ethics and epistemology, and the relation between the two.

Yet perhaps the most pressing need in education is for the clarification of specific issues that are relevant to key educational decisions. This task lends itself well to techniques of philosophical analysis. The need for making clear-cut distinctions, for pointing out the relations between apparently distinct issues, for drawing out implications, are all peculiar to the role of the philosopher.

The Philosophy of Education for Teachers

We must distinguish on the one hand between the philosophy of education as a disciplined mode of inquiry with a broad scope and almost infinite potentiality for depth, and the study of philosophy as a component in teacher education. The role of the teacher, and the limits of his area of decision, determine the way in which philosophy can contribute to his training. The future educational *theorist* would need to explore in depth the relations between philosophy *per se* and the study of education, the relation between philosophy of education and other disciplined modes of study within the field of education, and the limitations and potentialities of philosophy as a component in educational theory. This material would be of interest and value to the future teacher. He would need to be aware of these considerations, but he would not be expected to develop the skills and interests of the theorist. A course in the philosophy of education taught to administrators or school board members would meet a still different need. The relation between the aims of education and those of the community and the society would be a major focus; the establishment of priorities in educational planning and the criteria for these would also be central; the examination of over-all curricular decisions as they reflect the basic values underlying them would be another key problem. The issues treated in such a course would again be relevant to the teacher's concern. But he is primarily a practitioner. He must be able to use the discipline, knowledge, and method of philosophy in treating general educational problems, but his concerns center more directly on problems of *teaching*, as they can be approached philosophically.

The nature of a course in the philosophy of education is determined, then, by the structure of the discipline and by the future role that the student will assume. This role is the chief ground for delimiting and defining the content of a course in the philosophy of education. Thus the focus of a course in philosophy of education for teachers can be determined by examining the characteristics of the student who will be educated to be a teacher, the role that he will assume, and the qualities which the "finished product" is expected to exhibit.

For the purpose of this analysis we will assume that the student who is engaged in a program of teacher preparation is in the process of a liberal education. He is pursuing a program of studies aimed at attaining the knowledge and skill associated with the liberal arts and sciences and is cultivating the traits of mind characteristic of a liberally educated person. He possesses knowledge of the humanities, social sciences, and natural sciences and skill in investigating basic problems studied through those disciplines. He should also have some understanding of the complementary nature of those studies. Programs of liberal education are many, and educational experiments have shown that diverse patterns of preparation have comparable success in attaining the objective of producing a liberally educated person. The patterns of study are less interesting here than the skills and understandings which the student should possess. These are summed up most succinctly in the Harvard Report's description of those traits of mind for which a program of liberal studies should strive: to think effectively, to communicate thought, to make relevant judgments, to discriminate among values.[1]

Yet even if students have acquired considerable knowledge and skill prior to entering a program of teacher preparation, there will be a wide diversity in their interests and skills. This is due to the variety of college curricula with different emphases, and to the use of an elective system. Because of these factors we cannot assume homogeneity on the part of the students. Many will have studied no philosophy before and most will have only a passing acquaintance with it. Many who have studied philosophy will have forgotten much of what was learned. Thus the problem of teaching the philosophy of education is similar at both the graduate and undergraduate level.

In a sense, then, one must start from scratch. In another sense, the teacher of the course in philosophy of education begins with a disadvantage in that the students often arrive with prejudices concerning basic educational issues. These attitudes must be "unlearned" or modified if the course is to be successful. The student usually tends to think in stereotypes and to cling to beliefs originally accepted without due consideration. He is often inclined to accept personal experience or currently accepted practice as a directive. The belief in the validity and integrity of the traditional academic disciplines is a common prejudice of many liberal arts students.

1. There is a cogent discussion of these elusive qualities in the Report of the Harvard Committee, *General Education in a Free Society* (Cambridge: Harvard University Press; 1946), pp. 64–73. The development of these "traits of mind" is, of course, a major aim of the "professional" course in philosophy of education as well.

They consider these subjects to be sacred because they have been exalted so often by teachers and commencement speakers who offer an emotional plea rather than a philosophic rationale for their acceptance. If one is to maintain that there is value in the academic disciplines properly taught, as one would assume there is, a careful justification for that value is essential. Neither emotional attachment nor appeal to tradition are of themselves sufficient grounds for such justification. Many students subscribe to the cliché that value judgments are simply based on personal taste, or that "science" holds the ultimate answer to questions of policy. The student is often reluctant to consider new ideas and to arrive at definite commitments on issues which demand decision.

These are some of the difficulties facing the teacher of philosophy of education. They are in part counterbalanced by the genuine motivation of the students which stems from a clear professional orientation. Issues and principles which seem peripheral if not vacuous to the student with no professional goal in view take on a meaning for the future teacher. This factor, however, has its own drawbacks, for his clear-cut future role as a practitioner tends to narrow the student's interest to the merely practical. A major emphasis of the course in philosophy of education must therefore be on the relation between theory and practice, between immediate and ultimate concerns, between superficial and basic issues.

The task of the teacher of philosophy of education, then, is similar in some respects to that of the psychiatrist. His charges are reluctant to objectify their present beliefs because they fear that they cannot withstand criticism. They are reluctant, also, to introduce themselves to new possibilities because their present belief system is comfortable to hold. The instructor must, therefore, introduce problems, bring beliefs into the open so that inconsistencies can be revealed and eliminated, and attempt to free his students from prejudices by forcing the process of justification.

We expect the teacher to be an effective practitioner. Yet this does not entail merely developing competence in a limited and clearly defined set of skills which can be catalogued, such as skill in swimming or typewriting. For the teacher must cope with a very wide range of problems that are not solved by applying simple rules of thumb. In spite of the fact that the teacher's role is often defined by those who stipulate the aims of education, these aims are usually so general in character that they leave a wide area of interpretation for the individual teacher. In fact, it is quite often his responsibility to decide in what manner and to what extent his subject and his presentation of it will be *educative*. This in itself poses a wide ground for decision and responsibility. The teacher must be able to establish priorities. He must be able to decide when his pupils have acquired sufficient experience to be set free. He must be able to objectify the basis for his selection of the material to be studied, and to justify it. He must be able to transfer his belief in the value of that material to his pupils so that their enthusiasm for study can be nurtured. This involves understanding of theory, and skill in translating theory into practice.

This concept of the teacher's function suggests the role of philosophy in teacher education. Because of the nature of the discipline of philosophy, it can be most fruitfully employed in the area of analysis of issues and justification of beliefs. Philosophy is a meta-study in that it seeks connections among other disciplines, and examines basic assumptions and conclusions which stem from applications of other disciplines to specific problems. Philosophy, then, can function in several major ways: (1) in developing techniques of logical analysis in order to recognize fallacies; (2) in making explicit certain value assumptions and implications contained in theoretical discussions of educational issues; (3) in helping the student become aware of contingent conditions which are related to apparently isolated issues; (4) in helping the student recognize the extent to which some educational problems are in fact unique and *not* directly related to basic philosophical considerations; (5) in leading the student to a conception of his role and responsibility as a decision-maker; and (6) in leading the student to develop a consistent but tentative body of beliefs and principles which can serve as an anchor-ledge for his professional decisions.

The Course in the Philosophy of Education for Teachers

We can now turn to a discussion of the aims of a course in the philosophy of education functioning as a component in a program of teacher preparation. The postulation of these aims rests on our previous analysis of the discipline of philosophy, the field of education, the relation between philosophy of education and the other disciplined modes of inquiry into the field, and the future teacher's role. In general it may be stated that the aim of such a course is to use the methods of philosophy in order to explore problems central to the teacher's role, and to develop those understandings which will enable him to make more informed decisions within his area of responsibility.

There is a wide range of problems that confront the teacher. These problems have varying degrees of relevance to his essential role as a practitioner. Problems most directly related to this role are those which deal with teaching *per se* (What is subject matter? What is the relation between method and aim?). Another cluster of problems concerns issues which are directly related to teaching theory and practice but more general in character (What is curriculum? Why are some subjects more valuable than others?). These issues cut across a wider area of teacher responsibility. A third category of problems relates to the role of the teacher as an educator who is responsible for informed opinions, if not decisions, on issues of a still more general nature (What is the proper function of education in a free society? What are desirable and justifiable aims for the educational enterprise?). And finally there are basic philosophical issues which underlie many of the problems in each of these categories (How are values justified? What do theories of knowledge imply for methods of teaching? Do theories of democracy dictate educational aims?).

These problems are listed in order of relevance to the teacher's role as a practitioner. The latter problems are related less directly to that role but nevertheless highly relevant to a thorough consideration of problems of the first sort. These issues must be treated in a course in the philosophy of education because they are *logically* relevant to a proper understanding of practical issues, although to the student they may seem abstract, general, and unrelated to day-to-day teaching problems. The line of cognition in Plato's *Republic* distinguishes modes of understanding that are relevant to analyses of types of knowledge. These in turn can be helpful in formulating broad aims for education that control the objectives of instruction. This study of the line is not directly relevant, but ultimately relevant to practical teaching problems. Rousseau's philosophy is, superficially, the most impractical directive in the history of education, but his analysis of freedom and discipline, and the state and the individual, is relevant to the concerns of many teachers because these concepts are basic to their formulation of educational policy.

The major objective of the philosophy of education, then, is to help the teacher to make informed decisions within his proper area of responsibility and to evaluate his practice and the theory that underlies it. It remains to discuss the means for accomplishing this objective. A major aspect of the method of a course is the choice of material to be presented and studied. It is here that we see the intimate relations between the concepts of aim, subject matter, skill, and method. These are all interrelated, and they must be consistent with one another. Nevertheless, an analysis of these factors must proceed by discussing each separately for the purpose of clarity.

If we take the suggested aims of a course in philosophy of education to be valid, we must consider, then, four separate factors: the selection of those *principles*, theories and facts which are to be learned by the students (knowledge); the selection of those *skills* which are to be nurtured; the *organization* of the content of the course; and the *method* by which the material will be presented.

The Selection of Content—Knowledge. There are several bases for choosing the facts, principles, theories, and problems which will serve as the content of the course. Some content is included because it deals with significant contemporary issues that are of concern to the teacher. Its relevance is clear and obvious. One example of this type of content would be an analysis of some of the diverse factors that are involved in defining an "educative experience." It would involve the presentation of various definitions of "education," and several basic theories of education and teaching. On the other hand, some content is included, not because of its direct bearing on contemporary issues, but because it is *prerequisite* to an understanding of such issues. Thus a discussion of the relation between fact and value may be necessary to prepare the student for an analysis of educational "needs"—a concept that involves a complex relation between the two. Finally certain material may be chosen because it presents a rich field for interpretation or analysis. In many respects Plato's *Republic* is an outmoded document, irrelevant to our time and our society. Yet the complexity of the problems and the facility of analysis presented make it a model of philosophical investigation of basic educational issues. Its study greatly facilitates subsequent analysis of contemporary issues.

The principal criterion for selecting material to be presented, then, can be stated quite simply. That material should be chosen which will have the widest and deepest application to those problems that are of greatest concern to the teacher. The material must be logically central, and the principles discussed should be basic and axiomatic, affording transfer to a variety of specific issues. In attempting to work out a definition of "education" the student must consider such concepts as purpose, aim, control, and experience. These are notions that are basic to the discussion of unique and practical educational issues. To concentrate on the unique and practical, with its greatly limited application to other problems would be to engage in training in its most narrow sense. It is this type of concentration that has aroused so much criticism of teacher education, because it aims at learning rules of thumb (familiarly called the "bag of tricks") rather than the acquisition of a broad theoretical approach. The aim is an understanding of principles rather than rules. This would suggest that although the course aims at skill in practical decision-making, the content of the course might be highly abstract and theoretical, concentrating on those principles and problems which would have maximum *transferability* to practical areas. Thus Whitehead's provocative discussion of the "rhythms" of education, with all its paradoxes, serves as rich source material.[2] Gilbert Ryle's distinction between "knowing that" and "knowing how" sheds light on a variety of specific educational issues.[3] The material is central. Its applications are wide.

2. A. N. Whitehead, *The Aims of Education and Other Essays* (New York: Mentor Books, New American Library, 1957), pp. 27–40.
3. Gilbert Ryle, *The Concept of Mind* (New York: Barnes and Noble, 1949), pp. 25–35, 40–61.

The sources of material to be presented are various, then, stemming not only from writings on education but also from the classic works from the several academic disciplines. From philosophy, the discussion of theories of knowledge would be imperative. The student should be familiar with the differences in the treatment of the concept of experience in such authors as Plato and Dewey. The contrast between Rousseau and Locke regarding the role of the teacher in defining and inculcating beliefs and attitudes might be an example. But it is necessary to stress that these materials are studied in order to promote philosophical understanding rather than because of their historical or literary significance. Finally, material which presents contemporary educational issues in clear fashion must be included, both to inform the student and to ensure that he can draw relations between abstract theory and contemporary practical problems. The recent criticisms of educational practice by Arthur Bestor, Admiral Rickover, and Paul Woodring are helpful in this regard.

The Selection of Content—Skill. In the final analysis it is skill in philosophical analysis and interpretation which serves as the major aim of a course in the philosophy of education. All other facets of the course—the selection of material, the mode of organization, the method of procedure—are subsidiary to this major objective. Therefore the content selected should not only provide that knowledge necessary for an understanding of philosophical principles, but should also provide an opportunity for analysis and interpretation on the part of the students. The material chosen, then, should demonstrate both the complexity of educational issues and the ordering of that complexity. It should exemplify the presentation of adequate evidence and the use of logical rigor in arriving at justifiable conclusions. It should represent a rigorous study of basic principles and the valid implications which can be derived from them. In short, it should present a rich field for philosophizing which, with proper methodology, can culminate in the students' acquisition of skill in analysis and synthesis.

The body of available material is broad, ranging from statements on the principles of instruction in the secondary school to the logical analysis of such concepts as knowledge, experience, transfer, need, and adjustment, in our modern journals of philosophy, psychology, and sociology. It is unfortunate that the latter have been neglected, for the specialist studies in the disciplines often deal with concepts that are pertinent to the discussion of educational issues. The examples are many. A failure to be clear about the classical philosophic problem of the relations between causality, determinism, and freedom has plagued discussions of modes of instruction appropriate to an educational program that strives for the maximum freedom of its products. A failure to recognize the dangers of invoking the "naturalistic fallacy" of converting *what is* into *what ought to be* often hampers the study of educational aims. The clarification of such concepts as equilibrium, the means-ends relationship, or self-actualization, can be most helpful in eliminating pseudo-problems and clarifying important issues. To acquaint students with these analyses and principles would go a long way in developing their theoretical sophistication.

The Use of Material—Organization. The organization of the material chosen brings together the joint objectives of acquisition of knowledge and skill. A final ordering of the material is subject to a variety of factors, including the level of achievement of the students, the skill of the instructor, the choice of issues which are to be presented, and the specific principles and skills to be learned. The organization of material is, of course, directly related to the method of the course, and hence is dependent upon psychological as well as philosophical considerations. The former will be discussed presently. Here we can point to several logical factors which must be considered as prerequisite to the final organization of the course. These are derived from its aims.

One factor of utmost importance is the necessity for a constant awareness of the relation between knowledge and skill, so that the major aims of the course will be constantly kept in focus.

If the major aim is the acquisition of skill in the analysis, interpretation, and evaluation of educational issues, then problems must be introduced that test for these skills. Knowledge of principles is insufficient. It follows that problems of increasing complexity must be considered so that the student is given the opportunity to sharpen, modify, and refine his skills as the course develops. The organization of the course must turn, then, on this process of refinement and development.

However, it must be noted that this is only one factor among many which must be considered in the organization of material. Other relevant factors may drastically affect the final organization, the most important of which is the development of categories of understanding which are logically prerequisite to the acquisition of skill in analysis. Before students can interpret and criticize they must be aware of the richness and complexity of educational issues. In order to develop acuity in recognizing fallacies in argument, isolated simple examples must often be used in preparation. Material of increasing degrees of complexity must be introduced gradually. These logical considerations are factors that help to dictate the final organization of the course. This means, of course, that the study of problems of immediate or contemporary interest must often be postponed until students are sufficiently knowledgeable to confront them. For example, one of the student's major concerns is to develop a conception of his role. In order to do this properly he must have arrived at important decisions regarding the content of his instruction, the specific aims of his teaching, and their relation to broader educational aims. This suggests that careful study and definition of these concepts is prerequisite to the study of the complex notion of teacher role.

A final consideration in the ordering of material is the need to provide an opportunity for the student to develop justifiable beliefs to guide his decisions as a teacher and educator. The provision of this basis for decision is a major aim, and the course must be organized to provide such an opportunity.

The most important point to be made here is that the teaching of philosophy of education, like all other teaching in which the freedom of the learner is a prime factor, is an art. It is an art which can benefit greatly from the modes of inquiry and principles of understanding that can be derived both from the discipline of the subject and from the principles of psychology. Yet in the final analysis the mode of procedure is determined by a number of factors including not only the aims of the course and the principles of learning, but also the make-up of the class and the skills and preferences of the instructor. The theory underlying teaching informs the instructor's practice, but it does not determine it.

Since the major aim of the course is to develop skill in analysis, an opportunity must be given to practice it in both written and oral form. This implies that classes must be small enough to provide the opportunity for discussion and to allow the instructor to examine specimens of students' written arguments. This is merely one example of the importance of keeping the focus of the course constantly in mind. The major difficulty in courses in the philosophy of education is not in the adequacy of their objectives, but rather in providing a method of organization and procedure which will ensure that the objectives are actually being taught for and tested. It follows that there must be an insistence on open-endedness as well as commitment, on the acquisition of knowledge *and* the development of skill. And all of this demands a knowledge of the students in the course—their backgrounds, limitations, and abilities, so that a healthy tension can be maintained between the specific objectives of the course and the limitations of the students and the instructor.

It is clear that the role of the instructor of philosophy of education is a crucial, responsible, and active one. He must not only be aware of but also responsible for relating the field of philosophy to the practical problems of teaching. Indeed, in his teaching he must *demonstrate* the relation between abstract theory and concrete problems. And all of this must be done without indoctrination, or in any way destroying the freedom of his students, but rather by increasing the opportunity for that freedom. His role, then, is not unlike that which will be assumed by his students when they enter the classroom as teachers.

The teacher of philosophy of education is primarily a teacher of philosophy. Philosophy is his discipline. His field of interest is education. He must be schooled in philosophic techniques, be aware of their application to educational issues, and be interested in the application of these skills to the practical pedagogical problem of teaching students to be teachers. None of these requirements is less important than another in the process of developing a free, creative, and responsible teacher.

CHAPTER V

GEORGE W. GOETHALS:

Psychology for Teachers:
A Consideration of Priorities

At the present time, that which passes in most teacher-training programs as psychology for teachers is an academic and intellectual anachronism. While psychology has been seen for many years as one of the foundations of professional training, it is more often accepted by the student as a requirement than anticipated as a challenge. Whether it has paraded under the title of "educational psychology," "human growth and development," or "psychology for teachers," it has scarcely been a rallying point of intellectual ferment for the person entering teaching. What might be one of the most important incidents in the young teacher's whole intellectual experience usually is a triumph of tedium.

This essay takes as its point of departure the conviction that this situation has developed because of the assumption that there is a field which can be called "educational psychology." Obviously, the refusal to admit the existence of such a discipline represents a minority opinion, if the plethora of texts in educational psychology is taken as a valid criterion. However, within the past decade the idea of training liberal arts graduates to be teachers by way of the M.A.T. programs may be regarded as a decisive departure from tradition if not a major revolution. A similarly critical moment has been reached in the meaning that psychology can have for the potential teacher as contrasted with its traditional role. It is to the creation of this optimal experience that these comments are addressed.

It must be emphasized that what is being discussed is the concept of "optimal experience." In terms of present conceptions of the proper curriculum for teachers, educational psychology in the conventional sense is probably a perfectly harmless experience. While the student is not inspired, neither is he injured. However, to avoid considering what is involved in this optimal experience begs a fundamental question: Given a body of knowledge known as psychology, is there something which this discipline can offer which will be of real meaning to the future teacher? Unless it can be demonstrated that such is indeed the case, it might be better to do away with psychology completely. The future teachers in our schools have a right to expect more than the neutral in any course of study. Whatever they are asked to study must be intellectually challenging and personally replete with meaning. How can psychology for the teacher in training be a challenge rather than a chore, and in what ways can and should it have great personal meaning? To answer these questions requires a digression into some matters of history.

Trends in Teacher Training

In 1956 the author, in collaboration with Dr. Wesley Allinsmith, was asked by the Joint Commission on Mental Illness and Health to prepare a monograph dealing with the ways in which the rapidly expanding field of mental health had influenced the role of the school in American society.[1] In the process of carrying out this task we were struck with the very rapid and important shifts in emphasis that had occurred in teacher training.

At the simplest level of discussion, the past fifty years have been marked by the much cited and often scorned trend toward teachers' taking care of the needs of the "whole child." There was

1. W. Allinsmith and G. W. Goethals, *The Role of the Schools in Mental Health* (New York: Basic Books, 1962). See the chapters on school curriculum and on teacher training.

a consistent and growing emphasis upon the teacher's understanding the child as a person; furthermore, there were myriads of statements to the effect that the good teacher taught children rather than subject matter. To put the matter another way, there began to be a *psychological* priority in teaching.[2] The child came first. Whatever his needs might be, it was up to the teacher to discover and satisfy them. These might be intellectual, or vocational, or even emotional. The highwater mark of this trend is found in the 1950 White House Conference on Education which stated that the goal of education was "a healthy personality for every child." [3]

Quite generally, because this trend coincided with a growing preoccupation with social welfare, it was seen as being "good" and on the side of the angels. To attack openly and publicly something that was designed for the welfare of the child in a democratic society was tantamount to heresy. Until the late 1940's this interest in the welfare of the child remained axiomatic in American education, and teacher training began to reflect this by the inclusion of more and more materials pertaining to child development.

The criticism of this trend came from two quite different directions. One line of attack was that which is personified by the work of Bestor, who equated concern with the child not only with bad teaching but also with the intellectual erosion of American society.[4] These concerns with the child's welfare were seen as "frills" perpetuated in the American school by professional educators who at best seemed to have questionable motives. Another attack came from individuals who were friendly to the field of education but felt that a great mistake was being made in strategy. Because this criticism is extremely thought-provoking in itself, and central to the thesis of this chapter, some consideration in detail is required.

This latter line of criticism is best seen in the comments of David Riesman, Fritz Redl, and Margaret Mead.[5] While their point

2. P. M. Symonds, "Mental Health in the Classroom," *Journal of Social Issues*, XV (1959), 1.

3. Midcentury White House Conference on Children and Youth, *Proceedings* (Raleigh, N.C.: Health Publications Institute, Inc., 1950).

4. A. E. Bestor, *Educational Wastelands* (Urbana: University of Illinois Press, 1953).

5. These three papers, from very different points of view, give an ex-

of emphasis varies somewhat, it is possible to exemplify the theme. They share the conviction that society has changed rapidly in the past fifty years, and our knowledge about human behavior has been radically increased. The typical teacher in trying either to prepare a child for a role in a constantly changing social system, or to bring to bear the "newest and best" knowledge, faces profound frustration. The rapidly shifting social order means that what he teaches about the world one year is out of date the next. The new knowledge makes fiction out of last year's closely held truths. Unable "to keep up" or harassed by what Redl has called "the omnicompetence" demand, the teacher becomes inefficient not only as a master of subject matter, but also as a person who can cope with children on a personal level. The multiplicity of demands, roles, and conflicting expectations leaves the teacher without a plan of action or a philosophy of teaching.

What struck us about these comments was not their validity. This might well be debated. It was instead that in considering this reasoned presentation of a present dilemma, an extremely interesting and seldom-recognized facet of teacher training became clear.

Until relatively recently, teacher training has suggested three possible emphases. The first of these is that a teacher, to be prepared, needs to know his subject and know it well. If he is master of his specialty, he will be able to teach and teach well. A second point of view is that a teacher must be trained in such a way that he can prepare his students for life. Knowledge of a specialized nature is important, but not nearly so important as helping the child to find and effectively act in some social role in his society. The third approach takes a number of different forms but its central theme or core is the conviction that whether one is preparing the child to

---

cellent perspective to the problems of the teacher's role in contemporary society:

a. D. Riesman, "Teachers Amid Changing Expectations," *Harvard Educational Review*, XXIV (1954), 106.

b. F. Redl, "What Do We Expect of Our Teachers?" *Conference Proceedings* (New York: Bank Street College of Education, 1954).

c. Margaret Mead, *The School in American Culture* (Cambridge: Harvard University Press, 1959). The Inglis Lecture for 1950 was delivered by Margaret Mead on March 15 at Harvard University.

master intellectual skills, to find a vocation, or to understand his culture, the most important thing that can go into the training of a teacher is more and more content concerning child development. Knowledge of the child solves all problems.

At first glance, putting aside superficial prejudice, any one of these three approaches seems reasonable. In a benign way they are all concerned with aspects of the child's welfare. But a second look will reveal one thread of thought suggested by the comments of Riesman, Redl, and Mead. While it may be possible with a certain amount of inner security to feel that one has adequately mastered one's subject-matter field, it is not possible to feel equally secure about the world, which is constantly changing, and the knowledge that is constantly growing about the development of the child. While it is difficult to keep up with the best that is new in any branch of a subject, it is not an impossibility. High school courses, regardless of the sophistication that goes into their creation, are finite; however, the possibilities that exist about the social order and about the "best knowledge" relating to children are infinite. This is due to the dynamic nature of a technological social system and a field that is constantly generating new research.

Educational psychology therefore has tended to sensitize students to the vast fund of knowledge that is available without giving them any criteria for selecting what is most salient. Apathy develops because the student has no way of coping with an ever-increasing mass of detail, which he is usually told will be even more prolix in the near future. Not only are criteria of selection from the field of psychology itself left in a vague state, but also the uses of research findings in the classroom itself are left in limbo. The student turns away from his attempts to understand the child and assess his culture and falls into an increasing ambiguity.

In the consideration of teacher training programs and their relation to the mental health of the students, it was found that one very important departure, aimed at doing away with this kind of overwhelming ambiguity, lay in teacher training which would give as much attention to the psychology of the teacher as to the psychology of the child. In the most general terms, the proposition was that the better the mental health of the teacher, the better would be the mental health of the pupils in his charge. To put the matter another way, knowledge of the processes of personality remain fairly abstract when its dynamics are discussed in the abstract or when they are projected onto the child; however, when they are part of the experience of the teacher in training, priorities become established and order restored to what previously had been a chaos of general information about behavior.

When Allinsmith and Goethals originally considered this fourth approach to teacher training, their point of departure was to assess the way this practice in teacher education would, in the long run, affect the mental health and emotional stability of the child in the classroom. Their general conclusion was that the more integrated an individual teacher became, the more positive would be the effect he would have on his pupils. A corollary to this which may be even more important is that concern for the teacher's functioning at maximum level provides a way of establishing guidelines about what psychology can mean to the teacher in training generally, and more specifically to those aspects of psychology which are most relevant. In order to understand these emerging criteria of selection and inclusion, some matters pertaining to this history of psychology require attention.

Psychology and "The Third Revolution"

In 1948 Robert S. Woodworth published a revised edition of his classic *Contemporary Schools of Psychology*. This cogent little book, originally published in 1931, remains one of the clearest and most concise pictures of the history of psychology. It is of symbolic importance that when Woodworth presented his revised edition to the public he did not change two very important observations.

The first of these was that behaviorism, originating in America, and Gestalt psychology, originating in Germany, had their beginnings in the same year, 1912. Further, that all the threads that made up modern psychology were enunciated as themes between 1898 and 1912. Woodworth explains this revolution within psychology as the second important one in its history, the first being the influence of the physics of Galileo's time. This later revolution he feels was a consequence of the advances in analytic chemistry and the great strides made in physiology during the nineteenth century.

Woodworth's second observation was that taking into account all that had come about since this fertile decade and a half, no new schools of psychology had arisen either in Europe or America since 1912. Therefore, the themes and threads brought forth around the turn of the century at this moment of intellectual revolution both stimulated and delimited the scope of contemporary psychology.

It is always fascinating to speculate, from the historical point of view, what "might have been." It is a serious question whether Woodworth, whose perceptive scholarship has been demonstrated in many works, would have held to this latter statement if he had published his revised book five years later. For 1949 marked the start of another revolution in psychological thinking as dramatic as the one at the turn of the century. The components of this dramatic shift may be outlined in the following manner:

> The presentation by D. O. Hebb of McGill University of *The Organization of Behavior: A Neuropsychological Theory* in 1949.
> The publication by Erik H. Erikson of a collection of his papers pertaining to personality development under the title *Childhood and Society* in 1950.
> The publication in London by Nicholas Tinbergen of *The Study of Instincts* in 1951.
> The publication, also in London, of *King Solomon's Ring*, by Konrad Lorenz in 1952.
> The publication by John W. M. Whiting and Irvin L. Child of their cross-cultural research entitled *Child Training and Personality* in 1953.
> The meeting of the first Nebraska Symposium on Motivation and the publication of that proceeding in 1953. This symposium has continued to meet and publish its proceedings each successive year.
> The publication of the *Handbook of Social Psychology*, edited by Gardner Lindzey, in 1954.
> The publication in the *Harvard Educational Review* of an article by B. F. Skinner entitled "The Science of Learning and The Art of Teaching," in 1954.[6]

6. Robert S. Woodworth, *Contemporary Schools of Psychology* (New York: Ronald Press, 1948). The discussion by Woodworth is to be found in the first ten pages of his book. Proper citation of the newer works will follow as each is analyzed.

When Woodworth discussed the formation of contemporary schools, it will be remembered that he emphasized that psychology was markedly influenced by developments in other fields of science. The existence of new methods created radical rethinking about the kind of problems psychology as a science could attack. It might be stated that this was a revolution of method.

The revolution between 1949 and 1954 to which we have alluded is an upheaval of an entirely different kind. It is much more subtle and in many ways much more complex. If the earlier upheaval can be called one of method, this recent one may be called one of priority and salience. This is suggested in part by the fact that Woodworth talked about the formation of *schools* of psychology during a fifteen-year period, whereas this present list focuses upon *publications*. All of these works, however, accomplish one of two things: first, they may take a theme from existing knowledge and carry it through to its ultimate synthesis; or, second, they may with some new insight radically reorganize a fund of existing knowledge so that its priorities completely change. Quite obviously some of these contributions accomplish both.

The reason that most courses in educational psychology have become anachronistic is that they have failed to take into account either the shifts in teacher training or the new priorities within psychology. They have remained contemporary in that they have exposed the student to many of the ideas which would properly fall within the spectrum of psychology that Woodworth has defined as "modern," but they have not taken into account the issue of content saliency.

Psychology and Teacher Training

In the previous two sections I have suggested that in both teacher training and psychology there have been some shifts of emphasis or priority. While at first it may seem that these two changes have little in common, a careful second look reveals otherwise.

Teacher training for a time seemed to view the beginner as a kind of "empty organism" into which knowledge of various kinds was infused. As the general task of the school became broader, more and more information of various kinds—particularly that pertaining to the child's welfare—seemed necessary for the beginning teacher. A point was reached where many felt the teacher was being asked to try to master far too much knowledge for far too many roles, and a retrenchment was suggested. The teacher is now seen as a very alive person rather than as a void that required filling—an alive person who could best understand the psychological issues in another person's life if he had mastered these same issues in his own.

The discipline of psychology, particularly in the early 1940's, found itself possessed of a tremendous amount of empirical data pertaining to every aspect of behavior. The rich store was a consequence of two factors: first, of the great amount of psychological research generated during the Second World War, and second, of the availability to the competent research psychologist of many new sources of funds to execute further investigations. Data proceeded to build upon data. It was not until the last years of the 1940's and the early 1950's that the psychologist took the time to assess what all these data meant, how they were related, and what they suggested in terms of unified theory.

The link between teacher training and psychology, the situation which they had in common, was that they were possessed of weapons but had no strategy. The psychologist had more and more data which were not seen in perspective. The person training teachers saw an infinite amount of information available, all of which might be "good" for the trainee. Both fields were forced, paradoxically because of the richness of their resource, to take a hard second look at themselves. Making the teacher the focus of teacher training and reassessing the priorities of knowledge—both were aspects of the same phenomena. Both have elements of the revolutionary. Unfortunately there has been a minimum of communication between the psychologist and those concerned with the training of teachers. Therefore, both are inclined to be myopic about the other. The psychologist is usually very naïve about the new trends in teacher training and their implications. The trainer of teachers often assumes that what psychology has to offer him is still a mass of interesting but somehow rarified information. When this communication can be made more open, then it will be possible to have the trainee approximate what has been called earlier the "optimal experience." It is my hope that this essay can help to establish some lines of communication to bring this about. This will be accomplished by considering the meaning that these eight publications have not only for psychology as a discipline, but also, by extension, for the teacher in training.

It is extremely important that one matter be recognized as this is begun. While I believe that these publications either are classics or represent the most important trends at the present for a person considering the place of psychology in the training of a teacher, they are offered at the level of the strategic or the salient, rather than of the curricular. It is my firm opinion that any course of study in psychology for teachers which ignores these trends is largely a waste of time. However, the way in which these trends can be translated into a course of study are many. The range of priority will differ from person to person. The essential point is not an orthodox curriculum of study in psychology, but the development of priorities which can be used to determine a variety of curricula which will have impact upon the teacher in training, which include information that will be retained longest, and which have over time the most salutary effect upon both the teacher himself and the child in the classroom.

The article by B. F. Skinner in 1954 is the last in the chronology of revolution. It is treated first because it both carries on a tradition, that of rigorous laboratory behaviorism, and makes radical suggestions about the role of the teacher in the instruction of the child. Skinner's central thesis is that it is not possible for the teacher in the typical classroom to reinforce, or "shape," the behaviors that he feels are desirable. Therefore, the amount of learning that could be accomplished in any period of time is but a fraction of that which is possible. Skinner feels that the solution to this problem, at a time when this condition is being made more acute by greater numbers of students, is for the teacher to employ mechanical aids such as teaching machines. When this proposal was made, Skinner was well aware of the objections which would be taken to his proposal; and his rebuttal speaks for itself: [7]

> Some objections to the use of such devices in the classroom can easily be foreseen. The cry will be raised that the child is being treated as a mere animal and that an essentially human intellectual achievement is being analyzed in unduly mechanistic terms. Mathematical behavior is usually regarded, not as a repertoire of responses involving numbers and numerical operations, but as evidences of mathematical ability or the exercise of the power of reason. It is true that the techniques which are emerging from the experimental study of learning are not designed to "develop the mind" or to further some vague "understanding" of mathematical relationships. They are designed, on the contrary, to establish the very behaviors which are taken to be the evidences of such mental states or processes. This is only a special case of the general change which is under way in the interpretation of human affairs. An advancing science continues to offer more and more convincing alternatives to traditional formulations. The behavior in terms of which human thinking must eventually be defined is worth treating in its own right as the substantial goal of education.
>
> Of course the teacher has a more important function than to say right or wrong. The changes proposed would free her for the effective exercise of that function. Marking a set of papers in arithmetic— "Yes, nine and six *are* fifteen; no, nine and seven *are not* eighteen" —is beneath the dignity of any intelligent individual. There is more important work to be done—in which the teacher's relations to the pupil cannot be duplicated by a mechanical device. Instrumental help would merely improve these relations. One might say that the main trouble with education in the lower grades today is that the child is obviously not competent and *knows it* and that the teacher is unable to do anything about it and *knows that too.* If the advances which have recently been made in our control of behavior can give the child a genuine competence in reading, writing, spelling, and arithmetic, then the teacher may begin to function, not in lieu of a cheap machine, but through intellectual, cultural, and emotional contacts of that distinctive sort which testify to her status as a human being.

7. B. F. Skinner, "The Science of Learning and the Art of Teaching," *Harvard Education Review,* XXIV (1954), 86; reprinted by permission. For a full treatment of the teaching machine issue see D. Porter, "A Critical Review of a Portion of the Literature on Teaching Devices," *Harvard Educational Review,* XXVII (1957), 126.

There is a simple job to be done. The task can be stated in concrete terms. The necessary techniques are known. The equipment needed can easily be provided. Nothing stands in the way but cultural inertia. But what is more characteristic of America than an unwillingness to accept the traditional as inevitable? We are on the threshold of an exciting and revolutionary period, in which the scientific study of man will be put to work in man's best interests. Education must play its part. It must accept the fact that a sweeping revision of educational practices is possible and inevitable. When it has done this, we may look forward with confidence to a school system which is aware of the nature of its tasks, secure in its methods, and generously supported by the informed and effective citizens whom education itself will create.

Now the interest in teaching machines, or what is often called "programmed instruction," has probably far surpassed even Skinner's fondest hopes.[8] However, there is a question raised in this situation that goes far beyond the existence of this new vogue. The query may be asked in a number of ways, but in essence it is this: How and why did Skinner get away with it?

The question is only partially facetious. Periodically, laboratory psychologists have been asked by those concerned with professional education to translate their laboratory findings in the classroom. While these requests have often been honored, the translation is usually extremely forced. The educator comes away with the feeling that the "psychology of learning" in a formal sense has little use in the class.[9]

Why then did Skinner, as hardheaded an empiricist as can be found in the ranks of American psychology, meet with such success? The explanation seems to lie in certain factors relating to Skinner's position generally and to a realization that developed once this position was understood. Skinner has always held that it was

8. A. A. Lumsdaine and R. Glaser, eds., *Teaching Machines and Programmed Learning: A Source Book* (Washington, D.C.: National Educational Association, 1960).

9. Probably the closest success in this direction is the 41st Year of the National Society for the Study of Education. Even in this very interesting monograph under the chairmanship of T. R. McConnell the issue seems forced. "The Psychology of Learning," *Yearbook of the National Society for the Study of Education* (1942), 41, Part II.

premature at the present state of knowledge to make claims for a theory of learning.[10] Instead, he has insisted that research be directed to the way in which behavior can be made to vary under different conditions of reinforcement. This way of looking at things openly permitted *behavior* in the classroom to be considered, rather than some laboratory orthodoxy of *learning*. Paradoxically, because Skinner did not present a learning theory, his ideas about learning were more easily accepted. He did not ask the teacher to think about learning in the abstract; instead he asked that behavior be considered with care and precision. This, however, is but part of the story.

The most important matter that is involved here psychologically is that by its very nature Skinner's stance was, in and of itself, permeated with the strategic attitude: something is manipulated to cause a change in something else. As this attitude became clear to the person interested in educational research, a startling fact became obvious. This was that the process of learning, in a broad sense, was not necessarily the same thing as the psychological manipulation of instructional materials. Skinner's work provided a scientific basis for the construction of a curriculum, particularly in the so-called "skill" subjects. It opened the way to a science of instruction closely related to the research of the laboratory. It suggested that the active process of instructing someone might be on a quite different continuum from the more general question of how and why the student learns.

The most valuable contribution that any scientific undertaking can produce over and above its "results" are its implications for division of labor. Skinner was not only suggesting a technology of instruction, he was also clarifying and making more efficient the role of the teacher. The teacher was to be supplemented by the machine, not replaced by it. The psychologist in turn has before him a clear and specific mandate as to his role in relation to education: the careful programming of materials so that optimal learning can take place.

If the work of Skinner suggests a psychology of instruction

10. B. F. Skinner, "Are Theories of Learning Necessary?" *Psychological Review*, LVII (1950), 193.

which can make a bridge between the classroom and the laboratory, the work of Donald Hebb is extremely provocative in its discussion of the way learning capacity develops generally. While Hebb's work is in some ways speculative, it is a classic in the sense that it attacks the "why" of theories of learning from a direction entirely different from Skinner's.

In terms of learning, Hebb's book raises a question that has concerned psychologists and social scientists for many decades, and will probably concern them for years to come. This is the degree to which the behavior of any animal is *species specific*. Can we, given data collected in the laboratory on infrahuman animals, extrapolate from them theories about the human being? [11] To put the matter another way, is man's learning on the same continuum as that of the rat or the pigeon?

Hebb's answer to this question, which is fundamental to anyone who is going to be involved in teaching, is extremely subtle since it both supports and rejects the concept of animal data. Hebb supports the notion of animal study with vigor, not only in this book but in a later article written with W. R. Thompson.[12] However, his support of animal data is somewhat sardonic and antithetical to the usual. Hebb would employ data, particularly on various levels of mammals, to show systematically the way in which behavior of primates is profoundly different from that of the lower animals. True, the same principles, such as reinforcement, may be involved; but their salience to behavior may differ greatly from species to species. Thus there may be common elements in behavior, but they are subject to modification in a particular species.[13]

Hebb maintains this position by a careful reassessment of knowl-

11. F. A. Beach, "Experimental Investigations of Species Specific Behavior," *American Psychologist*, XV (1960), 1. This is an extremely fine summary of the problem with an excellent bibliography. It is useful not only in understanding this issue as it applies to Hebb, but also as it applies to the ethologists who are also discussed in this chapter.

12. D. O. Hebb and W. R. Thompson, "The Social Significance of Animal Studies," *Handbook of Social Psychology*, ed. Gardner Lindzey (Cambridge: Addison-Wesley, 1954), p. 532.

13. C. S. Ford and F. A. Beach, *Patterns of Sexual Behavior* (New York: Harper and Brothers, 1951). The work of Beach and Ford is important in that it raises the question not only of species differences in learning but also

edge from neurology and comparative psychology. He feels that what is involved in learning something cannot be separated from a consideration of the structure of the central nervous system. This structure not only sets the limits of what can be learned—scarcely a new idea—but the speed and manner in which it is learned, in Hebb's theory a revolutionary discussion indeed: [14]

> But, for widely differing phylogenetic levels, a hierarchy of "intelligence" (or psychological complexity: McBride and Hebb, 1948) can be assumed, which corresponds to gross differences (1) in size of the cerebrum, or (2) in the proportion of afferent to internuncial neural tissues. In the lower vertebrates, the cerebrum is small, and the afferent systems are massive in comparison with the internuncial. Within the mammalian series, there are differences both of absolute and relative size of association cortex which may be assumed (in the total absence of any exact data) to have a relevance to the greater speed with which the "lower" species can learn to respond selectively to the environment, and to the comparative simplicity of the behavior when it is fully developed.
>
> These anatomical considerations draw attention to another point. The learning ability of higher species at maturity is not merely the capacity for a greater number of associations or for associations that involve finer sensory discriminations. The behavior also shows a less direct control by the stimulus of the moment, from the immediate environment. In larger association areas the central phase sequence can be more complex: it must still be organized and ultimately controlled by the relatively smaller sensory projection areas, but the phase sequence can escape the direct control more frequently and for longer periods. The possession of large association areas is an explanation both of the astonishing inefficiency of man's first learning, as far as immediate results are concerned, and his equally astonishing efficiency at maturity.

For the classroom teacher this idea of *two* stages being involved in the learning process, particularly when the human being is concerned, has a central value. While we have often criticized in psychology the tendency to anthropomorphize behavior, Hebb's work

the way in which higher animals in particular may have to learn most, if not all, of their behavior. This raises the further issue of whether the higher primates, including man, have to "learn how to learn."

14. Reprinted by permission from D. O. Hebb, *The Organization of Behavior*, copyright © 1949 John Wiley & Sons, Inc., New York. (Note in particular Chapters Six and Seven.)

may help the teacher to avoid "adultomorphizing" the learning of his students. Human learning, particularly of new material, is agonizingly slow.

Probably the most thought-provoking conceptions developed by Hebb have to do with his discussion of the intimate relationship between learning, the perceptual capacities of the organism, and motivational structure. These should be read and pondered by any person who has the sublime arrogance to try to teach another. Two of these ideas require comment even in an overview such as this.

The first of these is the discussion of what all teachers are concerned with, namely, "set" learning. That is, learning that requires the attention of the student. Hebb points out that *attention* is a very complex phenomenon involving a transaction on the part of the organism between his internal physiological structure and the perceptual input from the environment. If these ideas were included in the training of teachers, "holding the class" would be a much less mysterious matter.

The second of these ideas is Hebb's careful discussion of what it means for man to be an emotional animal. The place that emotions play in human beings is not discussed here in the usual psychoanalytic framework, but rather from the point of view which suggests that man has the capacity for profound irritability or reaction potential. The implications of this emotional dimension both socially and developmentally are central for thinking about factors that can effect learning within the classroom.[15]

The work of Tinbergen and Lorenz, while related to some of the ideas Hebb discusses—particularly those pertaining to species differences—is included for additional reasons. The ethologist has aroused some questions which in many ways are as central as those suggested by the problem of species-specific behavior. One series of questions focuses on problems of methodology; another, on the dynamics of learning.

The ethologist has been insistent that the behavior of any or-

15. D. C. McClelland, J. W. Atkinson, R. A. Clark, and E. L. Lowell, *The Achievement Motive* (New York: Appleton-Century-Crofts, 1953). The second chapter of this book provides a very detailed discussion of the intimate relationship between emotion and motivation. It further suggests the fact that all motives, particularly in higher animals, are learned.

ganism be studied under conditions which are as close to its natural habitat as possible. He postulates that any given animal is uniquely equipped to cope with its natural surroundings and the only way to make any reliable comments about its behavior is as a consequence of field observation.[16] If the animal is taken into the laboratory, only a portion of the behavior can be observed because the stimulus configuration is so very different; in fact, serious errors in conclusion can be made.[17] This information parallels the interest in American psychology in the effect that observation itself has upon a subject.[18] For the teacher in training, it raises the question of how much he really knows about the behavior of a child; to what extent is the behavior of the student in the classroom a valid representation of the student as a person. Teachers sometimes tend to feel omniscient concerning their students, and this material can help to make them somewhat more conservative.

The aspect of Lorenz and Tinbergen that is most arresting, however, concerns their discussion of an aspect of learning or, more properly, a dynamic pertaining to learning. This is their exegesis of critical phases and of imprinting. In their work with animals, Lorenz and Tinbergen found that during an animal's life cycle there seemed to be periods of time when it could, optimally, learn a particular behavior. If this behavior was not learned at that time, one of two things could occur: first, the animal might learn a completely inappropriate response, such as learning to follow a human rather than his own group; second, once this time had passed it was impossible, later, for the animal to incorporate the behavior into his repertory of responses.[19]

16. N. Tinbergen, *The Study of Instincts* (Oxford: University Press, 1951). And K. Lorenz, *King Solomon's Ring* (London: Methuen, 1952).

17. Carpenter, C. R., "Field Study in Siam of the Behavior and Social Relations of the Gibbon (Hylobates Lar)," *Comparative Psychology Monographs*, XVI, No. 5 (December, 1940). Also by Carpenter: "Characteristics of Social Behavior in Non-Human Primates," *Transactions of the New York Academy of Sciences*, Series II, IV, No. 8 (1942), 25.

18. The so-called "stimulus value of observation," also known as the Hawthorne effect, has been discussed by industrial psychologists in particular.

19. See J. M. S. Itard, *The Wild Boy of Aveyron* (New York: Century, 1932); Itard's original report was completed in 1806, and was sent to the French Minister of the Interior. Also J. A. L. Singh and R. M. Zingg, *Wolf-*

Hebb, in his discussion of von Senden's cataract patients, shows the profound difficulty that can occur for man if his sequence of learning is thrown "out of phase" even when the task is very simple.[20] As suggested above, probably the most dramatic material available is that which pertains to feral children. However, the most important meaning of these data from the ethologist is the perspective that they may give to the Freudian theory of the neurosis. The psychosexual stages of development, the vicissitudes attendant during their course, the dynamics of regression and inappropriate fixation, all imply something that is very close to the notion of the critical period.[21] Thus Lorenz and Tinbergen's work is linked to some nuclear problems in learning, and also to some of the central assumptions of psychoanalysis.

The final conceptualization that Lorenz and Tinbergen both put forth is, like much of Hebb, important philosophically as well as psychologically. Man tends to assume that he stands at the apex of a Darwinian order of things. Too often this is equated with naïve notions about simplicity and complexity. What the ethologist places before us in this connection is the fact that both man and the lower animals can have extremely complex behaviors but with very different wellsprings and social implications. The lower animal can have, as a consequence of highly developed patterns of instinctive behavior, extremely complex responses which appear to be almost unlearned. Social problems are "automatically" solved. Initial learning is instantaneous and probably painless. Yet these patterns, despite their complexity, have almost no flexibility. Man on the other hand has to learn almost all, if not all, of his behavior. This means great effort and frustration in relation to primary learnings. Once this has been accomplished the variability and creative insight of man can find new solutions to myriads of problems. Yet man is left with his

children and Feral Man (New York: Harper and Brothers, 1939); and W. Dennis, "The Significance of Feral Man," *American Journal of Psychology,* LIV (1941), 425.

20. D. O. Hebb, *The Organization of Behavior,* pp. 111–112.

21. World Health Organization Study Group on the Psychobiological Development of the Child, *Discussions on Child Development,* ed. J. M. Tanner and Bärbel Inhelder (New York: International Universities Press), Vols. I, II, III (1958).

emotions, an evolutionary anachronism which often makes him ignore that which he has learned. Man is a prisoner of the flexibility of his learning; the lower animal a prisoner of his rigid patterns of response. Both are complex, but for very different reasons. Man and the ant have equally complex societies, but they operate out of dynamics which are antithetical. Lorenz and Tinbergen force the beginning teacher to ask searching questions about the nature of complexity, both personal and social.

It was mentioned that with the notion of the critical period a bridge was built by the ethologist to psychoanalysis as well as to learning. It is to the former that I wish now to turn, through a consideration of the work of Erik Erikson.[22] Erikson sees himself and his work in a novel perspective:

> One may scan work after work on history, society, and morality and find little reference to the fact that all people start as children and that all peoples begin in their nurseries. It is human to have a long childhood; it is civilized to have an ever longer childhood. Long childhood makes a technical and mental virtuoso out of man, but it also leaves a lifelong residue of emotional immaturity in him. While tribes and nations, in many intuitive ways, use child training to the end of gaining their particular form of mature human identity, their unique version of integrity, they are, and remain, beset by the irrational fears which stem from the very state of childhood which they exploited in their specific way.
>
> What can a clinician know about this? I think that the psychoanalytic method is essentially a historical method. Even where it focuses on medical data, it interprets them as a function of past experience. To say that psychoanalysis studies the conflict between the mature and the infantile, the up-to-date and the archaic layers in the mind, means that psychoanalysis studies psychological evolution through the analysis of the individual. At the same time it throws light on the fact that the history of humanity is a gigantic metabolism of individual life cycles.
>
> I would like to say, then, that this is a book on historical processes. Yet the psychoanalyst is an odd, maybe a new kind of historian: in committing himself to influencing what he observes, he becomes part of the historical process which he studies. As a therapist, he must be aware of his own reaction to the observed: his "equations" as an ob-

22. Reprinted by permission from Erik H. Erikson, *Childhood and Society,* copyright © 1950 W. W. Norton & Company, Inc., New York.

server become his very instruments of observation. Therefore, neither terminological alignment with the more objective sciences nor dignified detachment from the clamoring of the day can and should keep the psychoanalytic method from being what H. S. Sullivan called "participant," and systematically so.

While other psychoanalysts have seen an analogue to the historical process in the study of the clinical case, none has seen himself so pungently as Erikson as being influenced by it and a part of it at the same time. Often one projects an image of the social scientist as beyond influence, an objective landmark in the confusion of technological complexity. Erikson will have none of this. As the child and his parents are, for better or worse, influenced by cultural pressures—which after all are part of this same historical process—Erikson sees his relationship to his patients, his work, and his theoretical convictions as a personification of the inevitability of history. Erikson is not merely a contributor to knowledge; he is a participant in the actions of his time, which are the data of knowledge.

Earlier, I made the remark that Skinner's work was of value to the educator or the person concerned with teacher training because it took a stance which suggested the strategic pose. Over and beyond the intellectual value of his work was a way of viewing the world, a *Weltanschauung*. Erikson too suggests a view of the world and by implication a way of calculating one's relationship to it. Here is no plea for quiescence or the easy solution; instead there is the commitment to the ultimate participant relationship to a world in flux. If Erikson had made no contribution to theory, which he has, if he had offered no ideas about method, which he does, his ideas would be valuable simply for the aid they give an individual in estimating his role behavior or, in Jung's terms, his possible actualization and personification in present society.

From the point of view of theory, Erikson represents a synthesis.[23] He is the embodiment of those who were profoundly influenced by Freud's insights but not blind to his shortcomings. In the course of his work he has tried to show how man's personality

23. D. Rapaport, "A Historical Survey of Psychoanalytic Ego Psychology," introduction to Erik H. Erikson, *Identity and the Life Cycle: Selected Papers* (New York: International Universities Press, 1959), pp. 5–17.

is an intricate balance of the somatic, the cultural, and ego organization. Unlike Freud he has refrained from defining integrated personality in terms of a unitary consideration. While the ego is important, man's integration is a complex balance not only of the factors mentioned above but of accidents of personal history and momentary situation, which can make any one of these primary in its influence.[24] This suggests to a person working with others that the organization of personality is a fluid situation open to determination by a variety of sources which may range from the personal to the purely physical.

While Erikson's inclusion of cultural factors as determinants of personality structure was a common revision of orthodox Freudian theory, there are two other ideas upon which only Erikson has elaborated to any extent. First, Erikson insisted that the development of personality was not, as Freud had suggested, largely determined early in life. An individual's identity was something which was open to modification throughout his total life cycle. Second, and even more important, this development was carried out not only in relation to the culture generally, but also specifically in relation to *significant other persons.*[25] Therefore at times parents, peers, teachers, lovers, and one's own children could be relatively more or less significant.

These conceptions make psychoanalytic theory alive for the person who is in teaching. The darkness of Freud's concern with pathology is replaced by a lyric sense of the communality of man and the ways in which people can influence each other both for good and bad. Even more important, by discussing the total life cycle, the teacher can have a fairly realistic idea of the problems the child faces at different ages, from early childhood through adolescence, and can thus assess the role which it may be best to adopt.

However, as stimulating as these issues may be, they are largely

24. See Erikson, *op. cit.*, pp. 19–43.

25. E. H. Erikson, *Identity and the Life Cycle: Selected Papers* (New York: International Universities Press, 1959). See also: H. S. Sullivan, *The Interpersonal Theory of Psychiatry*, ed. Helen Swick Perry and Mary Ladd Gawel (New York: W. W. Norton, 1953).

academic. They are important in the sense that they provide a version of psychoanalytic personality theory which, while highly sophisticated, is clear and comprehensible to the beginning student. But the most important element in Erikson's theory is the way in which his thinking accomplishes one of the goals suggested early in this paper: that is, to make psychological issues part of the student's personal experience. How this comes about is best suggested by a statement from Erikson himself: [26]

> I know very well that this shift in conceptual emphasis is dictated by historical accident—i.e., by the revolutions that are taking place in our lifetime, affecting our personal fortunes as well as the symptoms presented and the unconscious demands made on us by our patients. To condense it into a formula: the patient of today suffers most under the problem of what he should believe in and who he should—or, indeed, might—be or become; while the patient of early psychoanalysis suffered most under inhibitions which prevented him from being what and who he thought he knew he was. In this country especially, adult patients and the parents of prospective child patients hope to find in the psychoanalytic system a refuge from the discontinuities of existence, a regression and a return to a more patriarchal one-to-one relationship. . . . The study of identity, then, becomes as strategic in our time as the study of sexuality was in Freud's time.

This statement not only gives the teacher in training an insight into the central shift in psychoanalytic theory, but even more important, it suggests that his own life cycle, the child he is teaching, and the culture as a whole are bound together in a common task which is the search for identity in a personal and historical framework. To suggest that this observation relieves the teacher's anxiety misses the mark. It may well increase it. But at least it makes clear what there is to fear and in the process it dissipates the cloud of ambiguity. The teacher, by seeing his place in history, can begin to act in such a way as to introduce control into that history.

The meaning that the work of Whiting and Child, Lindzey, and the various symposia on motivation can have for the beginning teacher is of an entirely different kind from that of the materials

26. E. H. Erikson, *Childhood and Society*, pp. 239ff.

discussed so far. Lindzey's handbook is not read. It is consulted. But in consulting it the student can become aware of how the slow work of research proceeds to test theory. Also, in reviewing the work of various specialists, he can see the way in which the field of psychology is not a neatly delimited discipline at the present time; but, in the best sense of the word, a social science which draws from a variety of sources. The papers of the Nebraska Symposium, which are highly technical, when taken in perspective show the way in which theory is slowly and painfully generated. Whiting and Child exemplify not only research, but the way in which problems as elusive as the values a person internalizes may be subjected to rigorous test.[27] Less space has been given to these works, not because they have had little influence, but because they are more technical and therefore can be considered supplemental to the works here treated in more detail.

The Teacher and Psychology

The person who takes the responsibility of teaching psychology to one who in his own right is going to teach has a finite amount of time in which to organize an infinite amount of material. I have tried to suggest criteria that may help to determine what could be taught. It is my conviction that a knowledge of the areas that have been suggested will make psychology a more rewarding experience for the person in training. It will be noted that I have included both the speculative and the rigorously scientific, the humane and the objective.

It is somewhat of a contradiction to end a paper or an article with the idea which was its true genesis. Yet in this case I feel it is appropriate. Margaret Mead, who occasionally can come very close to wisdom in the midst of her many writings, once summed up our problem today more succinctly and in a sense more opera-

27. For supplementary information, read in: Judson S. Brown *et al., Current Theory and Research in Motivation: A Symposium* (Lincoln, Nebraska: University of Nebraska Press, 1953); J. W. M. Whiting, and I. L. Child, *Child Training and Personality: A Cross-Cultural Study* (New Haven: Yale University Press, 1953), G. W. Allport *et al., Theory and Method,* Vol. I of the *Handbook of Social Psychology* (Cambridge: Addison-Wesley, 1954).

tionally than anyone else: "We need to teach our students how to think, when you don't know what method to use, about a problem which is not yet formulated." [28] It is to that end that I see psychology having a place in the training of teachers.

28. Margaret Mead, *The School in American Culture* (Cambridge: Harvard University Press, 1959).

THE EDUCATION OF THE SCHOLAR-TEACHER

CHAPTER VI

GERALDINE MURPHY:

The Teacher of English

EVERY now and then in ordinary conversation, we use some word that doesn't say what we wanted to say. We know, because our listener doesn't respond violently enough—or he responds too violently! We try again and a look of surprised disgust tells us that at last we've produced the effect we wanted.

We are constantly "trying out" words in this fashion. As children we would not let people "put words in our mouths." We tried hard to make words express our little ideas. Now when we write letters, we have many "second thoughts." And usually before we make an important request, we rehearse our "speech." The more our fate hangs on our words, the more conscious we become of how we are saying what we are saying. We carry on an inner debate: "Should our sentences ask, or tell, or command? Should our words soothe or irritate? Should we be boldly direct or cautiously circular? Should we open with an attention-getter or close with a punch line?" Court cases and friends are won or lost by the way things are said.

We arrive at many of our judgments on others from their use of words. We call people clear or muddled, clever or dull, alert or tiresome because of the way they express what they say. When someone uses the "grand manner" to say the trivial, we laugh— behind his back, if he is serious. We sense when a speaker is "talking out of both sides of his mouth." And we are shrewdly aware of the shadings of inner contradiction in saying one thing and meaning another; we call it evasion, or understatement, or diplomacy, or lying. A single word can bare a soul and tip us off on the depth of our "naïve" acquaintances.

Everyone, too, has some fun with words. We enjoy an accidental rhyme, a chance alliteration, a slip of the tongue, a double meaning. And we always have some favorite word-child for our friends to mock and parody. We tease with words, withholding and withholding the point of a story. We "top" another's outlandish comparison, or we leave listeners to puzzle out our new version of some old cliché. We never quite get over being intrigued by the rhythms and sounds of words.

Day in day out words dare us to try to make them say what we want them to say. Every now and then they deceive us into thinking we've mastered them—they let us turn an exact phrase or strike a pleasing sound. But it's all a ruse, for, as speakers and listeners, we spend our lives in a running battle with words. We're often losing. We are, for instance, always asking our listeners verbally or by gesture to "know what we mean." We are always repining that we can't express the experiences we have had. We "could write a book"—if we could only write. We are, furthermore, frequently aware that we've missed the point in what the speaker said. We smile vaguely at the joke we didn't get, or alas, we think we've gotten it when in truth we've "seen" only what's above the waterline.

Too often as we listen to our friends or to the speakers in novels, plays, poems, and essays, we are verbally both hard of hearing and nearsighted. We hear and see only the general outline, so we miss the experience. We are worse off than if we were verbally deaf and blind, because, having the outline, we mistakenly think we have all. In the world of words, we are often "have-nots," underdeveloped and so underprivileged.

It is the English teacher who is charged with the responsibility of making us "have's" in the world of words. His is the difficult task of helping each student develop his sense of language so that he can become a competent writer and a responsive reader. A competent writer or speaker is one who puts words together in such a way as to produce some desired effect. He can, in other words, express his own ideas and his experiences precisely and adequately. A perceptive reader or listener is one who responds to words in this way or that because of the certain manner in which they have been put together. He can, that is, undergo the experience expressed by reacting properly to the words. The common denominator of reading and writing is sensitivity to language. It is this that the English teacher must try to get students to intensify. The prospective English teacher must be educated to fulfill his responsibility economically and effectively.

What kind of education would help him?

As we offer our answer to this question, we shall be keeping our eyes on what knowledge, skill, aptitude, and sensibility the teacher must have if he is to help students develop a command of language. We are not trying to accommodate our proposals to the currently accepted undergraduate course patterns for English majors. We are not trying to limit changes to tinkerings with the façade or minor renovations. We are trying only to suggest what *ought* to be if the English teacher is to be prepared to discharge his responsibility. Our proposals are entirely feasible. But following them may overthrow the "system." Perhaps we need that radical a change.

An English teacher must have an acute sensitivity to the ways words work together. Such a sensitivity is not learned, as a fact or the spelling of a word or the way to bake a cake is learned. It is developed gradually by continual noticing, much as a feeling for color, texture, sound, or style is developed. The teacher must slowly become aware, on one hand, of the ways context affects the sounds of words, their meanings, and the associations "they drag after them" and, on the other, of how a word affects the sound and the sense of the context.

The teacher's consciousness of the ways individual words function should gradually expand to include first an awareness of the interplay among clusters of words and then a feeling for the ways that sentences and large compositional units work together and against one another. As his sensitivity extends to ever larger configurations of language, it simultaneously becomes more discriminating and more subtle. The development of this kind of response to language can be promoted by studies that direct the prospective teacher's attention to a wide variety of word patterns of increasing scope and greater refinement. An English teacher's undergraduate courses in literature and in composition must be such studies; they must, above all else, intensify his sensitivity to language. For that is his most crucial need.

Courses in Literature

The focus of the literature courses should be the reading of works of literature as works of art. It should not be study *about* literature. In the freshman year, the prospective teacher should begin immediately to learn to respond to language as an artistic medium. His introductory course in the reading of literature should be a disciplined approach, because learning to react to conscious arrangements of words demands care, concentration, and precision. A course that encourages emotional catharsis, irrelevant reactions, and sweet rhapsodies is not useless; it's detrimental. It gives a false impression of what perception of an art consists in and requires.

An introduction to reading literature should be comprised of a sequence of readings carefully arranged to emphasize successively various aspects of the literary use of language. We stress "emphasize," for in no case should works be *used* merely to exemplify metaphor, or paradox, or variation in rhythm, or anything else. Works of literature, like all works of art, are integrated wholes. Emphasizing one aspect is highlighting for a moment's attention one effect of a unified whole. Once the beginning reader's attention has been directed to a certain aspect, he should be expected to continue to notice it whenever and however it appears in later readings. So, as his discernment of some new aspect of a work of literature is being initially encouraged, sensitivities previously encouraged are being broadened, varied, and intensified. For example, his feeling for the connotation of words is being continually developed while he is being introduced to the way metaphor controls a work. Gradually, the student will begin to respond simultaneously to each of many different aspects in whatever way the work demands.

If such a highly conscious approach to reading works of literature seems synthetic, then so is our usual approach to the "reading" of people. In each encounter with people, we are shown some facet of human nature. Let us suppose that on one encounter we "meet" deceit. We probably never meet deceit in the same shape again. Nor do we expect to. From our brief encounter, we get a generalized sense of deceit, and when we meet it again in quite different guise, we "know" it. We are not interested in detecting it in order to prove we could identify it; what we want is to see how it "works" in this new situation. In a similar way, we encounter "paradox" or "irony" or any other aspect of literature; we develop a sense of the aspect. We are not interested in it in the abstract, but only in the way it "works" in each unique situation.

Although we do not want to stretch this analogy between human characteristics and the formal devices of literature too far, we should note that our getting to know deceit does not mean that we lose all our other sensitivities to human nature or that we are hardly capable of developing any new ones. Deceit holds the center of the stage for a moment, then becomes merely another awareness that we hold in escrow until some new encounter calls it forth. The same is true of our sense of metaphor, or parallelism, or any other aspect of literature.

The way in which the introductory course in reading literature is taught determines whether the prospective teacher learns to analyze works mechanically or to bring a work to life in new ways at each reading. Close reading is mandatory. But if a work is read as an artistic whole, such concentrated reading does not lead to murderous dissection. Rather it enhances the chance of a proper perception of the work. In fact, without close attention to the words of the work, the reader cannot hope to undergo the experience of the work at all. A proper response to "these words in this order" *is* the "Open, Sesame!" to the experience of the work.

Rather than offer *a* pattern for an introductory course in the reading of literature, let us say that any course pattern is probably adequate if, on one hand, it takes into account the requirements and the limitations that the nature and functions of literature place on the reading of it, and if on the other hand, it is organized to encourage beginning readers to react ever more discriminatingly to the language of literature. In other words, the course must respect the integrity of literature, and it must be planned and taught to develop a sensitivity to, not a knowledge about, literature.

Many different paths can lead to essentially the same end. One excellent approach to critical reading is, however, suggested by Reuben Brower's *The Fields of Light*.[1] This approach, which leads through a close study of the imaginative structure of works to the central meaning, is the basis of a systematic introduction to literature offered by Mr. Brower and his colleagues at Harvard. They prove that, given a staff of responsive readers and imaginative teachers, a course in close reading need not be a prolonged post-mortem nor a groping for fancy handles to hold poems with. This approach really encourages the kind of noticing that acute perceptions are "made of."

If a prospective teacher of English could have only one course in literature, it should be a well-organized, well-taught course in the reading of literature. Such a course takes precedence over all other courses in literature. A student must be able to read literature discerningly before he can criticize it, evaluate it, or value it. Refined reading is a prerequisite to all of these activities and to all studies *about* literature. One can, of course, study the history of literature, the history of criticism, literary theory, or critical theory without first being able to read works of literature. But to do so is to ignore the fact that the work of literature antedates and dominates any body of facts related to it or any theory derived from it or from the study of it. Such bodies of knowledge are ancillary to the work. The work is the *raison d'être* for all of them. They would not exist unless there were first works of literature, and they have little significance unless what they are describing has first been experienced. A course that develops a responsive reader of literature is the central course in literature for the prospective teacher of English—and everyone else.

Natural aptitudes for literary perception probably vary. Not all who take such a course will become highly sensitive or equally sensitive readers. But, as our opening remarks tried to suggest, all

1. New York: Oxford University Press, 1951.

people seem to have some feeling for language, and this natural awareness, whatever its initial degree, can be intensified by disciplined attention to the ways words work together in literature.

If a course in the reading of literature came at the very beginning of an English major, it could have several salutary side effects. It could, first of all, disabuse students of the idea that their major—literature—is just another body of knowledge. They would soon realize that they can know "who wrote what when" or "which critics said what about a certain work" and still be quite unable to read the work on anything but the literal level. They would understand that reading a work of literature and knowing about one are two different things. It is the wise student who knows his major is an art, not a special branch of history!

Such a course could, secondly, discourage obtuse literalists from majoring in English or considering the teaching of English as a career. The course could screen validly. Thirdly, it could explode the all too prevalent myth that a sensitive response to literature consists in a mild nausea, a rise in temperature, or a momentary ague. As Seymour Chatman points out: [2]

> There is a serious danger that some of the best minds coming into the university find literature unpalatable because they have picked up the notion, in high school and elsewhere, that poetry is supposed to be very vague and elusive. It goes without saying, of course, that this is quite untrue; that poetic language is not only extraordinarily complex but also extraordinarily precise; that the responsible and successful poet is just as careful about the structure of his discourse as the most thoroughgoing logician; that even in Romantic poetry it is necessary to recognize the difference between vagueness of *feeling* and the precision of language in which these feelings are depicted. . . . The greatest service modern teachers can perform is to convince our more technically minded students that they do not have to give up any sense of intellectual discipline when they take up a poem; that, far from it, they should be prepared for an experience which is just as intellectually demanding *and* satisfying as that afforded by scientific discourse.

2. *Style in Language,* ed. Thomas A. Sebeok (Cambridge and New York: MIT Press and John Wiley & Sons; copyright © 1960 by Massachusetts Institute of Technology), p. 278. Chatman's italics.

The introduction to literature that we have suggested would make clear to the student that the perception of literature demands attention, discipline, imagination, and detachment. He can experience the work only if he approaches it freely and allows it to direct his responses. And it is only by undergoing the experience of the work that he can have the enjoyment, the pleasure, the sense of rightness and fulfillment that are the peculiar values of perceiving works of art.

What courses in literature should follow such an initial course? The prospective teacher of English needs separate courses in the reading of poetry, of fiction, and of drama. In other words, he should have a concentrated reading of each genre. These courses might be organized in various ways. They might be arranged historically to stress differences among writers or to emphasize the evolution of the form. They might be planned so that each work read would reveal an increasingly subtle use of language. Or the works included in such courses might be clustered by themes, in order to dramatize stylistic variations. But however these courses are arranged, they should be specialized extensions of the introductory course in the reading of literature. The number of works included in each of the genre courses should not exceed what can reasonably be read with care, vital attention, and a play of imagination.

As readers become more sensitive, they become more interested in how the work produces the effects they are experiencing. They turn back to the work for a closer, more conscious "noticing." By doing this repeatedly, the reader gradually becomes somewhat of a practical critic. He needs names to talk about what he continually notices, and he redefines critical terms so that they describe the formal devices that produce the effects. He begins to distinguish between extrinsic data that can elucidate a work and information that is interesting but irrelevant to experiencing the work. In other words, he starts to develop a critical theory of his own in the same way that critical theory was developed.

The reader should not refer to professional criticism until he has made both his own unbiased responses to works and his own initial critical reflections. The use of formal criticism in connection with the reading of works should begin after the genre courses. And courses in the history of literary criticism—like that suggested by

Bate's *Criticism: The Major Texts* [3]—or in types of criticism—like that suggested by Hyman's *The Armed Vision* [4]—should be deferred until they can function as organizing contexts for the various theories and types of criticism with which he has become familiar. These courses are of most worth when they can place his own critical views and the formal criticism he knows in the tradition. It probably takes three years to effect such critical seasoning.

Period courses or general surveys of literary history should be postponed until students are able to read literature with sufficient sensitivity to perceive the poems, plays, and novels of a period as dramatic representations of the values of the period. When we speak of works of literature as dramatic representations of values, we are not referring so much to the mores depicted in the works or to the subject matter the writers selected. We are referring, rather, to the attitudes that certain uses of language imply. In early seventeenth-century American literature, for example, the homely metaphors, the logical framework, the "plain style," the sentence rhythms like long combers one gently overtopping the other suggest more about the religious attitudes of the time than the subject matter of Wigglesworth's "The Day of Doom" does.

Until students can read works of literature well enough so that style suggests the "mind and spirit" of the age, they are not really ready to grasp the significance of works of literature as the products and the reflections of this or that society. As the direct representation of value, literature is a peculiar kind of social document. If students are not experienced readers of literature, they may confuse works of literature with other kinds of social documents and read them as if they were history or sociology or ethics. And if they read works of literature referentially or normatively, they miss the unique kind of insight into an age that only works of art can give. Period and survey courses should be taught so as to emphasize the relationship of the work of literature to its social context. Students would probably not be ready for such courses much earlier than their junior year.

Too many survey courses are simply heroic efforts to "make it"

3. Walter J. Bate, *Criticism: The Major Texts* (New York: Harcourt, Brace, 1952).

4. Stanley E. Hyman, *The Armed Vision* (New York: A. A. Knopf, 1948).

from *Beowulf* to Virginia Woolf or from the *Bay Psalm Book* to *The Neon Wilderness* in two harried terms. Too many survey courses simply stretch the students' memory span, burden the pedant with learned lumber, and give the dilettante some handy quotable quotes. This is regrettable. For only the survey course allows the reader to see works in both their local and their total context, so that he can come to understand the work within the confines of its own age and grasp its significance in the literature of the language. No one can evaluate works of literature or interpret evaluative judgments intelligently without such knowledge of literature. A good survey course, therefore, plays a vital role in the understanding, criticism, and evaluation of works of literature as works of art.

An English major who has successfully completed the course pattern we have outlined would now be prepared as a reader, as a practical critic, and as a student of literary history for some advanced forms of literary study. He is ready, for example, to read the works of an individual writer intensively, concentrating on his development as a writer or on the ways he expresses his age. Courses centered on the prose and poetry of Milton, the poetry of Pope or Wordsworth or Yeats, the major plays of Shakespeare, the novels of Hawthorne, James, Melville, or Conrad would be the appropriate type. These are only suggestions. Such courses might very well emphasize or concentrate on one or two works of the writer.

Our English major would also be ready to do comparative studies of the styles of two or more writers. His courses might deal with the Restoration dramatists, or such groupings as Dryden and Pope; Shelley, Keats, and Byron; Hawthorne, James, and Eliot; Joyce, Mann, and Proust; Browning and Arnold, the American Transcendentalists, or the novelists of the Victorian period. The variations of this sort of study are manifold. Writers can be grouped so as to show baldly graphic or extremely subtle stylistic differences. The design of these courses is limited only by the reading sophistication, the imagination, and the teaching skill of the instructor.

Studies in the works of individual writers and groups of writers form the apex of our pyramid of literature courses. By the time the student begins these studies he will have read many of the works of the writers he is concentrating on, and furthermore, he will probably have read some of the works several times. Is this overlapping a mistake? Of course not. We are talking about works of art. The student may "have" an historical statement after one contact with it, but one "long look" would never give him the "Mona Lisa." With a hundred looks he would not possess it; he would simply have a multitude of ever new relationships with the painting. The same is true of a work of literature. The more relationships he can have with it before he begins an intensive study of it the better.

If, for example, he read *The Tempest* first in his genre course and again in his survey course, his reading of it in connection with his study of Shakespeare's plays would be just that much more satisfying. As he read the play these several times, he would sense more and more the amazing gamut of human experience that is unified in this drama. He would feel less and less that each reading was exhaustive or ultimate. Each reading would resemble each meeting he might have with a great human being. On the first meeting, the student knows only that he's met "someone." His second meeting simply enhances his interest. The person begins to reveal an astonishing complexity. Successive contacts slowly disclose a personality that is a rich harmony of very diverse human experiences. The student concedes that he'll never really "know" this extraordinary person, and for that reason, the meetings continue to be illuminating and rewarding.

Throughout the pyramid of courses we propose, the prospective teacher would be constantly intensifying his sensitivity to language. His early critical reading of literature would make it possible for him to read responsively and pleasurably works of greater literary quality as he moved on to the study of particular genres, to criticism, to literary history, and finally to specialization in particular writers. The teacher would be well read in the only way that matters: he would have *undergone the experiences* of a wide variety of works of literature.

From responsive reading that is both broad and intensive, he would know what literature is and what its functions are. He would never mistake art for a body of knowledge. He would be well aware that literature is not ethics, psychology, sociology, or history. He would never think that one could enjoy the values of literature by studying about it. He would not, in short, have any of the misconceptions that distort and disvalue much of the reading of literature in our high schools. He would come to the teaching of literature with the ability to read sensitively just about any work put before him. And reading literature responsively is the *sine qua non* of teaching literature.

Courses in Writing

If the prospective teacher is a sophisticated reader of literature, he is intensely sensitive to the ways words are put together. He has the perceiver's feeling for the artistic organization of language. If he is to be a competent writer, he must develop an artist's feeling for the aesthetic organization of language. He must learn how to put words together to make them produce the effects he wants. That is what effective writing is. The student's English major must include at least two full courses in writing. If these courses stress putting living words together in ways that make them say what the writer wants to express, it matters little whether they emphasize expository writing or descriptive and narrative writing. They should include all three.

Composition is essentially a struggle to make language express an idea or an insight. The struggle both helps the writer clarify what it is that he wants to express and shows him how he can exploit words to make them serve his purpose. By painstaking trial of now this word now that, now one ordering now another, the writer develops both an acute sensitivity to words as units of meaning, sound, rhythm, and syntax and a respect for what language can do when it is ordered with precision and imagination.

Whether the composition courses emphasize expository or "creative" writing is probably less important than that they be systematic. A carefully developed sequence of writing tasks is essential. Each exercise should reinforce what has been taught through the preceding exercises, should stress the form or principles currently being studied, and should anticipate the next task. There are available models of such carefully devised writing programs. Richard

Sewall's paper, "The Content of Student Writing," [5] offers an integrated series of writing exercises. And the organization of topics and readings in Martin and Ohmann's *Inquiry and Expression* [6] suggests several different useful sequences of writing tasks.

Writing should be frequent, but the papers should not exceed two or three pages. Assignments of this length insist on tight organization, meaningful transitions, syntactical constructions that speak for themselves, and words chosen and placed for maximum "mileage." Frequent short papers give the beginning writer repeated opportunity to work intensively on a manageable piece. And, of course, they give the teacher many chances for close criticism of the precision and effectiveness of the student's writing.

Ex post facto writing instruction may take many forms. Cooperative class correction of one or two papers from each writing is often instructive, especially if the exercise was sufficiently guided so that all papers are relatively similar in form. Even the examination of relevant professional models is useful if literal imitation of them is discouraged. But neither co-operative correction nor the study of models can substitute for an individual conference with the writer. This mode of writing instruction is good for all students, necessary for all English majors, and mandatory for all prospective teachers.

The individual conference helps the writer to see how he can improve the weaknesses and correct the faults of a particular piece of his own writing. And we would stress that the purpose of an individual conference is to help the writer to *see* how he can correct his paper. It is not to tell him how or to show him how. An instructor can tell him how by an end comment on his paper, and he can show him how by revising the paper for him when he reads it. The office of the individual conference is different from that of the other modes of writing instruction.

Since the office is different, the method varies appropriately. The teacher simply asks questions that focus the student's attention on

5. In *Essays on the Teaching of English*, eds. Edward Noyes and Edward Gordon (New York: Appleton-Century-Crofts, 1960), pp. 61–77.
6. Harold C. Martin and Richard M. Ohmann, *Inquiry and Expression* (New York: Rinehart, 1958).

one or two salient flaws. The questions are phrased in such a way as to *suggest* the flaw to him and to urge him to make some fitting change. Sometimes it is merely a matter of reading the sentence aloud to the student. He hears the lack of coherence, the pied tenses, or the dead words. During the conference the student is alerted to concrete examples of his own writing problems. He is, furthermore, internalizing a kind of critical questioning that pinpoints a problem and suggests modes of correcting it. And finally, he writes one or more new versions of the faulty construction then and there.

Writing courses do not aim to get students to learn either the abstract principles of writing or how to spot others' errors. Their purpose is to get each individual to be able to put words together so that they express whatever idea, attitude, or experience he wants to communicate. It is only by learning to improve particular pieces of his own writing that he will learn to write. Oftentimes, a student can list in abstract terms all his writing faults without having the slightest idea of what these faults look like in concrete words and phrases. He knows his faults because the end comments on his papers have repeatedly said, "Unity!" "Paragraphing!" "Spelling!" "Good idea ineffectively stated." He is like the man who knows he is a cheat and a liar because people have told him so, but he has no idea as to the particular acts he commits that justify their saying so. And he cannot, of course, correct his faults, for he has no notion of when he is committing them. Specific comments and individual writing conferences can help the student know his enemies—in the flesh.

The prospective English teacher must be aware not only of his writing problems but also of his fortes. He must know when he has succeeded and how he effected this success. Through critical reflection on concrete instances in his own writing, he must become conscious of the ways *he* bends words to create effects. Everything he writes should, furthermore, reflect his awareness of the differences that the choice of words and the ordering of them can make. He should demonstrate this sensitivity not only in the over-all organization of his critical papers but also, say, in the decision to slow up a series of adjectives by using "and's" instead of commas. He should show his sense of language when he is using words referentially to express an historical fact, a mathematics proof, or a scientific finding, as well as when he is using them to evoke an experience in a short story, a poem, or a one-page narration.

The writing courses should be taught so as to impress upon the prospective teacher that he is composing every time he tries to express something in words. He must realize that he sharpens his sense of language or dulls it by the way he chooses and orders words *each time* he does it. He must be made to feel he has defaulted whenever he yields to a cliché, an inaccurate word, a tired metaphor, or a careless tense sequence. Through his writing courses, he must develop a composition "superego."

Our proposals for the preparation of an English teacher have insisted on an education that should, above all else, develop the teacher's sensitivity to language. "Development" is what we have meant to stress. For, as our preface suggested, sensitivity to language is probably always a matter of degree. It can never be considered fully developed. It must be thought of, rather, as developing or declining. Our proposed program of three full courses [7] and ten half courses [8] in literature and two full courses in composition would make our English major exercise verbally day in day out. Under a continual demand for critical reading and precise writing, he would have maximum opportunity to develop his responsiveness to the way words work in literature and the way he works them in composition. Through these courses he would certainly also learn literary history, the theory of literature, the use of critical principles in the explication and evaluation of works, and the principles of composition, grammar, vocabulary, and writing mechanics. But these learnings would be subsidiary to his learning to read and to write. This is as it should be.

Works of literature preceded—and take precedence over—the theory of literature abstracted from them and the literary history written about them. Writing preceded the descriptions of grammar and the compilation of rhetorical principles, and the knowledge of

7. Introduction to Literature, Survey of English Literature, Survey of American Literature.
8. Three genre courses, criticism, three period courses, three special courses.

either of them is simply a possible means to effective composition. The English major whose literature courses have concentrated on works of literature as works of art is not likely to mistake a knowledge of the facts of literary history for an ability to experience works of literature. And the English major whose study of composition has centered on producing certain effects by ordering certain words this way and that will hardly confuse an ability to spell, punctuate, or cite grammar rules with an ability to write. To be clear on these crucial distinctions is absolutely essential for anyone who plans to become a teacher of English.

Electives

If an English major follows our proposed pattern of courses, then in a sixteen-course college program he would have six full-course electives. We shall suggest only four of these. They are courses that we think would give the student a broad yet relevant context for his English major. Each of the four subject matters is clearly connected with literature and composition and yet is clearly distinct from them. So while through the study of each the student is taken farther and farther from his field of specialization, the tie to his major holds. As the spokes in a wheel link the hub to the rim, these courses relate his field of concentration to all other attempts to understand man and his world.

A course in the perception of painting or music would help him understand the importance of the medium in all arts. He would see that it is the medium that determines what each art can express and how it can express it. It is the medium, then, that differentiates the arts and gives each its unique value. It is the medium that a perceiver must respond to if he is to have the experience the work of art expresses and the value that accrues from the experience. We suggest painting because, though it "represents life" almost as much as literature does, still, since it is a presentational art, perceiving it is quite different from reading a work of literature. We suggest music because, though discursive like literature, it "represents life" less than any other art.

The English teacher should also have a course in another language—the language of numbers. Radical as their differences are, mathematics and literature have much in common.[9] They are both "insights into the possible" rather than statements of the probable or the actual. Both are ideals of orderly structure, both are intrinsically interesting, both discipline the human imagination. But mathematics is formal and abstract; it expresses its insight into the possible in signs that, as "self-effacing means" to something else which lies beyond them, can be substituted for one another. Literature is sensuous and concrete; it expresses its "alternative to the actual" in symbols, which though conventional have associations and surface. They cannot really be substituted for one another, and every time they are re-employed they "must wear their symbolic expressiveness with a difference." The qualities of the sign and those of the symbol suggest the nature and the limitations of each of these insights into the possible.

An English major should also be familiar with the writings of Freud, Jung, and related psychologists. Personality psychology has affected modern literature and criticism more than any other social science. A course in theories of personality would be a useful supplement to studies in literature. Such a course would also make clear the fundamental distinction between the purpose of psychology and that of literature. Even in its most "imaginative" form, psychology purports to be a *description* of human behavior, not a dramatic representation of possible human experiences. No prospective teacher who understands this difference will be caught plumbing the depths of Macbeth's unconscious or interpreting *A Tale of Two Cities* as a slow fulfillment of a death wish.

Finally, every English major should be conversant with the various modes of exploring and expressing human experience. The student needs to know that there are many approaches to the same human experience; he should be aware of what these approaches are, how they differ from one another, and what the value of each approach is. He needs to know that guilt, for example, can be dra-

9. In this section I am indebted to Dorothy Walsh, "The Cognitive Content of Art," *The Philosophical Review*, LII (1943), 441–445.

matically represented in literature, in sculpture, and in painting, that it can be described in psychology, analyzed in ethics, and defined theologically.

A course could be organized around certain persistent human ideas or experiences that have been expressed or explored in various ways. Ideas like "individualism," "evil," or "equality" might form points of reference for examining through pertinent documents the methods that history, anthropology, art, biology, and philosophy, for example, use to understand human concerns. If the idea or the experience is held constant, then the variation of the approaches to it both in the kind of truth they offer and in their methods of arriving at it becomes clearer. This is obviously not just another "great books" course.

Through this kind of course the student would begin to recognize how his own major field fits into the spectrum of modes of expressing human experiences, and he would see how these essentially unique modes relate to and complement one another. He would realize that only literature expresses experience through the medium of language and that no other mode of expressing experience could really substitute for it. It is important for a student to realize the place of his special study in the scheme of things, and it is crucial for a teacher to know which mode of approaching experience he is offering to his students and why he bothers.

Our proposed undergraduate program consists of an integrated pattern of fourteen full courses. A student's previous studies would, of course, suggest what adjustments he should make in our pattern and how he should "spend" his other four half-courses. After six years in secondary school, why shouldn't a student have as academic capital three years of history, two or three years of science, and three or four years of some modern language? In college, he should be able to spend his freedom on courses in philosophy, intellectual history, or linguistic science, or in reading the *literature* of the modern language he knows. He should, in other words, be setting what he learned in secondary school into a meaningful context.

We warned the reader at the outset that we would not attempt to stay acceptably close to existing undergraduate programs. We have not tried to reflect what is but to suggest what should be.

We did not start out with the assumption that there is a pattern. But we have assumed that an education needs a clear focus and an identifiable relatedness. Majoring is choosing the mode of expressing and exploring human experience most germane to one's own aptitudes. Concentration need not be isolation. In fact, a major cannot be truly understood except in relation to all other modes. On one hand, they give it a context, and on the other, it is the point in terms of which the student sees the similarities, the differences, and the unique values of all of them.

If a prospective English teacher has had the kind of undergraduate major we have suggested, he has been educated to educate himself. If he has never read Joyce, no matter. He can begin tonight. His courses aimed at developing sensitivities and abilities that would prepare him to cope with a wide variety of similar tasks of increasing difficulty. A sensitive reader, he can extend the scope of his reading at will. He can experience any work he chooses to read. And he can reread with ever fresh experiences. A competent writer, he has learned to be his own critic. He has developed two crucial abilities, and they have freed him. He needs no academic high priest to mediate the mystery. He is ready to "go it alone." He does not *really need* any more formal courses in literature and composition. His undergraduate major suffices. He may still enjoy hearing some stimulating critical lectures or engaging in a lively seminar, but when he finishes college, all he needs to do to become a teacher of English is to learn how to teach English in high school. If he takes a graduate year, "his work is cut out for him."

Unless an English major has become both a sophisticated reader of literature and a competent writer by the end of his undergraduate years, he most certainly must become both before he begins to teach English in high school. So he must have as much further study as is needed to develop these abilities. And he must be willing to take elementary "working" courses in reading and in writing. Such courses should take precedence over any other subject-matter preparation he may need or desire. Knowing how to read and how to write are surely necessary conditions for teaching others how.

Having to insist that prospective teachers of English meet these requirements seems almost comic. And yet, until very recently no one seemed to notice that many English majors have little sense of the importance of "putting these words in this order" and little "ear for writing prose." And may we notice here that too many English majors have little awareness of the significance of "these words put in this order" and little sensitivity for reading literature.[10] The prospective teacher's deficiency in writing has received more notoriety than his inability to read literature has, because the first is more easily discovered and because improving the teaching of composition in high school is the current "cause." The indignation of the colleges and the public has made it so.

But the lack of notoriety does not mean that the teacher's inability to read literature is any less important or any less deleterious in its effects on high school students. It simply means that since high school students do not try to sell in the market place their ability to read literature, there has been less notice of the fact that many excellent students not only cannot read a work but do not even know that they cannot read one. For obvious reasons, the public has discovered that Johnny can't read, that he can't spell, and that he can't write. But it may never find out that he can't read literature either. So it may never pressure teachers to prepare to teach him. But whether the public moves or not, programs that purport to prepare English majors to teach English in high school are obligated by their very purpose to make sure that prospective teachers can not only write competently but also read literature responsively.

The Fifth Year

For twenty years now there have been fifth-year programs designed especially to improve the subject-matter preparation of prospective high school teachers by offering them another year or half-year of course work in their major field. In the case of the English major, it has been generally believed that his subject-matter

10. In August, 1961, the Commission on English, CEEB, officially noticed that inservice teachers needed retraining in both composition and literature. At this writing I do not know whether or not the Commission noted the *same* sort of deficiency as I mention here.

preparation is adequate if he has covered the conventional period courses in literary history and the "standards": Shakespeare, Milton, and Chaucer, perhaps. If he hasn't taken these courses, he spends his fifth year filling in the "gaps." How often has anyone thought to ask whether the emphasis in these courses was on reading works or on learning about them? The assumption has been that the English major is a major in literary history, rather than in literature, and that there is a certain body of information he must know. When he has "covered" that, he "knows literature." What he really knows is, of course, literary history.

As our proposal shows, we agree that the prospective English teacher needs to know literary history, but we hold that this kind of knowledge of literature is neither primary nor most central. All types of knowledge *about* a work of literature are ancillary to the experience of it. "First things should come first." Before we can decide whether or not a prospective teacher is prepared as far as his subject matter is concerned, we have to consider what the nature, the function, and the structure of the subject matter are and then what facets of the subject matter are most central, which are prerequisites of others, and such related questions. In this way, we can discover what is essential to knowing the subject matter, what is necessary, what desirable, what peripheral. We can see the importance of each aspect of the subject and the relationships among the aspects. After such an analysis, we can better decide whether or not the teacher is prepared in the crucial aspects of his subject matter. Such an inquiry would save us many misjudgments. On the very practical level, we would never, for example, think that one teacher's ability to identify every allusion in a poem was as important as another teacher's ability to suggest how these allusions worked in the poem.

Perhaps no prospective teacher will have the English major we proposed. Most major programs will probably diverge from it in varying degrees. Our general recommendation would, of course, be that each prospective teacher spend his graduate year bringing his total English preparation as close as possible to our proposed undergraduate program. If, for example, he is adequately prepared in both reading and writing but has not had certain period courses, he should study those periods in formal courses only if the courses available treat works of literature as artistic expressions of the relevant society. But if these courses are simply fleeting glances at titles hung on a time line, then prospective teachers who are already competent readers would be far better served by a reading course in the period. Using some good general text—like *Major British Writers* [11] or *Major Writers of America* [12] or Matthiessen's *American Renaissance* [13]—as a spine for his study, the student should read or reread the major works of the period, referring to related critical and specialized historical studies as he requires. We are suggesting that bringing his total preparation in English close to what we have proposed is not merely a matter of covering the same ground, but of covering it in the same way.

If the teacher is generally well prepared, he may feel he needs—which usually means he would enjoy—a course in exposition or narrative writing or the writing of poetry. Or he may long to do a detailed study of some writer that the high school curriculum will likely be innocent of. In his graduate year the well-prepared student should be encouraged to follow his bent, to indulge his whims and have fun.

The pattern of undergraduate courses we proposed would be desirable for every English major, whatever his future plans. It is in no sense a special vocational preparation for a high school teacher of English. Graduate study in all fields is, however, really specialized preparation for certain occupations. And the patterns of study within a field should be differentiated accordingly. The prospective high school teacher and the candidate for the Ph.D. in English do not have similar needs, for they do not have similar goals. Their programs of study should reflect this difference. The Ph.D. candidate must narrow his studies so that he can become highly competent in several areas of literature and definitively expert in one. In this area, he must make an original contribution. The high school English teacher doesn't need to know which library holds the letters

11. George B. Harrison, ed. (2 vols., New York: Harcourt, Brace, 1954).
12. Perry Miller, ed. (2 vols., New York: Harcourt, Brace, World, 1962).
13. Francis O. Matthiessen, *American Renaissance* (New York: Oxford, 1941).

of James Joyce or where the original manuscript of Benjamin Franklin's *Autobiography* is. He doesn't need to be invincible in any particular areas of literary knowledge. He must, instead, be intensely sensitive to the ways language is used to evoke and to express experience. He needs to have read broadly and penetratingly. He must have "felt his way" through many books and through the same books many times. He needs to have written frequently and consciously. Many times he should have taken some "bare little fact" out of his own experience and forced words to express it. The prospective teacher is not preparing to be a literary critic or a literary historian. He must "know his subject" in the way a high school teacher needs to know it.

The Meaning of Teaching

No one can teach what he does not know. But a person can "know a subject" and not know how to teach it. "Knowing a subject" does not imply knowing how to teach it. A prospective teacher can, in fact, be a very sensitive reader and a competent writer—he can even know "how he does it"—and still not know how to try to get students to learn to read literature and to write ably. With few exceptions, the English major needs help to learn how to translate what he knows into teachable terms. This translation is a very difficult task, first, because teaching is not merely telling students something; it is trying to get them to learn it; [14] second, because "trying to get students to learn something" is a very complex skill, and last, because what must be taught in high school English is not simply data but the ability to read and to write. Let us now look more closely at each of the three conditions that make it difficult for a teacher to translate his knowledge of English into teachable terms. Seeing what the problems are may facilitate understanding the kind of "help" in the teaching of English we shall later propose.

First, giving students the interpretation of "Dover Beach" is not teaching literature; telling students the principles of composition

14. For this concept of teaching, see Israel Scheffler, *The Language of Education* (Springfield, Illinois: Charles Thomas, 1960), p. 67ff and Chapter V.

and what a good theme is is not teaching composition. Teaching is not transmitting information to be recorded and repeated on request. Teaching is questioning, suggesting, objecting; and it is encouraging the students to question, suggest, and object. It is refuting opposed interpretations, admitting variant readings, and offering critical insights for evaluation. Teaching is not rhapsodizing on the transport felt through aesthetic appreciation or on the release self-expression brings. A teacher is not an entertainer, nor a scholarly *poseur,* nor a frustrated preacher. A teacher is not trying to prove to his students that *he* knows how to interpret a poem or to write one. He is trying to get them to learn how. The teacher makes his own knowledge, skill, and aptitudes serve his attempts to get students to learn whatever he is teaching.

The teacher is never standing between the student and his work. He is always bringing the student to the novel or to the writing task. He reads so that the student hears the voices in the story, not the teacher's voice. He provokes the student to a "sudden insight" on how to remodel his sprawling paragraph. The teacher "looks over the student's shoulder" and encourages him to notice this, and this, and now that. The student must "see it" himself. The teacher counts that day lost when he tells the student what the writer is doing or how the sentence must be rewritten. The teacher longs for the day when students can read and write on their own, better perhaps than he ever did.

Teaching, then, is trying to get students to learn a certain thing, and this is a very complex skill. Like many complex things, however, it can be described in a deceptively simple way: the teacher has something in mind he wants students to learn, so he gives them some materials that will help them to learn it, and some directions on how to use the material, and when they have completed the task, he finds out whether or not they learned the thing he had in mind. Just three easy steps. Only rubbing a lamp could be simpler. It is only when we go behind the scenes that we see the number of prior decisions that each of these three actions demands.

The teacher cannot simply have "something in mind" that he wants students to do. He must ask himself, "What should be the general aim of this lesson if the long-range aim is such and such?"

"On what grounds do I think so?" "What particular version of that general aim would be best for this class?" "What are my reasons?" The teacher cannot simply give materials and directions, he must first ask himself, "If this is what the aim is, then what materials would it be *valid* for me to use to achieve it? Of these materials, what would be *feasible* in this class?" "Why do I think so?" "If this is the aim and these are the materials, what teaching methods *may* I use?" "How do I know?" "Of these methods, which method or methods would be most effective in this class?" "What suggests this to me?" Finally, the teacher cannot evaluate in just any convenient way. He must ask, "How *may* I test to see whether or not the class has achieved the aim?" "Of these ways, which would be most feasible and useful in this class?" "Why?"

These questions make clear that in no case can the teacher "do as he likes regardless." For every judgment he makes, he must give himself reasons that are objectively acceptable. He is forced to decide responsibly. To do this, he must know what factors he should take into account in his decision, which factors take precedence, and of the justifiable alternatives he can choose from, which one or ones could actually be implemented in the particular class he has in mind.

We can best suggest the difficulty of responsible decision by showing what is involved in just one concrete decision on materials. The question confronting the teacher is: "If the aim of the lesson is to help the class *sense* the ironic in literature, which poem should I choose to achieve it?" In order to answer this question, the teacher would, first of all, have to know a goodly number of "ironic" poems —know them as one knows something he has read freshly many times. Secondly, from working with the class, he would have to have discovered such things as, how sensitive a response to language the class as a whole had, what subtlety it could grasp, whether the class was ready to read a work in which the situation itself is ironic or in which the attitude toward the situation is ironic, what intensity of ironic experience the class could "tolerate," and how close to its own adolescent experience the work could come without tempting the students to "dissolve" the experience of the work into their own lives. It takes all these deliberations to arrive at just one decision: that the poem read should be this poem rather than any of the others considered.

Yet choosing material is probably the simplest decision the teacher makes. It is far simpler than deciding either on appropriate methods for teaching the material or on fitting ways for testing the achievement of the aim. A teacher may, for example, decide that he will use close questioning as his method, because the aim is this, the work is that, and the class is so. But this conclusion is only the beginning. He must decide, then, what the actual questions will be—and why, in what order they will be asked—and for what reason. In other words, he must come right down to practical matters and say, question by question, what he intends to do in the class-room. The same is true of decisions on testing.

Even these few illustrations of what a teacher must know and must be able to do suggest that teaching is a complex skill. And, of course, we have glanced at planning only. We have not even mentioned what the teacher must be capable of doing when he takes his plans to the classroom.

Finally, teaching English in high school is an especially challenging task because the primary aim is not to get students to learn facts but to get them to develop abilities. They must develop a response to the language of literature sensitive enough so that, within their capacities, they will be able to read with literary value any work they wish. They must learn to write competently enough so that they will be able to express appropriately any idea, attitude, or feeling they desire to express. These abilities are not simple, mechanical skills. Even in their elementary forms, reading and writing are two of the most complex activities a student learns to perform.

The English teacher must know how to help students develop the ability to read responsively and to write ably. Telling a student how to develop an ability is not helping him develop it. The teacher must be able to devise sequences of tasks or exercises that will, first, lead the class to experience the effects of various arrangements of words and then will help them to see how writers produce these effects. The exercises must begin with arrangements the class is quite familiar with, though perhaps unconscious of, and they must range—often in "baby steps"—to the most subtle configurations. The teacher must, in other words, be able to "program."

Developing abilities to read and write requires much shrewder questioning, much more ingenious planning, more imaginative approaches, examples, and analogies than does teaching information about literature and composition. It is far easier to teach a student to name arrangements, to define critical terms, to recite the "five steps to good paragraphs," or even to recognize literary devices in context than it is to help him develop a feeling for the way words act together or an ability to compose words so that they behave as he wants.

The difficulty of designing teaching practice so it will actually lead to the achievement of aims such as we are discussing may account for the surprising hiatus we frequently observe between what a teacher says he is aiming for and what he is actually doing in the classroom. He may say, for example, that he is trying to develop the students' ability to read critically, but we find the class memorizing poems, or relating their life experiences to the last two lines, or making anthologies of poems they thought good—for "God and country" reasons! Making teaching practice constantly reflect the aim is a very challenging business, and when the aim is the development of such abilities as reading and writing, the difficulty is multiplied many times.

A Course in the Teaching of English

The discussion of the last few pages suggests not only why the English major needs help in learning to teach "what he knows" but also what sort of assistance he needs. In general, it is of two kinds. The first is help in understanding what reading and writing consist in and in devising a variety of justifiable and feasible means for getting students to develop these abilities. A good "working course" in the teaching of English can offer this kind of assistance to the prospective teacher. The second type of help complements the first: it is assistance in learning to use in live classes the methods he has devised. Only guided classroom teaching can provide him with a real opportunity to try out and adapt his teaching plans. The prospective teacher needs both a course in the teaching of English and practice teaching.

This twofold preparation for teaching might be organized into a three-part sequence. It might begin with the "working course" in the teaching of English, during which the student, first, would develop a "position" on the teaching of literature and the teaching of composition to guide his practice, and secondly, would work out in a variety of vicarious teaching situations how the principles he holds would affect his practice. At the midpoint of this course, the student should begin observing live classes, for he needs to "try out" from the back of the room his dry-run planning. He can do some imaginary teaching at a safe distance. Finally, at the end of his "working course," he should begin teaching English in terms of the "position" he shaped for himself and taught vicariously during the course and his observation.

While he is practice teaching, the student should get all the informed critical assistance he needs to bring whatever pupils sit before him to and through the work of literature and the writing task. Classroom practice is not just the end of an integrated three-part sequence. It is the reason for the student's going through the other two parts. The "working course" and observation are necessary preliminaries to actual teaching. But it is only in the classroom that the student can prove that he *can* teach English effectively without violating the nature of the subject matter.

The prospective English teacher needs both the theory of the "working course" and practice in the classroom. If a "working course" in the teaching of English is not extended into guided classroom teaching, then the course is like a prolonged rehearsal of a show that never has a trial run. The show goes directly to Broadway "with all its imperfections on its head." If, on the other hand, classroom teaching is not preceded by a good "working course," then the teacher goes into the classroom without really thinking through what he is trying to do with what he knows, why he is trying, and how he might be able to do it successfully without distorting the subject matter. It is unrealistic to suppose that he can coolly think through these matters either while he faces thirty students—or in the panic of the night before. Confronted with such situations, he will do whatever he can to survive.

If he has no preliminary "working course," where does he develop a set of principles to guide his practical decisions? Is he supposed to abstract a theory from his classroom practice? A theory for teaching composition and literature validly? Unlikely. A prospective archer may correctly induce from actual trials a theory for mastery in archery. He cannot mistake failure for success. He hits the bull's-eye, or he doesn't, and he won't construe the movements associated with his failures as the principles of archery. A prospective teacher can mistake failures for achievements. He can think his ability to excite and involve students in irrelevancies and tangents is an ability to teach literature. He may take what "worked," whether it is allowable or not in terms of the subject matter, as a principle to be applied in future situations. Most, if not all, beginning teachers need to know how to translate subject matter into justifiable and workable plans before they begin practice. Otherwise, when they go into a classroom, they may practice "telling," or "courage," or "being at home with a class," but they probably will not practice teaching.

Elsewhere we have offered a scheme for guiding classroom teaching,[15] so we shall not discuss that part of the prospective teacher's preparation here. We shall instead concentrate on the form and content of a good "working course" in the teaching of English.

The form of the course is important. It must be conducted so that the teacher will develop *for himself* an explicit, consistent, valid "position" on the teaching of literature and the teaching of composition. This "position" is essentially a statement of principles which will govern to some extent every decision he makes, even such decisions as to ask this question rather than that at a particular moment in a lesson. This "position" should not be a "received dogma." The assaults of the classroom are too great to expect that a teacher will hold fast to what he is not convinced of and committed to. And he must feel committed to act in accordance with

15. "The Prospective Teacher as Observer," *The Journal of Teacher Education,* XIII, No. 2 (June, 1962), 150–156.

his "position" even when carrying it out demands hard work and ingenuity. The teacher must know what he thinks and what he believes in, and he must come to his "position" by arguing the crucial issues out with himself. The gradual development of a "position" on the teaching of literature and the teaching of composition is a most important aim of a good "working course" in the teaching of English.

During the course, the teacher should be confronted with the crucial questions in the teaching of English in a logical sequence. He must answer each of these, after he has assessed as many alternative answers as possible and has selected one that he can defend and commit himself to. Reading and discussion may enlighten his decisions, but the teacher must arrive at his final choice himself. And after he has chosen, he should make a brief statement of his choice and his reasons for it. Nothing invites clarity, precision, and reappraisal more than writing the answer down.

So much for the process of formulating a "position." Now let us see what issues he must decide about. For economy, we shall discuss the teaching of literature only. And the first questions are, of course, "What is a work of literature?" and "What are the functions of literature?" The teacher can arrive at answers to these questions in one of two ways: by reflecting on his own experiences with literature and inducing from them his own theory of literature or by examining the answers several established theories of literature have given to these questions and choosing the answer or answers that seem most adequate. The first course is far preferable, but it is open to only those English majors who have reading experiences to generalize from.

When these initial questions are answered, the teacher must find out what the various branches of the study of literature are, and he must determine how they are related to one another and what values the study of each branch can afford. After he has arrived at answers to these questions, the teacher will know not only what the possible areas of study are, but which must precede and which must follow, and which is most central to the study of literature as a whole. He will be ready to decide which studies of literature it would be most justifiable and most valuable to have high school students engage in. He must have decided on these matters before he can decide on aims for the teaching of English in high school.

By this point in the "working course" the teacher's "position" has really taken shape. He is now ready to apply it in some practical decisions. His first opportunity is in the stating of some general aims for the teaching of literature. He does not "look these up" in books. His previous deliberations on the nature, the functions, and the values of literature advise him on what these aims can and should be. When he has made his decision, he should say what he is trying to get students to learn, as simply and as clearly as he can state it.

If the teacher's theory of literature is to guide his practice, then his general aims must be working aims, not just hollow ideals. And if these aims are to be working aims, he must understand what they involve precisely enough to spell them out eventually into a series of particular aims that will direct his classroom teaching. Understanding what general aims involve demands taking a close, analytic look at them. What do we find if, for example, we take such a look at one of our own general aims, cited earlier: "to try to get students to read literature sensitively"? We see right off that we are aiming to develop abilities, not convey information, and we ask what differences that might make in our teaching practice. We see that it is "reading literature" that we must teach, and we want to know what that demands on the reader's part that, say, reading factual prose does not. What does "sensitively" mean? And how can "reading literature" be analyzed into its constituent abilities? How are these related to one another? Such questions would help us understand what was involved in our general aims, and the answers to them would usually help us decide on some "flight of stairs" —a set of particular aims—that will lead to achieving the general aim.

In order to spell out general aims into a series of particular aims, then, the teacher must analyze the general aim to see what the knowledge or skill he cites consists of and how its parts are organized. But when this is done, a very practical question remains to be decided: in teaching the knowledge or skill, is it best to follow the logical organization of parts or does effective teaching require quite another kind of organization? If it does, the teacher must be capable of devising one. This, in brief, is the kind of inquiry he must make into his general aim before he can set up particular aims that can guide his teaching step by step.

Setting up a sequence of particular aims—whether for a few weeks, a term, a year, or a high school English course—is a very difficult task. It is difficult, on one hand, because the teacher is pioneering. There are no useful models. General aims have so often been merely lovely sentiments and pious hopes that few teachers have ever seriously tried to derive particular aims from them. Most teachers have nodded courteously to the platitudes and have set up, as stop-gaps, short-range aims apropos of whatever they were doing. So when the prospective teacher sets about analyzing his own general aims to arrive at sequences of teaching aims, he is tracking an unexplored land. And he tends to fear his own findings. Setting up particular aims is difficult because, on the other hand, the teacher is blocked by his own past experience. He is unconsciously tied to the way he has been taught the same or a similar skill or knowledge. He finds it hard to conduct an unbiased inquiry. Like the "mind over matter" painter, he cannot see what is there because he knows too well what "ought" to be there.

All prospective teachers must be encouraged to be bold and open-minded enough to admit what an inquiry suggests, however radical the finding may seem. This is especially necessary if the inquiry shows that the natural structure of the knowledge or skill is not a suitable teaching structure and that they must devise a new structure. If, for example, the aim is "to get students to become responsive readers," inquiry may show that, though connotation is the logical first step, the first thing that must be taught is that the experience represented in the work of literature is a selection that is curtailed, stretched, and ordered to produce an effect. An understanding of artistic selection, then, becomes the first particular aim in the sequence the teacher will set up.

The sequence of particular aims a teacher arrives at is really the organization he thinks will move students step by step toward achieving the general aim. As with the general aim, the statements of particular aims must be concrete, and the teacher must know what behavior every verb he uses refers to. If, for example, he uses the word "understand" rather than "know," he must be able to tell specifically what difference his choice makes in terms of expected behaviors. Moreover, he must be able to say why with a general aim of, for example, "to teach students to be responsive readers," he chose to state one of his particular aims as "to develop a sense of the ironic," rather than "to understand irony." He must be prepared to point out what difference, if any, using the first aim rather than the second would make in the teaching plan he would develop for classroom use. The prospective teacher must be constantly aware that soon he must translate each of his particular aims into plans of action that he could use in high school classrooms.

When the teacher has come this far in his "working course," he must begin to "teach" the "position" that he has been shaping. He must develop a series of models—complete teaching plans for individual lessons or sequences of lessons—that will detail ways that one or two of his particular aims could be achieved. Although developing a few questions or sketching out a fragment of a class lesson has illustrative value, partial planning of this sort would not be appropriate practice for a beginning English teacher. Planning must always be the shaping of a significant whole, each part of which is essential and fitting in itself and in the total context. In order to plan realistically, the teacher should at this point in the course begin systematic observation of a live class, preferably the one he will teach.

The development of teaching plans raises new questions: What content would be appropriate to achieving this aim in this class? What methods would bring these students to and through the content in such a way as to achieve this aim? How can the progress of the students be estimated? The prospective teacher must defend in terms of his "position" the choices of content, methods, and testing procedures he makes. He must be able to offer reasons for shaping the lesson as he did, for emphasizing one phase of the work being read rather than others. He must know what each question is supposed to elicit, what each written paper is supposed to accomplish, what each analysis is supposed to achieve. He must be able to account for a sequence of questions being arranged in a certain order, for certain passages being read, and for the way in which they are to be read. He must tell how today's study relates to yesterday's and leads on to tomorrow's. This is only a sampling of the kinds of questions a prospective teacher must learn to ask himself about every plan he ever creates. He must always be prepared to explain and defend exactly why, given his aim and his class, the design of his lesson, over-all and in every detail, is as it is.

The way in which the prospective teacher must develop his teaching plans in this course forces him to deal with philosophical and psychological considerations *simultaneously*. He is not permitted to create a philosophically justifiable plan which he will "psychologize" later in the classroom. He must, rather, set down only those questions that *are* both justifiable and feasible. The prospective teacher's plan represents decisions made after a consideration of all relevant factors: the nature of literature, the aim, the work, and the students. The plan is his considered opinion of what philosophically *and* psychologically he ought to do.

The insistence on this kind of unified planning is neither trivial nor idiosyncratic. It is unrealistic to suppose that a beginning teacher —or even an experienced one—can organize content for teaching or can convert subject matter into teachable form, as he stands before a class. Whatever his respect for the integrity of subject matter or for teaching justifiable content by valid methods, if he has not a feasible plan, then, confronted with a class, the teacher will do what he can.

Furthermore, definitive planning such as the teacher learns to do through these model lessons, frees, rather than inhibits, him. If he has pored over the material as thoroughly as he must to plan this way, if he has thought through the various schemes for handling a lesson, and the many ways of phrasing a question and such, it is *less* likely that he will be confronted in the classroom with anything that he has not considered and somehow anticipated. Such planning will help him overcome the major bar to useful discussion in literature classes: it will help him recognize which comments are relevant, which tangential.

Security and freedom in teaching are earned by thorough preparation. If excellent lecturing demands careful preparation and conscious design, then the teaching-learning situation in a classroom with thirty students involved could hardly need less. That a lesson should be almost an improvisation of undefined sorts is the curious conclusion of those who confuse discipline, form, and order with authoritarianism and rigidity.

During the time that the teacher is developing his model teaching plans, he should have short, intensive, "dry-run" practices in using a wide variety of teaching techniques, so that he would never be prevented from teaching his "position" because of ignorance of possible techniques or a lack of skill in using those he knew. The teacher should, for example, know how to question analytically, how to develop "continuing" questions that will unify the study of longer works, and how to move from denotative questions to connotative. He must be able to decide what is discussable and to design discussion questions; he must know when and how to synthesize and how to summarize. He must know how to use critical writing in the study of literature. So while he is working on his model plans, he should be practicing these techniques and a host of others on poems, short stories, and plays of increasing complexity.

To conclude the "working course," each teacher should develop, for immediate use in his own practice teaching, an extended, detailed model for several weeks' work. This might be a model for teaching a period of literature, the reading of poetry, the works of one or more authors, or an individual work. As the teacher develops such a model, he will be confronted with every problem that planning involves. This will be his chance to make many interrelated decisions in terms of his "position." He will be conducting the "full orchestra." He will be forced to exercise many teaching skills in the complicated ways that real life in the classroom requires. Developing this model challenges the teacher to demonstrate his ability to make each question, each work, each test a fitting and necessary part of a large, consistent, meaningful whole.

In our description of the "working course" in the teaching of English, we have confined our discussion to literature in the interests of clarity, economy, and concreteness. In the actual course, composition would get its fair share of the time. During that half of the course, the prospective teacher would develop a "position" on the teaching of writing through the examination of questions that range from the nature of linguistic acts to ways of getting the reluctant student to "carry off" his paragraph with style.

Both the literature and the composition sections of the course are designed to help the teacher to arrive at a justifiable and feasible "position" and to learn to teach in the light of it. This course will not tell the teacher what to think or how to do anything. It asks him to put his head in his hands and think hard about the nature of literature and the nature of composition, about their functions, and about the crucial problems in the teaching of each. He must know his subject fundamentally in order to think through these problems, and thinking through these problems gives him a firmer hold on his field than he has ever had.

Writing is making something out of language. Reading is perceiving the thing made. Writing is creating; reading, re-creating. Both the maker and the perceiver must have an intense sensitivity to language. It is this sensitivity that the education of an English teacher must help him to develop, to understand, and to be capable of developing in others.

JURGEN HERBST:

The Teacher of History

> What we seek in history is not the knowledge of an external thing but a knowledge of ourselves.
>
> —Ernst Cassirer

> We may propose to use practice work as an instrument in making real and vital theoretical instruction; the knowledge of subject-matter and of principles of education. —John Dewey

The education of which I speak in this chapter is the process of intellectual growth which I deem the desirable professional preparation for the aspiring high school teacher of history. While intellectual growth is lifelong, I am dealing here primarily with the history teacher's training in a program of graduate professional education. I assume that the future teacher is an American college graduate who has majored in one of the fields commonly taught by members of the arts and sciences faculty. He has taken courses in history, the social sciences, and the humanities, which may or may not have been supplemented by work in education. When he enters a graduate program of professional education, practical questions relating to choice of courses arise at once. Should the future history teacher take more and advanced work in history, or should he concentrate on related disciplines, such as government, economics, or the history of art and of science? Should he rely on his college studies in these academic disciplines and turn his attention to educational subjects, such as the history and philosophy of education and psychology? Should he have practical training in teaching methods, classroom administration, legal problems of education, and curriculum development? How much time should he spend teaching his subject in nearby high schools? All of these questions may be subsumed under a general heading: What do we consider a desirable professional graduate education of the future high school teacher of history?

The history student in a graduate program for teacher education knows that he learns history in order to teach it, and that he studies education in order to teach well. Teaching history to him is the vocation by which he expects to earn his living. He assumes that his instructors supply him with knowledge that is of practical value. Thus he studies psychology in order to understand his students and his own function in the classroom. Having been told that many high school principals will expect him to teach modern European history and realizing that he is ill-prepared in this field, he enrolls in a European history course. He may desire, also, to take up work in labor relations once he has learned that many a history teacher is called upon to teach "Problems of Democracy." The future history teacher thus perceives that all his studies are of vocational value to him, including those of his undergraduate years in college.

But is the study of history a strictly vocational enterprise? Do all of its components supply the teacher with information that is of direct practical applicability in the high school classroom? How much information learned in a college course on "The Great Historians from Herodotus to Ranke," for example, will the teacher inject into his world history course in grade nine or ten? And what will he do with the "History of Civilization before Pericles" in his senior class on modern European or American history? If the study of history were to have a narrowly vocational purpose only, the teacher might argue that he could or should dispense with college courses of the kind listed above. Yet such argument is not accepted for any student of history—whether he be in a liberal arts college, a teachers' college, a state university, or a graduate school of arts and science or of education. Students of history are required to gain a comprehensive understanding of history as a subject-matter field. They are advised to study history for a more general, rather than a narrowly vocational, purpose. For future teachers, in particular, the study of history must be both a vocational-preparatory and a liberalizing enterprise. What is meant by the latter will become clear, I trust, in the course of this chapter. The implications of this assertion for a statement on a program of desirable professional graduate education for teachers of history are two: (1) We must show that vocational and liberal elements of education can be fused to yield the desired professional training. (2) We must show how this fusion takes place in the education of the history teacher. To show how the fusion of vocational and liberal elements of education comes about naturally in a desirable program of teacher education we shall begin our discussion with an analysis of the nature of history as a subject of instruction.

History as a School Subject

In the most comprehensive sense of the word history is everything that has happened in the past. Brief reflection will show that such definition of history is irrelevant to our discussion. We simply are not informed about everything that has occurred in the past. Even if we were, we could scarcely hope to utilize this mountainous burden of information for instructional purposes in high school or college.

Our task is to define the nature of history as a school subject, and here we confront history first as recorded data of past human events. Such data may be ancient tools or coins which bear silent testimony to the accomplishments of bygone generations. They may be documents written on paper or parchment, engraved on stone, or impressed upon metal. They may be nothing more than a sign —the cross on a Roman wall—or they may be statements of several pages in length, such as *Magna Charta*. Again, they need not be documents in the historian's meaning of original sources. They can meet the eye as textbook tables of dynastic genealogies, or as space-fillers in our newspapers.

History as recorded data of past human events, however, is only one form in which history as a school subject is known or studied. Much more frequently the student encounters the meaningful narration of selected historical data, presented in his textbook and in historical works. Here the data are embedded in the author's narrative, and are endowed with meaning through the descriptive or explanatory context. History as a school subject now appears in the form of historical writing. To recorded data is added historical scholarship and interpretation.

History as recorded data of past human events and as interpretive narration presents problems that are alike, essentially, both to the history student in high school and to the future teacher of history as graduate student. But the latter encounters history also as a field of knowledge that he will have to teach. To put it another way, the future teacher not only studies and informs himself of the meaning with which historians have in the past endowed historical data, but he himself will also, in preparation for his lessons, endow the facts with meaning. Unless he intends to cite verbatim the texts of others, he himself cannot but engage in historical interpretation. The future teacher thus encounters history as a personal challenge to the correct narration of historical data and their meaningful interpretation.

Lastly, the history teacher will re-create past history in the classroom. His interpretation of selected historical data, presented in the classroom, now becomes the object of discourse. The students will react—some positively, some negatively; some verbally, and others silently—to the interpretation the teacher presents. In the course of this exchange the teacher may modify his own interpretation and, if the lesson is successful, the teacher and his students together will re-create a fragment of history in the classroom.

If, then, we attempt a definition of history as a school subject we discern four aspects of history, each distinct by definition, yet all merging into one another in the teacher's study and presentation in class. History as a school subject comprises selected recorded data of past human events, their narration in the works of scholars, the teacher's own interpretative narration, and the re-creation of history in the classroom. One of the first demands on a program of professional graduate education is that its history students become conscious of the four aspects of their subject. Only when students understand the theory of their subject matter can they be expected to meet the varying challenges and situations of daily classroom teaching, and can they succeed in integrating their theoretical knowledge with their practice. Before we proceed to discuss the practical requirements desirable to stimulate the fusion of theory and practice, let us turn to a somewhat fuller exploration of the four aspects of history as they affect the education of the history teacher.

History as recorded data of past human events is the basic tool of the history teacher. The history teacher must have a reasonably full knowledge of historical data. While he need not strive for encyclopedic knowledge, his studies should have equipped him with a ready familiarity with dates and names. He should not be misled into associating Henry the Navigator with the British Navy, nor should he place the Hohenzollerns in Sicily. The Meiji period has no connection with the Incas of South America, nor does the history of the Holy Roman Empire include the exploits of Caesar. Historical categories, too, are elementary tools of the history teacher. Feudalism is found in the United States only infrequently, and capitalism is a term ill suited in discussions of Greek history. While it is hardly worth the time to draw up lists of names, dates, periods, and categories which the teacher is expected to know, the subject matter of high school history is still small enough in compass to require of the history teacher a basic professional vocabulary that can compare in depth and breadth with that of a teacher of French or chemistry.

To master history as recorded data of past events requires two further accomplishments of historical understanding. First, the teacher must realize that the data he encounters do not constitute the complete record of past events. Data are selected both by accident and by choice of the selector. A Greek vase or a Hebrew scroll may accidentally be uncovered and preserved. A document may be kept or discarded by its discoverer because he deemed its content significant or trivial. Recorded data thus always represent a selection of records. Secondly, the data thus selected and preserved are symbols of historical facts. They are not the facts themselves. The coronation of Charles the Great was a unique historical event that took place in 800 A.D. This event, as are all facts of history, is past. What is present still is the memory of this event given to us in symbolical form as an historical datum. Unless an event takes place in the present, the student of history never encounters the unique events of history but always their records in symbolic form. Unlike the physicist the student of history cannot observe the events he studies. The uniqueness of historical events prevents the historian from repeating observations and experiments. His task is to report from recorded data.

Only rarely, however, does the teacher encounter historical data in isolation. If he has access to a museum he may see a Roman coin under glass. From a chronological table he may learn that the Pilgrims landed on Cape Code in 1620. Yet his study of history yields more than data concerning historical events. The facts and events of which the data are symbols are related to each other through the historian as author. The fact that the Pilgrims landed in 1620 is acknowledged in the histories of George Bancroft and of George Trevelyan. Bancroft comments that with this event "democratic liberty and independent Christian worship started into being." Trevelyan remarks that the Pilgrims came "asking only for land, of which there was abundance." The event referred to is the same, yet the stories told differ. One concerns political and religious developments, the other speaks of economic motivation. Turning his attention to the problems raised by differing historical interpretations, the student enters the field of historiography.

The historian as author interprets his data within a conceptual framework that he, the historian, has devised. This framework does not arise automatically from the data, but is superimposed upon them by the author. Every historical narrative or analysis is thus a synthesis of data and interpretative framework. This is why "histories" differ from each other even though the data they incorporate may be identical. In reading historical works the student must learn to distinguish the data from the interpretation. The future history teacher will come to appreciate this difference by familiarizing himself with past and current historians and their interpretative frameworks. For his high school course in world history the future teacher should understand the views of Thucydides, Polybius, Gibbon, Vico, Ranke, Lord Acton, and Mommsen. His knowledge of American history should encompass a knowledge of the concepts of history of Cotton Mather, George Bancroft, Herbert B. and Henry Adams, Frederick Jackson Turner, James Harvey Robinson, Charles Beard, Carl Becker, the Schlesingers, and Daniel Boorstin.

But just as encyclopedic knowledge of historical data is neither desirable nor sufficient, so it does not suffice simply to acquaint the future teacher with a number of historical interpretations. Such information, no doubt, adds sophistication to the teaching of history, yet it constitutes but another series of data, albeit of a different order. Historiography, properly approached, not only shows that historians interpret factual data; it also demonstrates that through their interpretations historians, too, make history. The controversies aroused by Charles Beard's *Economic Interpretation of the Constitution* may serve as an example of the historian as a maker of history. They show Beard as a human being and citizen who holds views on the nature and course of history, which make his book a document of the social and intellectual history of his own time and its publication an event in American history. The student learns from the study of historiography that history is human history in a twofold sense: It is made and recorded by human beings. It records past events of human history, and in accomplishing this the record itself becomes an event and a datum of human history. The student soon perceives that the writing of history is anything but a sterile occupation with the past.

The study of historiography extends this recognition of the historian as both reporter and maker of history to the function of scholars in other disciplines. It inquires not only: What is history and what does a historian do? It asks also: What is science and what does a natural scientist do? What are the humanities, and what do professors do in that field? These questions lead the student to perceive the differences and the common ground of the many fields of scholarship. Natural scientists, philosophers, professors in the humanities, and social scientists all seek to discover previously unknown facts and to express them clearly, logically, and meaningfully. In doing so they organize and interpret their data. While they may differ in the varying degrees of emphasis they place on the discovery, explanation, and creative interpretation of data, they all base their scholarship on the perfected techniques of discovery and the rational character of their interpretations and conclusions. The historian claims for himself the prestige of scholarship because his methods of source criticism and documentation are scientific, his narrative corresponds to what he believes were the historical facts, and his analysis is internally consistent and allows the reader to check the conclusions against the known data and against the demands of logic. The student of historiography should be encouraged to compare the historian's claim with that of other scholars. Only by comparative evaluation of the field of history and the historian's work can the student gain the comprehensive understanding of history that he needs.

Instruction in historiography should therefore include a general introduction to the problems of scholarship in the various areas of humane and scientific learning. Such a comparative approach is of particular relevance to the history teacher in the case of the social sciences. In the great majority of American school systems history teachers are expected to teach the Social Studies and, in particular, the Problems of Democracy course. The teacher finds himself forced to refer back to his undergraduate and graduate studies in political science, economics, sociology, and anthropology. He wrestles with the question whether he is dealing with data and concepts that demand an approach different from the one he uses in his history classes. He wonders just what this difference is, and how he is to change his method of teaching. He finds that although in Problems of Democracy he deals primarily with contemporary problems, he cannot and does not consistently exclude historical considerations. The problems of industrial arbitration and of federal debt management, for example, are contemporary as well as historical. Social, political, and economic issues are not restricted to either past or present. Instruction in historiography therefore ought to explore the interrelations of the various social sciences and of history in the context of the whole field of scholarship dealing with human affairs. Only then does it perform a function that fully justifies its place in the training of future history teachers.

The third aspect of history as a school subject concerns, as we have said above, the teacher's own use of historical and historiographical data. It is not enough for him to know his data. He will have to transmit these data in the classroom, and it is his task to relate them coherently, logically, and meaningfully. Let us suppose that he is about to teach a number of lessons on the Civil War. He is acquainted with a sufficient number of historical data. He also knows that some authors have seen in the war a clash between fundamentally different economic systems, that others have viewed it as a moral conflict over the issue of slavery, and others again have emphasized the war as a legal issue over opposed constitutional intrepretations. Furthermore, the teacher is well aware of the conflict among historians who deemed the war inevitable and those who thought it repressible. He can derive no comfort from the frequently heard and no doubt well-meant advice to stick to the "facts" and leave the interpretations alone. He knows this is impossible. The attempt to follow this advice consistently would lead to the suicide of the teacher as teacher and to his degradation into an "Information, Please" machine. The teacher is a human being with likes and dislikes, opinions, and—yes, prejudices, too. By making use of historical interpretations in the classroom he achieves at least one positive result, namely, that his own views do not appear as the only possible ones. By consciously and conscientiously working out his own interpretative framework the teacher embarks upon the only promising journey to replace his prejudices with well-formed and rational opinions, and to show his students how they, as rational human beings, may decide for themselves among different historical interpretations. Instead of running away from the problem of historical interpretation—a futile effort, anyway—the teacher faces the issue deliberately. From a receptive collector of historical information he turns into a teacher of history.

What considerations should guide the teacher in his attempt to work out an historical scheme of interpretation for use in his classroom? How can he assure himself, his students and their parents, that he will not parade his prejudices in class under the guise of "historical interpretation"? Where may he find the line that separates his professional freedom as a scholar from pure personal arbitrariness? How can he justify to his school board and to his community his academic freedom in the high school classroom—a freedom that he can rightly claim and that he enjoys in many of our school systems? On what scholarly duties does he base his scholarly rights?

We may derive these duties as corollaries of the aspects of history already discussed. As a student of recorded historical and historiographical data the teacher must remain faithful to his sources, must not contradict or distort them by willful omission, factual falsification, or contextual misrepresentation. The data, insofar as they have been duly verified, are sacred. The German high command in 1918 was convinced and acted upon the conviction that the war was militarily lost. The stab-in-the-back story, encouraged later by the Nazis, was a legend, not a documented factual account. The first and fundamental rule of history teaching demands adherence to the verified data. As an interpreter of historical data the teacher must adhere to the rules of logical thought—right reason, as the ancients called it. This demand does not imply that the teacher subscribe to the dictum that history as it happened is logical. Historical facts are neither logical nor illogical; they just are. The teacher may well hold with Henry Adams that history is "in essence incoherent and immoral," that it is "a tangled skein that one may take up at any point, and break when one has unravelled enough. . . ." But when he teaches history he will find it impossible to reach his students unless he has given much thought to the logical ordering of the materials he intends to present. His carefully prepared lesson plan will become his indispensable aid. In planning his lesson the teacher creates order out of what may appear chaotic and nonlogical. The logical ordering of data is the indispensable prerequisite for effective communication. And what is good teaching if it does not begin with clear, logical communication?

Teaching as the art of effective communication brings us to the consideration of the fourth aspect of history as a school subject: history as the re-creation of past events in the classroom. What are the implications of this concept of history, and what duties does it lay upon the teacher? Analogous to our recognition of the author-historian as a maker of history, we find that the high school teacher makes history in the classroom. Here history is made in the context of the teacher's professional experience. Each lesson taught gives him new insights into history and into teaching. As a result the teacher will never teach the same lesson again in identical fashion, not only because he will face different students, but also because the lesson taught has become part of his own history. In addition, the teacher makes history for and in the experience of his students. To them a history lesson is history over and beyond the factual data and their meaning as presented by the teacher. It involves them as responding human beings, arouses their curiosity, and comes to life as part of their personal experience. It follows that besides historical and historiographical data the teacher must know himself and his students. He must understand the psychology of high school students and of the learning process as it affects them and himself. He must realize that students are more than receptacles of factual data. They are human beings who respond in many different ways to his words, and who through their responses likewise endow data with meaning. To address his students in his lessons as responding human beings and to "make history" in the classroom the teacher must know how to exercise his profession as an art in effective communication.

For teacher and student alike the data of history have more than informative value. To live minds, and particularly to the minds of adolescents groping for emotional security, historical data are of existential significance. Let me return to a previously cited example to illustrate my contention. Confronted with Bancroft's and Trevelyan's comments on the landing of the Pilgrims, a twelfth grader may well ask: "Well, now, did the Pilgrims establish democracy, or did they ask for land?" Many a history teacher will be tempted to pass off the question by saying that the Pilgrims did both. If the teacher does this, he holds fast to his data and fully answers the student who wants nothing but the "correct" answer to be duly reported back in the next quiz. If, however, the teacher has been successful as a teacher of history, his student craves for more than the "correct" answer. He betrays a searching anxiety over the meaning of the Pilgrim story. He asks whether his ancestors were motivated by love of freedom or the desire for wealth. He wrestles with the question whether America stands for liberty or for security sought after through the acquisition of material gains.

For the student the historical question regarding the Pilgrims carries significance for his understanding of his country and himself. This is what I mean by the student's existential concern. In answering the student's question in full awareness of its meaning the teacher shoulders the responsibility of his profession. He faces the moral nature of history teaching. He transcends teaching as a vocational skill and exercises the privileges and duties of a liberal profession.

The teacher who with his students strives to re-create a moment of history in the classroom finds that the duties of his position are moral ones. His painstaking accuracy in the use of sources, his skill in the art of communication are now joined by his attempt to reach his students at their deepest awareness and to liberate them to fresh thinking on their own. This attempt calls for the teacher's responsible use of his psychological judgment. He must avoid indoctrinating his students with his personal views, he must not overtax their capacity to understand, and he must not underestimate it either. Above all, he must keep in mind that it is the needs and questions of his students—not his own—that he is trying to meet. He must be committed to evoke, recognize, and respond to his students' quest for values to live by. He leads his students to the data, challenges them to organize and express them rationally, and then encourages his students to relate these organized data to the questions they face. Both teacher and students share the facts as their common historical heritage. Each sees them related to himself and to his fellows as a living, personal, and common possession. History no longer remains an alien body of knowledge to be memorized, but a living bequest full of meaning to each individual student. Once the teacher has made history come alive, once he succeeds in re-creating it as a meaningful possession for his students, then, in his hands, the teaching of history contributes to the maturity of high school students, enriches their lives, and helps them grow into responsible members of their community and nation. The study of history has become more than a strictly vocational enterprise. In theory and in practice it is part of a liberal, that is liberalizing, education. It re-creates the past, brings it to life, and relates it to the lives of students. Information about the past becomes a guide for the future.

Professional Education for History Teachers

In the preceding section I have argued that history as a school subject encompasses both vocational and liberal elements of education and that in the training of the history teacher these two elements are to receive equal stress. I now propose that these two elements be emphasized simultaneously throughout the teacher's training and that we cease telling our students to pursue their professional education by adding education credits to subject-matter credits as though these credits were real and meaningful building stones of their education. History and education credits cannot be added together arithmetically and their sum then be taken as evidence for the desired education of the history teacher. If we persist in such bookkeeping, we only tend to encourage the student's estimation of history as dry, tedious, and leaning toward obscurantism, and his contempt for education as an academic variety of gadgetism conceived by professionals who found the standards of other disciplines too demanding.

The fusion of liberal and vocational education in the training of the history teacher follows as a logical and natural consequence from the nature of history itself. Historical accounts always have been composed with regard for the reader. Thucydides, for example, wrote the history of the Peloponnesian War as "a possession for all time." The historian as author is concerned both with data and with readers who will use his books in his own lifetime and long thereafter. The historian as author needs vocational training in both research and writing, and his research and his writing receive direction and purpose from a liberally educated mind. Substitute teaching for writing, and the historian as teacher does not differ from the historian as author. The history teacher takes his data, and seeks to communicate them meaningfully to his students. For him history as data and teaching as communication cannot possibly be separate and different entities. His education as a teacher of history must see to it that he takes each newly learned datum of historical information as a problem of communication in the classroom, and that he checks each problem situation in the classroom against the historical sources at his disposal. The division, then, between history and teaching is artificial. How can we overcome it in a program of teacher training?

I have argued above that teachers of history are to be conscious of the four aspects of their subject as an academic discipline and that these four aspects are distinct by definition, yet merge into one another in the teacher's study and teaching. History as recorded data and history as historiography represent knowledge that we expect our student-teachers to receive from regular college history courses. The future teacher of history, however, cannot stop here. He must bring his own vocational concerns into his college history courses. He must be encouraged to view his college class not merely as a source of historical information, but as a demonstration in teaching. He ought to wonder why the professor selected particular questions for discussion and dropped others, and why he was or was not successful in presenting a particular topic in his lecture. As a future teacher he should be given the opportunity to discuss these questions with the professor of his course. He will also discover the incidental bonus he receives when through his pedagogical questioning he learns more historical data than he thought possible before.

This approach to the study of history for the future teacher assumes two things: First, that the entire faculty of the university—in particular the staff of the college history department and the educators of the teacher-training program—are in agreement on the needs of the future history teachers, and are willing to meet these needs. To ask a student to discuss the pedagogical problems of his professor with the professor himself presupposes prior agreement on the part of faculty members to view their students as future colleagues in teaching. Secondly, it assumes that the future history teacher receives the kind of theoretical instruction set forth in this chapter at the beginning of his graduate studies in a program of teacher education. From the outset the student must understand the theoretical basis for the fusion of history and teaching. Only then can he apply this fusion in all his activities as student and teacher. To accomplish this there is need for instruction in the "Principles of History," instruction that each history major in a program of graduate education for teachers should receive during his first semester.

The key concept around which instruction in the "Principles of History" may be organized is history as a scholarly activity. The future history teacher studies the work of historians in order to understand the problems of historical writing and teaching. He studies historiography as a demonstration of different ways in which historians have responded to the challenge of meaningful organization and interpretation of historical data. He is asked continually to evaluate critically the historian's presentation of his data, that is to say, the future teacher is encouraged to view the historian's problems as his own. He is, furthermore, asked to acquaint himself with the problems of scholars in other disciplines, and to evaluate the relevance these problems and their solutions have for him as a teacher of history. Ever since the 1890's American social scientists have been hailed as indispensable helpmates of the historian. Should not the teacher inquire: What do the social scientists do? How "scientific" is their science? Inevitably, these questions lead to others: What is science? When history becomes "scientific," does it then become a science? What about the humanities and the arts, and their relationship to history? It is a truism that one cannot fully understand a subject of inquiry if one persists in seeing it in isolation. Thus one cannot understand history unless one compares it with other academic disciplines. One cannot find from the contemplation of the work of an historian whether it is scientific or artistic, unless one has a fairly clear notion of what science and art represent. The "Principles of History," then, as a part of the instruction of future history teachers must include in its scope the principles of scholarship.

Instruction in the "Principles of History" is a theoretical field. The student learns about the nature of history, and comes to view the teaching of history as a problem in communication and reconstruction. Complementing this theoretical instruction he should receive training in a course dealing with the "Teaching of History."

Here he learns that a battle may be described with all the verbal skill that a teacher can muster, but that it may also provide an object lesson in applied geography if the teacher chooses to analyze the movements of troops by reference to a detailed map of the battlefield and its surroundings. Again, students may be assigned to demonstrate and criticize the decisions of field commanders, and may be sent to the library to acquaint themselves with the political, logistic, and climatic factors, and the commander's past experience that helped shape his actions. In many teaching situations the teacher may want to forgo lectures and student reports in favor of the reconstruction of events through role-playing by the students. The teacher's choice takes into account the nature of the topic, the availability of teaching aids such as pictures, movies, tapes, maps, reference books, and the interests of his students.

Once the teacher's choice is made, his problem is how to translate his plans into practice. As every teacher knows, there are certain do's and don'ts in the classroom. When he decides on map work, he ought to be informed about the various ways of map-teaching. A physiographic map, obviously, is superior to a purely political map in demonstrating the influence of terrain on troop movements. The blackboard with an assortment of many different colored chalks allows the step by step construction of a map that may surpass in clarity if not in accuracy and beauty the printed wall map. The students, too, may develop their own maps on printed outlines or on white paper. For all these problems and for many more the "Teaching of History" course provides answers and instruction.

It is quite true that every teacher eventually perfects his classroom techniques through experience. Experience, however, is a hard taskmaster, and the beginning teacher does not have experience. Practical information is what he craves and needs. His theoretical instruction in the "Principles of History" will tell him which problem is an important one, but it will not, except in the most general sense, tell him how to approach it. The "Teaching of History," then, conceived as a course in practical information and related to the theoretical approach of the "Principles of History," is a necessary ingredient of the future history teacher's curriculum. It must help the new teacher build the basis for the growth of his own experience in the classroom.

The complementary aspects of the history teacher's education extend beyond the "Principles of History" and the "Teaching of History" to his liberal and his vocational training as well as his theoretical and practical work. On the theoretical side the student as history major is to widen his background in history and related disciplines. In his choice of courses he ought to be guided by his interests and the requirements of his future position. As a future teacher he should take work in philosophy, sociology, and psychology as these disciplines apply to education. The test of the student's theoretical education then lies in his practice in the high school classroom. Here the student-teacher is to demonstrate the recurrent fusion of the four aspects of history into one single, unitary lesson. In the lesson theory and practice are merged. Theoretical knowledge of history and education as disciplines of liberal scholarship, and practical skill in the techniques of teaching history are joined. Each alone, theoretical knowledge or practical mastery, is insufficient. The theoretician who fails to communicate and the master craftsman who has neither factual nor theoretical content to communicate are equally out of place in the high school classroom. The objective of history teaching always remains the re-creation of history true to the data, rationally expounded, and meaningfully related to the past, the present, and to the students. The history lesson at its best is always an achievement of artistic creation, a living, unitary whole, a comprehensive fusion of its factual and theoretical elements.

It appears, then, that practice teaching constitutes the final and most important step in the history teacher's education. In the high school classroom he puts to the test his knowledge and his skill. As a practice teacher or intern in teaching he performs all the functions of a regular teacher, but receives guidance and advice from his supervisors. His lessons are his attempts to fuse the liberal and vocational elements of his training. His supervisors are present to let him know how successful he is in his endeavors, where he fails, and how he may improve. Practice teaching is not the beginning of the teacher's actual career. It is rather the culmination of his professional training. It is not "work" in the sense of tasks performed by a professional teacher, albeit a new one, but a laboratory assignment carried out by an apprentice as part of his training.

As the well-taught lesson is the ultimate goal of the education of teachers, so practice teaching becomes the touchstone of a teacher-education program. Practice teaching must be an integral part of the teacher's training. It must not be allowed to be viewed as an afterthought coming as it usually does after the student has completed most of his academic work in the program. The student must not be handed over to schools which maintain no relation with the program, nor must he be entrusted to supervisors who have little or no knowledge about the aims of the program. The student-teacher must feel that practice teaching is related organically to his studies in history and related disciplines, and to the philosophy, sociology, and psychology of education. He must be able to see the connection that exists between the "Teaching of History" course and the day-to-day problems that he meets in the classroom. Practice teaching, in other words, should not send the student into a world altogether unrelated to his previous studies. His professors and instructors in the graduate program of teacher education should accompany him into the schools, and help him bring about the fusion of educational theory, subject-matter mastery, and pedagogical practice.

The chief responsibility for the successful integration of practice teaching lies with the faculty of the teacher-education program, and only secondarily with its students. Integration begins with the faculty, and is not to be left as inspiring exhortation to the students. This means that responsibility for practice teaching and its supervision rests on the academic historian as well as on the academic educator and the supervising high school teacher. It is not to be palmed off to high school teachers and administrators alone, or to be carried on by a specially hired staff of teaching fellows, retired teachers, and the like. The professor of history who teaches the "Principles of History" and the professor of education who is in charge of the "Teaching of History" are committed to the successful completion of their students' training. They therefore participate in the supervision of the student-teacher in the high school classroom. The benefits of such arrangement are substantial for professors and students. The historian escapes the seclusion of the academic classroom and profits from the all-too-rare opportunity of observing history taught to pupils unfamiliar to him. In the performance of his students as teachers the historian sees a test of his own effectiveness as a teacher. The educator is forced to test educational theory against the theory of history as a subject-matter field, and to view the techniques of teaching in the perspective of historical subject matter and its requirements. The student-teacher, finally, benefits from the educator's perspective on the problems of teaching, and from the counsel and advice he receives from a professional historian. By being urged constantly to analyze his teaching in the context of a theoretical framework common to himself and his supervisors, the student-teacher comes to realize meaningfully the relatedness of theory and practice.

Lest there be suspicion of a too theoretical or academic approach to high school practice teaching, let it be kept in mind that the student-teacher is also supervised by members of the high school faculty. To them the student-teacher turns for advice in many practical matters concerning his teaching of a particular class and the problems of classroom administration. From them he learns the daily routine of passes, disciplinary measures, and cafeteria duty. The supervising high school teacher ought to be a "master teacher" who has taught in many different situations, who is familiar with the different problems posed by general and college-preparatory classes, who understands the student-teacher's background in the "Principles" and in the "Teaching of History" courses, and who is aware of the sociological and psychological factors operating in the student-teacher's classroom. He advises the student-teacher on his lesson plans, and he accepts and guides him as a future colleague.

The practice teacher thus draws on the knowledge and experience of his high school supervisor and builds on the theoretical foundations of history as a discipline and of the teaching of history as a pedagogical activity. Through the participation and co-operation of academic historian, educator, and the high school "master teacher" can the practice teaching of history best achieve its goal.

Because practice teaching is an integral and crowning part of a program of teacher education, its supervision is the supreme assignment for the faculty and deserves and needs their best energies. For historian and educator the supervision of practice teaching remains the most demanding and most rewarding task of their work as instructors of future high school teachers of history.

We now return to our leading question: What do we consider a desirable professional graduate education of the future high school teacher of history? The answer is: An education which fuses the vocational and liberal elements of instruction throughout its course. It consists of studies in factual and philosophical academic disciplines—the "Principles of History," and courses in history and related disciplines; of theoretical and practical educational studies and assignments—courses in the philosophy, sociology, and psychology of education, and the "Teaching of History"; and of practice teaching. The questions raised at the beginning of this chapter concerning the students' choice of courses cannot be answered in a universally prescriptive form. For graduate students the choice of courses must be made individually after an evaluation of their undergraduate work in the light of the criteria established here. A student with a strong preparation in history should take graduate work in the related disciplines of the social sciences and the humanities. The "Principles of History" and the "Teaching of History" courses are to be required of all history majors, and further educational studies in the program should be theoretical rather than practical. The "Teaching of History" course and practice teaching with its tutorial conferences between supervisors and students supply the bulk of the practical pedagogical information the student can derive with profit from his graduate studies. Further practical training can be left confidently to the student's future experience. Given a firm theoretical background, the student will become his own best teacher. The fusion of the desirable elements of graduate professional teacher education should find its expression in the commitment of the historian, the educator, and the supervisory high school teacher to all aspects of the program. Organic integration is more than a fine phrase in the College Bulletin. It is the concern and assignment of students and professors alike. The results, we hope, will appear in the high school classroom. The ultimate goal is a more meaningful understanding of history and a deeper commitment to social responsibility on the part of our high school teachers and students.

NOTES: The quotations at the head of the chapter as well as the author's central inspiration for his views on the nature of history and on the relationship of theory and practice in the education of teachers have come from Ernst Cassirer's *An Essay on Man* (New York: Doubleday Anchor, 1953), p. 256, and from John Dewey's, "The Relation of Theory to Practice in Education," *Third Yearbook of the National Society for the Scientific Study of Education,* Part I (Chicago, 1904), p. 9. The reader will find Bancroft's and Trevelyan's statements on the Pilgrims in George Bancroft, *History of the United States of America,* thoroughly rev. ed. (Boston: Little, Brown, 1876), I, p. 246, and in George Macaulay Trevelyan, *A Shortened History of England* (New York, London, Toronto: Longmans, Green, 1942), p. 302. The quotations from Henry Adams are in *The Education of Henry Adams* (New York: Modern Library, 1931), pp. 301, 302.

THEODORE ANDERSSON:

The Teacher of Modern Foreign Languages

Introduction: Importance of Early Experience, Schooling, and Training

The education of the future teacher of modern foreign languages often begins with the first utterances he hears and learns to imitate. This may be his native language, which he may someday teach as a foreign language, or it may be a second language learned from birth in a bicultural situation. Lucky are those children for whom this first stage of language learning begins so early and continues for several years, long enough to become a permanent acquisition. A child in such a situation not only learns a language without special effort, he also acquires the mental set, habits of behavior, and sense of values of those around him. This process of learning a language in the context of its culture is a part of what is known as enculturation.

It is estimated that in addition to the million and a half Americans living abroad and in direct contact with other cultures we have in the United States some twenty million speakers of languages other than English. These provide a considerable reservoir of potential language teachers. In New York City one American citizen in ten is a native speaker of Spanish of Puerto Rican background. One Texan out of six has a Spanish name and can usually speak Spanish. Louisiana alone has some 400,000 speakers of French. Speakers of French in New England and in Louisiana, of Spanish in the New York area and in the Southwest, of German in the Midwest, of Italian in many large cities, of Chinese and Japanese on the West Coast and in Hawaii, and of Russian, Polish, and the Scandinavian languages in scattered places represent such vast linguistic and cultural resources that we should be able to find among them enough prospective language teachers to supply the entire country.

A second opportunity to begin the education of the future language teacher occurs when the child who knows only his native language goes to school. His first teacher of a foreign language is in a strategic position to plant in him the seed of a special interest in languages; and, with his first thought that he may one day like to teach, the pupil's observation of his teachers becomes more conscious and more critical. As teachers we too often fail to keep the possibility of a career in teaching attractively before our students. And in our teacher-training programs we often overlook the usefulness of these twelve to sixteen years of daily observation of teachers and school administrators.

The third aspect of the education of prospective teachers, the period of training, is our main concern in this chapter. This training may occur in a liberal arts college, in a school of education, in a teachers' college—now coming to be called a state college—or in a graduate school. We shall not describe existing programs, for they are changing and many of them are unsatisfactory. Too many have been organized to satisfy state certification requirements, which are in turn inadequate. Instead, we shall examine the desirable qualifications of a language teacher and use these as a basis for discussing an adequate teacher-training program. In order to suggest as concretely as possible what a teacher should be able to do, we shall start by describing two visits to language classes, the first near the beginning and the second toward the end of the secondary-school course. We shall then sketch briefly the six-year sequence of language study which these two classes presuppose. And finally we shall enumerate the elements of a teacher-training program designed to produce teachers competent to teach languages in the way that the times require.

A Visit to a Seventh-Grade Class in Russian

Let us first visit a seventh-grade class in a large city high school. Here a young woman is teaching a first-year class in Russian. The teacher's parents were both born in Russia, came to this country shortly after the Bolshevik Revolution, met, married, and raised their children here. By speaking Russian in the home, they enabled their children to learn this language as a mother tongue. At the same time the children learned English from their playmates and later in school. Our teacher inherited from her parents a deep-seated respect for the teaching profession and chose to become a teacher—of English. With the revival of foreign-language teaching after the launching of Sputnik and the passage of the National Defense Education Act of 1958 (NDEA), school administrators began looking for qualified teachers of Russian. At this time our teacher, who was already licensed, decided to offer to teach her mother tongue.

Knowing little of modern theory and practice, she enrolled in an NDEA summer language institute. Here her experience was that of many a secondary-school teacher. At first she resisted all the talk about linguistic science, the primacy of speech over writing, and language as behavior. These concepts did not correspond to her own language-learning experience in school nor to that of her parents. She resolved to keep an open mind, however, and gradually she began to understand the new ideas and to find them acceptable. What finally won her over was the demonstration classes, conducted in the early stages entirely without writing and without grammar explanation. The children watched and listened to a native-speaking teacher, imitated his every utterance and gesture, gradually memorized by ear whole dialogues, created rearrangements of these, and acted them out with gusto. Fascinated by the speed with which the children learned, by their accurate pronunciation, and especially by their great satisfaction with this kind of learning, she decided that this was the way she was going to teach Russian.

And this is the way she is teaching today, some two months after the first class in early September. The class contains thirty pupils, an equal number of boys and girls. Fortunately modern electronic equipment and choral techniques have mitigated somewhat the difficulties of large classes. Today, for example, we find that fifteen of the pupils are working with such equipment at the rear of the room while the teacher is working directly with the others.

By plugging in a set of earphones and turning a button we may monitor any one of the fifteen pupils at the electronic stations. At the moment they are doing pattern practice. They listen to a model sentence in Russian spoken at normal speed by a native speaker. This sentence is taken from a dialogue concerning a situation in school. The teacher is conscious of the fact that the situation is more characteristic of an American school than of a Russian school, so she has questioned her parents about their school experience in Russia, and in fact she has persuaded them to record a dialogue on tape parallel to the one now being practiced but culturally more nearly authentic though perhaps a little out of date. This dialogue she will use on Friday, when she likes to vary the program. She will also make it available in the school library, where there are three magnetic tape channels and four tables with a total of twenty-four listening posts.

Let us return to our fifteen pupils wearing earphones and absorbed in what they are doing. This is their third contact with this dialogue, which they have by now memorized. Yesterday the teacher presented this material and showed the class how to practice. Last night the pupils learned the dialogue by listening to a disc taken home from school. On the disc two native speakers do the whole dialogue at natural speed while the pupil thinks of the meaning, reminding himself, if necessary, by looking at an English translation. Each pupil listens to the dialogue as many times as may be needed to understand but about three times on the average. Then the dialogue is broken into short but natural utterances, with pauses for repetition by the pupil, followed by a repetition by the speaker. This procedure is also followed several times, according to the pupil's need. And finally the pupil is assisted in memorizing the dialogue in the following way: The voice on the disc says the first sentence, then repeats, omitting the last word or two. The pupil accompanies the voice aloud and fills in the missing words from memory. The voice repeats the sentence, omitting a longer segment at the end, and again the pupil fills in the missing words. When only the first words in the sentence are left, a voice says, "Now say the whole sentence." The pupil tries. The voice repeats the sentence. The pupil imitates. The voice repeats again and the pupil imitates. And a third time the voice repeats and the pupil imitates. At this point the pupil stops the turntable and practices the sentence as many times as may be necessary for him to feel confident that he knows it. This same process is then repeated with each successive sentence in the dialogue.

At their listening posts the pupils are now busy practicing the various patterns involved. The voice on the tape gives a model in the foreign language: "Let's go to the library." Pupil: "Let's go to the library." Voice: "Gym." Pupil: "Let's go to the gym." Voice: "Post office." Pupil: "Let's go to the post office." Since the structure is kept constant and the vocabulary varied only within the limits of what has already been learned, the pupils are encouraged to make their utterances not only accurate in pronunciation, speed, intonation, and juncture (the way words are connected), but also to make them habitual, or automatic. Gradually the sounds, rhythm, intonation, and structure will become more familiar and will lose their strangeness.

By listening to another form of replacement or substitution exercise we realize that not all is mere rote repetition, though much rote learning is essential to mastering a language. The voice on the tape says, with convincing naturalness, "There are two girls sitting at the table."

Pupil: "There are two girls sitting at the table."
Voice: "Desk."
Pupil: "There are two girls sitting at the desk."
Voice: "Standing."
Pupil: "There are two girls standing at the desk."
Voice: "Boys."
Pupil: "There are two boys standing at the desk."
Voice: "Three."
Pupil: "There are three boys standing at the desk."
Voice: "Were."
Pupil: "There were three boys standing at the desk."

Thus, while remaining conscious of the basic pattern, the pupil is led to vary the elements in it. Each repetition at natural speed and with faithful imitation serves to fix more firmly the fundamental structure of the language. The pupil thus becomes conscious of "correct" or appropriate usage, but there is no explanation of grammar, no talking *about* language. Gradually the pupils realize that at this stage the question "Why?" makes no sense, that the answer is always the same: "Because this is the way speakers of Russian say it."

This exercise has taken fifteen minutes. In the meantime, with the other half of the class, the teacher has been reviewing day before yesterday's lesson by means of pattern practices and question-and-answer drill. This is the fourth time over this unit. The response to pattern practice takes place first with everyone responding, then with boys responding, then girls, then with one row or file or group responding, then another. Instead of leaving fourteen pupils inactive while asking a question of one pupil, the teacher uses the chain system. She has one pupil ask another, who answers and in turn asks the next question of the third, and so forth. This proceeds simultaneously in each row or file, while the teacher listens, encourages, or corrects, as needed. After this the class is divided into pairs, the teacher taking on the fifteenth child, each pair going through the entire routine. Finally, the teacher calls on several pupils in turn to give a brief oral composition in the form of an original rearrangement of the structures and vocabulary that have been learned. The pupils get their greatest satisfaction from this kind of manipulation, which enables them to show that they can already "use" the language. The teacher takes note of mistakes, corrects them inconspicuously, and plans supplementary drills for use in class on the points involved. At the end of fifteen minutes the two groups change places. In this way two thirds of the class time is taken up.

The teacher uses the last fifteen minutes to introduce to the whole class the new unit, which the pupils will study at home from a disc for at least half an hour in the way that has already been described. In class the teacher explains briefly in English the situation on which the new dialogue is based, models the dialogue, identifies the new structures, demonstrates the pattern practice, and begins the drill. She wastes no time "explaining" meaning or structure. Since the pupils must at all times know the meaning, they are provided with an English version containing a completely natural translation and as needed a literal explanation of an occasional word or phrase. The bell rings, the teacher goes to the door, says good-by in Russian to each pupil, and each one answers in Russian. As they scatter, we overhear snatches of dialogue in Russian, proudly spoken.

The reader will recognize the contrast between the procedure we have described and his own language-learning experience. In the class we have just witnessed the teacher talks less than 50 per cent of the time and each pupil is engaged in listening and speaking more than half of the time. In addition, every time he listens he must make a prompt response, so that hearing and speaking are intimately connected. This routine is strictly adhered to Monday through Thursday, the teacher informs us. Fridays are used for a weekly test and for varied activities of a less formal nature. In testing listening comprehension the teacher uses only the structures and vocabulary that have been studied, though the words may be recombined in a new order. Different voices are used, but a normal conversational speed is maintained. Pupil response is tested by recording the pupil's oral reproduction of a few expressions, recording his response to various stimuli, such as questions, commands, incomplete sentences, and pictures, and recording an original one-minute oral composition given without notes. The test takes five minutes. As the first fifteen pupils record their tests on tape, the other fifteen have a brief recess outside the room. After five minutes they change places and the whole test is over in less than fifteen minutes. The teacher may either monitor the performance of the pupils or review their tape later.

The teacher uses the remaining time to broaden the interest of the pupils by extending their vicarious experience. For the purpose of giving her pupils some understanding of Russian ways of life, she uses films, filmstrips, recordings, books, magazines, newspapers, and pictures. The teacher makes her collection available to the pupils in the classroom or in the school library. In this early stage these materials are mostly in English or are pictorial. The pupils enjoy especially occasional visits of a Russian student from a nearby university or of a Russian *émigré* in the community, who reminisces about his youth in Russia. In addition, the teacher records the talks made by visitors, special interviews with Russian speakers, or radio programs in Russian. The teacher's resourcefulness and enthusiasm have of course a good deal to do with her pupils' interest. Already one of her boys has said that he would like one day to teach Russian.

A Visit to an Eleventh-Twelfth Grade Class in French

The class we have just described is imaginary; it is a composite of elements observed or suggested in various schools. The class we are about to describe is authentic except in detail and has been observed by the writer.

This visit is to an independent boys' school, where a class in French literature is taking place in early May. It is a class called French V, which presupposes the *equivalent* of four years of French study before the beginning of this course. The head of the department has explained to us that not one of the twelve boys in the class has had a full four years of school French previously. Six of the boys started French in this school but by taking the "fast" sections on the first three levels were able to move into French V in their senior year. The other six are juniors who have had the advantage of living and studying in France or Switzerland for at least a year. Two of these were assigned to French III Special when they entered as sophomores and one to French IV. One will as a senior take advantage of an opportunity extended to outstanding students to take French VI as an individual reading course, choosing the works of Balzac as his project. He will confer with his teacher once a week for half an hour. In the course of the year he will read some twenty of Balzac's novels, will become familiar with the story of Balzac's life, and will gain some understanding of Balzac's world. He will become a skillful and perceptive reader and will learn to write quite effectively by doing each week a book report, which will be carefully criticized and corrected by his teacher. Near the end of his senior year he will take the Advanced Placement Test in French administered by the College Entrance Examination Board, will receive the top grade, and in the university of his choice will receive six credits for a literature course and be given permission to take junior or senior courses in stylistics, civilization, or literature.

But we are anticipating. Let us return to our French V class. The teacher and the twelve pupils sit around a large circular table. The teacher is a man in his forties, a graduate of one of the Ivy League colleges, a major in French, and obviously adept at speaking French though his accent is not native. He himself began studying French in another independent school at the age of fourteen, became interested in it, and showed unusual aptitude. Immediately after completing his military service, he decided to become a teacher. He has had no formal preparation for teaching, but his sixteen years of contact with many teachers, a deep-seated love of teaching, a broad knowledge of and taste for the French language and literature, and four years spent living in France and traveling in other parts of Europe have combined to make him a skillful and dedicated teacher.

Today he is discussing with his class Jean Giono's novel *Le chant du monde,* published in 1934. The teacher takes the first few minutes to summarize in French the discussion that has taken place in the preceding classes, to clarify some points that have been left in doubt, and to set the stage for today's discussion. Before starting, however, he gives the boys a chance to ask in French about difficulties they may have had in vocabulary, construction, or meaning. Three or four boys ask about specific points. The teacher lets other boys answer if they can do so quickly. Otherwise he answers himself. The teacher then selects two boys to write in French on the board summaries of the day's reading. The boys work without notes but have obviously prepared to do this if called on. As we watch, we note with what accuracy they write. While the two work at the board, the teacher asks the class to summarize orally the reading of the day. He interrupts frequently with questions intended to probe more deeply the boys' understanding. Once this is finished, the teacher concentrates the discussion on one aspect of Giono's art, considering today the role of nature in Giono's novel, the pervasiveness, the vividness, and particularly the personification of nature. The boys enter eagerly into the discussion, talk easily, and appear intensely interested. The teacher tells us afterward that he had prepared for this book by having the French Club show two films based on Giono's works, namely, *La femme du boulanger* and *Regain,* thus giving the class a vivid visual impression of Giono's country and the personalities of his countrymen. About five minutes before the bell, the teacher ends the discussion in order to criticize and correct the two compositions on the board, with the participation of the other boys. He then assigns the next chapter for reading and dismisses the class.

In our conference with the teacher we learn that the course started with a reading of *Madame Bovary* in an unabridged edition. After this warming-up period the class turned to *La chanson de Roland*. From this point on the course became a survey of French literature. One of the standard anthologies was used but frequently assignments of whole works would be made. The readings included —and this is an authentic list—*Aucassin et Nicolette;* a *fabliau;* excerpts from *Le roman de Renart; La farce de Maître Pathelin;* selected poems from Charles d'Orléans and Villon; an episode from Rabelais; an essay from Montaigne; selected poems from Ronsard and Du Bellay; excerpts from Malherbe, Boileau, La Fontaine, Descartes, Pascal, Bossuet, La Rochefoucauld, La Bruyère, and Madame de Sévigné; Corneille's *Le Cid;* Molière's *Le bourgeois gentilhomme, Les femmes savantes,* and *Le malade imaginaire;* Racine's *Andromaque;* selections from Montesquieu's *Les lettres persanes;* Voltaire's *Candide;* Diderot's *Supplément au voyage de Bougainville;* selections from Rousseau's *Confessions* and *Discours;* Beaumarchais' *Le barbier de Seville* and *Le mariage de Figaro;* selections from Lamartine, Hugo, Vigny, and Musset; poems of Leconte de Lisle, Banville, Hérédia, Baudelaire, Verlaine, Rimbaud, Mallarmé, and Valéry; and Gide's *Le retour de l'enfant prodigue.* Unlike many a college survey course, this one did not stop at the end of the eighteenth century or even at the end of the nineteenth century but carried right into the middle of the twentieth, ending with Camus' *La chute,* published in 1956.

All of these twelve students will take the College Entrance Examination Board Advanced Placement Test in French, and it may be predicted on the basis of past records that approximately three of them will receive a grade of high honors, four a grade of honors, four a grade of creditable, and one a grade of pass. Most, and perhaps all, will receive credit for the first college course in literature. At least seven of the twelve will be eligible to take junior or senior courses in French during their freshman year in college.

Not many schools in the past have offered a six-year course of language study, but such a program is sure to become increasingly common. The Connecticut State Department of Education Curriculum Bulletin Series No. V., *Foreign Languages, Grades 7–12* (Hartford, Connecticut, 1958), describes various ways in which such a sequence can be planned, and the bulletin issued in 1959 by the National Association of Secondary-School Principals, entitled *Modern Foreign Languages in the Comprehensive Secondary School,* also encourages school administrators to plan such a course of study.

The Six-Year Sequence of Foreign Language Study, Grades Seven to Twelve

We would do well at this point, in order to see the whole of the teacher's task, to sketch the main features of a course of study beginning in grade seven and continuing through grade twelve. The first stage is largely audiolingual because it emphasizes the training of the ear and the tongue, without the use of writing or print. Instead of discussion of grammar theory there is varied drill to help the pupil master the sound system and the structure of the language.

Stage two, in grade eight, continues to provide practice in hearing and speaking and continued exposure to culturally authentic materials. Here, however, reading and writing are commenced, both at the same time, provided they have not been begun in grade seven. The first objective is to learn to read and write the patterns that have already been learned by ear. Initially much of the reading is done aloud and should sound like natural talk and not a form of intoning. The spelling system is systematically analyzed and thoroughly learned by abundant writing exercises such as copying, written pattern practice, and dictation. In the second half of the year pupils should be able to read simple texts slightly beyond the limit of the vocabulary and syntax that have so far been learned. Likewise, once the spelling system is mastered, it will be possible to extend writing exercises to include dictation of somewhat more complex passages, the rewriting of passages with a change of person, time, and number. Controlled compositions, that is, compositions in which the pupil is told what to say though not how to say it, and brief original compositions by the student within the limits of the vocabulary and syntax that he has learned are also encouraged.

The third stage, in grade nine, continues and expands the earlier instruction in language and culture. To these objectives are added a brief summary of the grammatical structure of the language. By this time the pupil acquires a knowledge of basic grammatical terms. As he becomes increasingly familiar with structure and expands his vocabulary, his ear is trained progressively by the use of a variety of native speakers, by the inclusion of more rapid speech, dialogues, group conversation, telephone and radio discourse. To make the pupils more conscious of the way of life of other peoples, the teacher supplements culturally significant reading materials by pictures, filmstrips, films, recordings, and personal talks by nationals from the country concerned.

After the pupil has learned to read easily material he has first learned to understand and say and is ready to extend his reading horizons, the time has come for making use of edited or bilingual texts. At this point the chief obstacle to understanding a written text is lexical rather than structural. When he comes to a word or idiom with which he is unfamiliar, he should be able quickly to refer to the margin or the bottom of the page for the meaning. And a little later he should be taught how to use a bilingual text. The bilingual text, in which the original text is printed on the left and the English translation on the right, is as yet little used but may soon become an indispensable tool for learning to read, once the initial stage has been passed. The pupil must be trained to consult the English *only after* he has made a vigorous effort to understand the original text. The considerable amount of time saved by this procedure should enable the pupil to read much more and thus more quickly reach the point of enjoying his reading.

In the ninth grade the pupil's skill in writing should also increase considerably. In addition to dictations and controlled compositions, the pupil at this point writes summaries of his reading and continues to do original compositions on subjects within his linguistic grasp.

In grades ten, eleven, and twelve there is continued practice in hearing and understanding various types of speech, practice in speaking on more mature and complex subjects, reading, writing, culture, and literature. In these grades ear training might well include rapid, even familiar, speech, low-fidelity recordings, and broadcasts that have been partly jammed. Grammar at this point gives way to a careful analysis of the style of various worthwhile authors. The reading is substantial though appropriate to the age of the learners. It continues to reveal and illuminate cultural patterns and various aspects of contemporary civilization, and to provide historical perspective. For an appropriate guide to the study of literature, the *Advanced Placement Program: Course Descriptions* of the College Entrance Examination Board may be recommended.

The kind of language program we have sketched calls for highly qualified teachers, real professionals. Of course, not all teachers need to be able to teach at all levels. On the lower level they must be able to coordinate their teaching with that of the elementary school. They must in fact be ready to fit into the whole elementary-school-to-college language program. In the future an increasing number of language programs are likely to begin long before the seventh grade. Already many school systems are experimenting with such programs, all the way from kindergarten to grade six, with satisfying results where conditions are favorable. Assuming favorable conditions, a program which begins in the fifth grade could in grades five and six accomplish approximately what is accomplished in the seventh grade in our hypothetical program, but better. Pupils who have had such a program in grades five and six might then very well move directly into the eighth-grade language program. Pupils who have started their foreign-language instruction in grade three and continued it for four years might be expected to achieve, quantitatively, the equivalent of grades seven and eight. In the quality of their understanding and speaking they should be expected to do considerably better. They might therefore move straight into the grade-nine level of the language sequence. Children who have begun their language learning in kindergarten or grade one and continued through grade six would have acquired an even better grounding in understanding and speaking, but they would not have achieved significantly more in reading and writing than those beginning in grade three. Therefore they should normally not move into a language class higher than grade nine.

This kind of program, especially one beginning in kindergarten or grade one, would, if we had properly qualified teachers, supported by their school administrators and the community, help compete successfully with our European rivals, who for so long have had an advantage over us. Completely authentic mastery of the structure and sound system of a foreign language is normally acquired by a child only before age ten, provided the circumstances are highly favorable. Gaining familiarity with another way of life, especially if it must be done vicariously, requires a long exposure to the unfamiliar culture and the enlightened guidance of highly qualified teachers. And even the basic reading in history, civilization, and literature requires the six-year sequence we have described, as a minimum. Such a program would enable a student to do in college mature work in a second language as well as in English.

Qualifications of the Secondary-School Teacher of Modern Foreign Languages

At this point we are faced with a dilemma. Teachers qualified to teach this kind of program should ideally have been educated in the same way themselves. But we know that most of today's teachers started their language learning at the age of fourteen or fifteen and were raised in the grammar-vocabulary-translation tradition. We know also that their training has been inadequate since liberal arts colleges have been negligent of their teacher-training function, teachers' colleges have neglected academic competence, and neither has collaborated closely with the other. We find no comfort in the certification procedures of state departments of education. A recent survey of certification practices conducted by the Modern Language Association of America reveals that not a single state *requires* of teachers eligible for certification even the basic ability to understand and speak a second language. The Russian teacher we watched has a certificate, the French teacher does not, and yet both are equally competent. This observation and many others lead us to conclude that there is no necessary relationship between certification and qualification.

On questioning the Russian teacher concerning her preparation, we found her critical of her courses both in education and in foreign languages. We have seen that her experience in the summer language institute opened her eyes and made her dissatisfied with the traditional type of work in foreign languages. Some of her courses in education were valuable, she felt, but others contained too many trivia and had no direct bearing on the teaching problem. They therefore tended to disenchant her. The French teacher we visited said that he enjoyed his courses in French literature, acquired from them a taste for reading and a critical sense, but regretted that he had had no apprenticeship in teaching until he took his first job.

The testimony of these teachers and of many others suggests that the teacher-preparation programs in many of our institutions, whether professionally or academically oriented, are inadequate for our present needs. State departments of education do little to remedy this situation. Instead of stating requirements in terms of proficiency, they are content with paper requirements, and even these are minimally stated in terms of twenty-four or eighteen or even twelve semester hours in the language concerned. There seems little hope for improvement without a completely new approach. A key to a more successful system of teacher preparation is certification based on demonstrated proficiency and readiness to teach, no matter how these qualifications may have been acquired.

Fortunately the beginning of such a program has been made in the field of languages. In 1955 the Steering Committee of the Foreign Language Program of the Modern Language Association (MLA) prepared a definition of the subject-matter competence of secondary-school teachers of modern foreign languages. This statement, which has been published in many places, was endorsed by eighteen national or regional language organizations and may therefore be taken to represent the present consensus of the language-teaching profession. Competencies were defined on three levels, minimal, good, and superior. The Committee expressed regret that the present state of the profession made it necessary to publish minimal competencies.

It is one thing to define teacher qualifications; it is another to evaluate them. The MLA, under an NDEA grant, has developed some very effective tests to measure as objectively as possible these various competencies. As an initial step in their standardization, preliminary forms A and B of these tests were used at the beginning and the end of the summer language institutes in 1960. During the school year 1960–1961 they were revised on the basis of careful item analysis conducted by the Educational Testing Service and were made available to teacher-preparing institutions and school administrators.

The Training of the Secondary-School Teacher of Modern Foreign Languages

We have considered how the qualified language teacher may be expected to perform in the classroom. This versatile performance requires that the teacher possess, in addition to the essential qualities of character, personality, and taste, certain knowledge and skills, which have been defined. These expected competencies appear formidable to most of our present teachers, who have had neither the advantage of learning a second language in its cultural context nor that of an early start and a long sequence of effective language learning in school and college. For such teachers in service who desire to improve we need an effective remedial program.

Such a remedial program has been provided by the NDEA, which subsidized twelve institutes in the summer of 1959, thirty-seven in the summer of 1960, fifty-five in 1961, and eighty in 1962, in addition to several year-long institutes. These institutes have amply fulfilled their purpose of explaining to the profession the new theories and of demonstrating the modern practices.

The main purpose of the present chapter, however, is to describe the kind of program suitable for a candidate who wishes to prepare for teaching a modern foreign language in the secondary school. As we list the desirable components of such a program, we must not forget the trainee's possible early exposure to another language and culture (enculturation), and his twelve to sixteen years of observation of teachers and schools.

Let us now consider the course of a prospective language teacher who enrolls in a teacher-training program at some moment between his freshman year in college and his first year in graduate school.

Before such a candidate is accepted, the director and staff of the program should satisfy themselves that he has the necessary personal qualities, that he has a compelling desire to teach and a deep interest in the language and culture that he intends to teach, and that his basic mastery of this language is such that he can be expected by the end of the training course to qualify as at least "good" in all seven categories of the MLA qualifications.

Having been judged worthy of admission, the candidate should at the outset be assisted in appraising his strengths and weaknesses. This initial diagnosis will normally consist of a series of personal interviews and the taking of the MLA Foreign Language Proficiency Tests for Teachers and Advanced Students. Such interviews would reveal whether the candidate has had the advantage of childhood contact with another language and culture, when he first conceived the desire to teach, how much his formal education may have contributed to his vocational purpose, how conscious and critical he has been in observing his teachers and schools, how widely he has read on educational and related subjects, and whether he has any special interests or talents relevant to a teaching career. All of these factors make a difference and should be taken into account as the staff helps him plan his course.

The Proficiency Tests will help the staff to determine to what extent the candidate already has the qualifications defined by the MLA. The candidate receives credit for the knowledge and skills he possesses, and the director and staff prescribe a program to enable him to overcome his deficiencies. Such a program consists of courses, individual work, or a combination of the two. Thanks to the advent of the tape recorder, whole courses can be put on tape, and the independent type of student may prefer to work his way through such a course at his own speed, merely raising a question now and then in a seminar or a professor's office. Lists of readings and of other kinds of materials—recordings, films, filmstrips, slides, pictures—should be available. In fact everything possible should be done to free any student with the slightest spark of independence from the goosestep of our traditional practices. As soon as he feels ready, the student should be allowed to demonstrate his readiness by teaching in the classroom and by taking an alternate form of the

MLA tests plus any other tests the director and staff may prescribe. Having given satisfactory evidence of his proficiency, he should be recommended by the institution to the state department of education and be granted a license to teach.

Providing each candidate with an opportunity to acquire the knowledge and skills outlined in the MLA statement of qualifications and in a form to suit his individual needs requires a program of great flexibility.

To be able to understand and speak another language with a near-native proficiency, a teacher must normally have been exposed to the foreign language before the age of ten. A teacher who has had such an advantage can usually model the language adequately for his pupils. We do not mean to imply, of course, that access to our language classrooms should be limited to native speakers of other languages. This *is* an ideal to be strived for, but there are many competent and inspiring teachers of modern foreign languages—like the French teacher we watched in the independent boys' school—whose teaching is excellent and whose services are needed. But a teacher should be able to recognize when his speech is not authentic and should be ready to supply authentic models on tape and discs. There is no room for compromise here. German is what the native speaker of German talks, not what a foreign imitator has learned belatedly and artificially in the classroom. Of those who have begun their language learning in high school and continued through college, only the most gifted approximate native mastery. A deficiency in understanding and speaking may be remediable, but it requires long hours of practice in listening to and imitating native speakers. A course in advanced oral composition should be available, but much practice in hearing and speaking can be provided in the language laboratory.

The literate skills (reading and writing) are the ones which have been traditionally stressed. Our teacher candidate may therefore not need much special training in reading, but he will probably need instruction and demonstration in how to teach reading. He will learn that without sufficient oral preparation silent reading is unsatisfactory. He will learn the technique of listening to a recorded reading while following a text with his eyes. He will examine studies that have been made of the "density" of reading texts (number of new words per page) and will learn how to adjust the density to pupils' progress. He will learn how to train pupils in the proper use of bilingual texts. And he may have the opportunity to explore the use of the tachistoscope in speeding up silent reading.

Teacher candidates will certainly need practice in writing. Writing is one thing that cannot be learned from tape; it requires a native teacher who is skillful in criticizing written exercises of all kinds. In addition to improving his own writing skill, the teacher candidate will need to learn how to teach writing. The teaching of writing has in the past been quite unsatisfactory in the secondary school, for two principal reasons. One is the fact that secondary-school teachers have been overwhelmed with classes both too numerous and too large and so have not been able to check carefully on assigned written work. The second reason is that we have not used properly the various forms of written exercises available to us. An adequate teacher-training program should provide a candidate with a course in advanced composition, if needed, and with instruction in the various techniques of teaching writing.

On the subject of grammar our teacher candidate will, if he has had the traditional instruction provided by teachers of English, Latin, and modern foreign languages, need to learn the newer concepts of linguistic science and the application of these concepts to the teaching of a second language. He must realize clearly that instead of studying grammar first and then language, as has so often been done in the past, pupils should first learn appropriate usage by direct imitation of authentic models. Only after having learned to use the basic structures of a language is one ready to learn how to analyze and describe the grammar of a foreign language. The procedure is similar to that used in learning one's mother tongue. By the age of five and a half the average child understands and speaks his mother tongue in perfect conformity to the cultural group within which he lives. In the primary grades of school he normally learns the basic elements of reading and writing and in the intermediate grades he learns, we hope, modern grammatical terms and concepts. His study of the structure of a foreign language should follow the same course and should provide him with the labels necessary to talk about language structure with an understanding of its classes, forms, and relations. This fundamental part of the teacher-training program can be provided in courses called "Introduction to Linguistics" and "The Application of Linguistics to Language Teaching." Mature students should naturally not be required to take these courses if they prefer to do the readings privately and take a rigorous examination on the subject.

Among the competencies of a modern foreign-language teacher the most controversial is knowledge of culture. The word itself causes confusion. For our purposes it will be sufficient to distinguish two general meanings, one which has long been traditional, especially with humanists, and the other representing the newer point of view of social scientists. According to the latter, culture involves the regularly patterned way of life characteristic of a society, or people living, feeling, thinking, evaluating, acting together. According to the former, culture involves the things that people have produced, the things which we would be proud to have produced if we had been in their place, the outstanding achievements of a people, particularly in the arts. In the past, language teachers have been primarily concerned with the second of these definitions, and among the arts mainly with literature. The MLA qualifications statement suggests that in our day this exclusive concern with literature is no longer adequate. This is not to say that literature is not important. Literature is in fact the only art form directly related to language. It would be tragic if literary study did not continue to attract ever increasing numbers of foreign-language teachers. What is needed, however, is a great broadening of interests in order to make room for some language teachers who will concern themselves with other aspects of culture, whether it be history, geography, economics, politics, or social institutions. Foreign-language teachers have hitherto been either totally oblivious of culture in the social-science sense or have had a very superficial view of it.

Future modern language teachers therefore need first of all a clear idea of the culture concept. They will then gradually have to learn how to apply this concept, just as they are learning to apply the concepts of linguistic science, to their language teaching. The kind of understanding that is involved may be acquired in various ways. One of the best is by living among the people whose language one teaches, and particularly during one's early years. A person with such an experience comes closest to identifying himself with another culture. But feeling oneself to be part of another culture is not sufficient. One should become conscious of it, be able to talk about it, if one is to be successful in making younger learners in turn aware of it. We may say in summary then that the ideal teacher should be able to represent another culture and should be able to make his pupils sensitive to another way of life. This requires great delicacy and intelligence if one is to avoid superficiality.

Language reflects culture, both through the words which arbitrarily represent meaning and through the structures which combine words. The language learner can early be made aware how radically these differ from English and be led to understand that other nationals organize their experience in completely different ways, as revealed by their language. Fortunately the audio-visual materials which are coming into wider use can assist greatly in bringing other peoples right into our classrooms, where we can both see and hear them in characteristic activities. The number of films, filmstrips, and tape recordings of good quality that are now available is limited, but the few that we have suffice to show that young learners are stimulated by seeing the immediate connection between the language they are studying and the life of the people who speak this language. In the future, materials selected for our language teaching must meet as rigorous a test of cultural authenticity as of linguistic authenticity. Furthermore they must at every stage in the modern language course be appropriate to the age and experience of the learner. It is in the field of culture that the future language teacher finds his greatest challenge and his greatest opportunity. To acquire competence in this field our teacher candidate should have the choice of taking courses on the "Introduction to the Social Sciences" and "The Application of the Social Sciences to Language Teaching" or of reading the substance of such courses on his own in preparation for an examination.

Professional preparation to teach a language should remain, as it now generally does, in the hands of language specialists, although a complete program for learning to teach requires the collaboration of professional educators. Readiness to teach a modern foreign language presupposes an understanding of the nature of language, best interpreted by linguistic scientists; of the process by which a foreign language is learned, which psychologists are only just beginning to investigate; of the relation between language and culture, which cultural anthropologists, sociologists, and social psychologists can help us understand better; of the best available methods and materials for teaching in a modern manner; and of the tests available for evaluating various aspects of language learning in accordance with the objectives which have been established. Ideally, the desire and ability to conduct research and experimentation in the field of language learning and teaching should also be part of the language teacher's equipment. To help the prospective teacher with his professional preparation, a training program should offer a course on "The Teaching of Modern Foreign Languages," but again let us emphasize that the candidate who chooses to read and study by himself rather than take the course should be encouraged to do so.

The program we have described constitutes only a part, though a major part, of the training of the teacher of modern foreign languages. Another major part of his training falls in the area of what is commonly called professional education. It includes such elements as an understanding of human growth and learning, of the place of the school in our society, of current educational theories and practices, of evaluation and experimental design, and of an apprenticeship in teaching, in which professional and academic educators should share supervision. Unfortunately there are still lacking a satisfactory working definition of qualifications in the field of professional preparation and tests to measure as objectively as possible such qualifications. This lack is one of the chief obstacles to rapid progress in the field of teacher education. Let us hope that our colleagues in professional education will undertake without delay to fill this gap in our educational system.

Summary and Conclusion

Let us consider some of the implications of the principles and practices which we have outlined. In the preceding pages we have considered the training program to be only the culmination of the teacher's early language-learning experience and his exposure to a culture other than his own. Indeed we may safely affirm that a college or graduate-school program for the training of a language teacher has little chance of producing highly qualified teachers if entering students are not already equipped with at least the basic language skills of understanding, speaking, reading, and writing. The acquisition of these skills presupposes a long sequence of effective language learning, at the very least a six-year program beginning in grade seven and continuing through grade twelve. There are, to be sure, known cases of qualified teachers who did not begin their language study until senior high school or even college, but they are exceptional in their interest and aptitude. Under normal circumstances not even a six-year sequence is sufficient to guarantee a near-native command of a second language, for we have noted that the average person does not learn to speak a second language without accent and without constraint unless he is exposed to this language in its cultural context before the age of ten.

A respect for these basic principles concerning the nature of language and the process of language learning suggests the need that we reconsider the whole structure of teacher education. If we agree that the hard core of a language teacher's qualifications is mastery of language and cultural awareness, we are bound to accept certain implications. For one thing, we should recruit far more of our teacher candidates from among those of our citizens who have learned a second language in its cultural context. This in turn requires the preservation and constant replenishment of our linguistic and cultural resources. It should require only a moment's thought to realize that a United States citizen who is equipped to use two languages skillfully is more valuable to himself and to his country than one who is not. And yet, at the same time that our Congress appropriates millions of dollars to promote more and better language learning, our schools systematically suppress the knowledge of languages other than English in children who come to school so equipped. It would be easy to cultivate other languages if our citizens valued these languages and wanted to preserve them.

The technical problems are not difficult. Many children in bilingual communities still enter school able to understand and speak a language other than English. At this point they are ready to learn the elements of reading and writing that language, which now we withhold from them until grade nine or ten, by which time they have lost their desire. Let us by all means provide this opportunity to read, at the psychologically proper moment. While learning to read and write in their mother tongue, these children would learn everything else in English along with the English-speaking children, except reading and writing in English, which could be delayed slightly until they were ready. One of our educational inconsistencies is that we are careful not to plunge our English-speaking children into reading until we are sure they are "ready" even though they have lived in an English-speaking environment for six years. With non-English-speaking children we show no such scruples as we plunge them into the reading of English, a *foreign* language. In schools where some of the children speak English as a mother tongue and also another language there is an unusual opportunity for effective language learning. While the children who speak another language are learning to read and write their mother tongue and learning to understand and speak English, the English-speaking children have the opportunity to learn to understand and speak the second language of the community. As the children play together, they can teach each other a second language under something approaching ideal circumstances.

Not only do we fail to exploit our national supply of teachers of other languages; we have also so far failed to develop on a large scale the exchange of teachers with other countries. Here too is a potential source of native-speaking teachers with the additional advantage that they have been well educated and can represent their culture authentically. Such exchanges would of course require on both sides a thorough orientation in the prevailing school philosophy and practices.

In discussing the training part of our teacher-education program we have emphasized the desirability of a flexible program conducted co-operatively by language educators, social scientists, and professional educators. The collaboration of social scientists is needed because the study of language—or linguistics—is a social science as well as one of the humanities. The collaboration of professional educators is indispensable, for they are most intimately concerned with educational theory and practice. The best basis for a satisfactory collaboration is, we believe, the acceptance of the principle that a teacher's qualifications when satisfactorily demonstrated should be recognized no matter how they may have been acquired. The experience and education of teacher candidates vary widely. But concerning what they should be able to do in the language classroom we have, as far as subject-matter is concerned, reached a workable consensus. What we now urgently need is a similar working definition of what a teacher needs to know and be able to do on the professional side. This is not nearly so difficult as it seems. There are well defined fields of knowledge, such as the place of the school in our society, the principles of human growth and learning, evaluation and experimentation, and teaching apprenticeship. All of these have been the subjects of courses and textbooks. By mobilizing its best thinkers the educational profession could therefore conceivably agree on a definition of knowledge essential to the teacher. A demonstration in the classroom of readiness to teach could be carried out in the presence of the supervising teacher and principal of the school and of a language educator and a professional educator from the teacher-training institution. A teacher whose basic knowledge has been validated by examination —whether or not he has taken specific courses—and whose readiness to teach has been demonstrated satisfactorily to such a committee as we have indicated above should, we believe, be recommended forthwith by the training institution and be granted a license to teach by the state department of education.

We have sketched the principal aspects of the education of the qualified secondary-school teacher of modern foreign languages. Is his education complete as he steps into his first regular classroom? Certainly not, but if his own teachers have been successful and he has in him the stuff of a teacher, he will think of his first class as the beginning rather than the end of his education. He will want to continue reading and speculating, and he will want constantly to improve his teaching by means of research and experimentation. And finally he will want to collaborate with other professional-minded teachers in improving unremittingly the quality of American education.

Suggested Readings

Balakian, Anna, "Certification Requirements for Modern Foreign Language Teachers in American Public Schools (1959–60)," in *Publications of the Modern Language Association of America,* LXXVI, No. 2B, May 1961.

Birkmaier, Emma, "Modern Languages," *Encyclopedia of Education Research,* 37th ed., Chester W. Harris, ed. New York: Macmillan, 1960.

Brooks, Nelson, *Language and Language Learning: Theory and Practice.* New York: Harcourt, Brace, 1960.

Carroll, John B., "Research in Foreign Language Teaching," in *Handbook of Research on Teaching,* N. L. Gage, ed. New York: Rand McNally, 1961.

————, *The Study of Language: A Survey of Linguistics and Related Disciplines in America.* Cambridge: Harvard University Press, 1953.

Chapin, Miriam, *How People Talk.* New York: John Day, 1945.

Cleveland, Harlan, Gerard J. Mangone, and John Clarke Adams, *The Overseas Americans.* New York: McGraw-Hill, 1960.

Cornelius, Edwin T., *How to Learn a Foreign Language.* New York: Crowell, 1955.

Delattre, Pierre, "A Technique of Aural-Oral Approach," in *The French Review,* January and February, 1947.

Desberg, Dan, "Structural Linguistics and High School Language," in *The Classical Outlook,* November 1959.

Dostert, Leon E., "Foreign Language Reading Skill," in *Journal of Chemical Education,* March 1955.

Duff, Charles, *How to Learn a Language.* Oxford: Blackwell, 1948.

Freeman, Stephen A., "A Report on the 1959 Summer Language Institutes," *Hispania,* March 1960.

————, "A Report on the 1960 Summer Language Institutes," *Hispania,* March 1961.

Gouin, François, *The Art of Teaching and Studying Languages.* London: George Philip and Son, 1912.

Hall, Edward T., *The Silent Language.* New York: Doubleday, 1959.

Haugen, Einar, *Bilingualism in the Americas: A Bibliography and Research Guide.* American Dialect Society, Gainesville, Florida; University of Alabama Press, 1956.

Hutchinson, Joseph C., *Modern Foreign Languages in the High School: The Language Laboratory.* Washington: U.S. Office of Education, Bulletin No. 23, 1961.

Jespersen, Otto, *How to Teach a Foreign Language.* London: Allen and Unwin, 1956.

Johnston, Marjorie C., "Foreign Language Instruction," in *Review of Educational Research,* April 1961.

————, ed., *Modern Foreign Languages in the High School*. Washington: U.S. Government Printing Office, 1958.

Lado, Robert, *Linguistics Across Cultures*. Ann Arbor: University of Michigan Press, 1957.

Langer, Susanne K., chapter on language in *Philosophy in a New Key*. New York: New American Library, 1948.

Marty, Fernand L., *Language Laboratory Learning*. Wellesley: Audio-Visual Publications, 1960.

Mathieu, Gustave, "Language Laboratories," in *Review of Educational Research*, April 1962.

Modern Language Association of America, *MLA Selective List of Materials*. New York: MLA, 1962.

————, Reports of Surveys and Studies in the Teaching of Modern Foreign Languages, New York: MLA, 1959–61.

Moulton, William G., "Study Hints for Language Students," *Modern Language Journal*, October 1952.

National Association of Secondary School Principals, "Foreign Languages in the Comprehensive Secondary School," in NASSP *Bulletin*, June 1, 1959.

National Education Association and Modern Language Association, *Modern Foreign Languages and the Academically Talented Student*. Washington: NEA, 1960.

O'Connor, Patricia, *Modern Foreign Languages in the Secondary School: Pre-reading Instruction*. Washington: U.S. Government Printing Office, 1960.

Parker, William R., *The National Interest and Foreign Languages*, third edition. Washington: U.S. Government Printing Office, 1961.

Penfield, Wilder, and Lamar Roberts, *Speech and Brain Mechanisms*. Princeton: Princeton University Press, 1959.

Politzer, Robert L., "On the Relation of Linguistics to Language Teaching," *Modern Language Journal*, February 1958.

Stack, Edward M., *The Language Laboratory and Modern Language Teaching*. New York: Oxford, 1960.

Starr, Wilmarth H., "Foreign Language Teaching and Intercultural Understanding," *School and Society*, March 19, 1955.

UNESCO, *The Teaching of Modern Languages*. Paris: UNESCO, 1955.

U.S. Office of Education, *Source Materials for Secondary School Teachers of Foreign Languages*. Washington: U.S. Office of Education, 1962, Circular No. 27001A.

————, *Useful References for Teachers of Foreign Languages*. Washington: U.S. Office of Education Circular No. 509.

CHAPTER IX

FLETCHER G. WATSON:

The Teacher of Science

Academic Preparation

What preparation in the sciences should a future science teacher have? In the period since World War II a number of committees and individuals have published comments and specific suggestions. Most of these have been essentially in agreement. In 1947 the AAAS Co-operative Committee on the Teaching of Science and Mathematics published a detailed analysis as part of the Steelman Report, *Science and Public Policy*.[1] A summary of this report also appeared in *School Science and Mathematics*, "The Preparation of High School Science and Mathematics Teachers." [2] Almost simultaneously those professors directly responsible for training future science teachers made similar proposals.[3]

In 1953 a group of professors and supervisors concerned with science teaching made an analysis of the actual preparation of teachers then in the classrooms of the country. The discrepancy between what was desired and the actual preparation of the employed teachers was stark and stimulating.[4] Subsequently, Watson directed

1. See Vol. IV, *Manpower for Research*.
2. Vol. 46 (1946), 107.
3. *Science Education for American Schools*, Forty-fifth Yearbook of the National Society for the Study of Education (Chicago: University of Chicago Press, 1946), Chapter 16.
4. F. G. Watson, Paul Brandwein and Sidney Rosen, eds. *Critical Years Ahead in Science Teaching* (Harvard University Publications Office, 1953).

attention to the necessity of spelling out what particular courses a future teacher should take.[5] If recommendations are left only in vague terms of semester hours, quite marginal courses may be taken while those essential to the beginning of a comprehensive knowledge of the subject field might be bypassed.

In 1959 the AAAS Co-operative Committee published a second report,[6] and in 1960 a slightly modified version appeared, "Preparation of High School Science Teachers." [7] These latter reports are quite specific in terms of the amount and nature of the study recommended.

Simultaneously, and with knowledge of the recommendations being made by the AAAS Co-operative Committee, the National Association of State Directors of Teacher Education and Certification in co-operation with the AAAS prepared a parallel statement on the preparation of teachers of science and of mathematics.[8] This committee was more concerned with what the prospective teacher needed to learn than with the titles or duration of courses. They observed that "the subject-matter portion of the curriculum for future teachers should be selected and organized on the basis of consideration for and study of the needs of teachers in the schools." This suggests, as Watson has elaborated elsewhere,[9] that it is time we considered teaching as a socially important career involving thousands of college graduates, and began planning programs specifically for their preparation, rather than insisting upon the time-hallowed pat-

5. F. G. Watson, "Course Requirements for Future Science Teachers," *Scientific Monthly,* LXXXV (1957), 320.

6. "Recommendations for the Preparation of High School Teachers of Science and Mathematics," *School Science and Mathematics,* LIX (1959), 281.

7. *Science,* CXXX (1960), 1024.

8. "Guidelines for Preparation Programs of Teachers of Secondary School Science and Mathematics," Recommendations of the Teacher Preparation-Certification Study of the National Association of State Directors of Teacher Education and Certification, and the American Association for the Advancement of Science; 1961, available from AAAS, 1515 Massachusetts Ave. N.W., Wash. 5, D.C. See also F. L. Fitzpatrick, ed., *Policies for Science Education* (New York: Bureau of Publications, Teachers College, Columbia University, 1960), Chapter 10.

9. F. G. Watson, "Preparation for Teaching Physics in Secondary Schools," *American Journal of Physics,* March 1962.

tern of majors and minors intended to prepare students for admission to graduate schools in a narrow field of study.

To accomplish their stated purposes, this committee developed eight guidelines; for each subject area they were spelled out in more detail than can be given here. The eight guidelines, with added comments, are:

I. The program should include a thorough, college-level study of the aspects of the subject that are included in the high school curriculum. (If taken literally, this would imply that no major changes in the subject areas of the secondary school curriculum were anticipated for many years. Actually, major changes are likely to develop within a decade.)

II. The program should take into account the sequential nature of the subject to be taught, and in particular should provide the prospective teacher with an understanding of the aspects of the subject which his students will meet in subsequent courses.

III. The program should include a major in the subject to be taught, with courses chosen for their relevance to the high school curriculum.

IV. The major should include sufficient preparation for the later pursuit of graduate work in one of the sciences or in mathematics. (Items III and IV will, in many colleges, impose a narrow pattern of study upon the student in an undergraduate program.)

V. The fifth-year program should emphasize courses in the subject to be taught. (This assumes that the basic pedagogical study is completed in the undergraduate program. Actually a number of universities are offering fifth-year programs for prospective teachers who have completed an undergraduate program majoring in science; for them the pedagogical study necessarily comes in the fifth-year.)

VI. The program should include work in areas related to the subject to be taught.

VII. The program should include preparation in the methods especially appropriate to the subject to be taught.

VIII. The program should take into account the recommendations for curriculum improvements currently being made by various national groups.

Modifications of many of these guidelines are made in separate discussions concerned with preparing teachers for junior high school science courses (grades seven, eight, nine) and for the obviously eclectic "earth sciences." Since already about twice as many teachers are involved in science for grades seven, eight, and nine as in the more specialized and elective courses for the upper grades, and since the number of teachers for science in grades seven, eight, and nine is expanding rapidly as more schools are requiring more instruction in these grades, it would seem more appropriate to design the basic program for the teaching of these grades and then add one or more specialities.

Beginning with the AAAS Committee report in 1946 most writers have agreed that one half of the undergraduate program of a future science teacher should be committed to the study of science and mathematics. Normally this would amount to about sixty semester hours in a four-year program. At least introductory course work in five major fields—biology, chemistry, physics, earth science, and mathematics—would be expected of all future science teachers. Thereafter specialization, but with appropriate supporting courses in other areas of science, should be encouraged in the biological sciences, or the physical sciences, or the earth sciences (geology, astronomy, and meteorology).

The desirability of introductory study in each of the major science fields can be justified on two bases. First, the sciences are now all so closely interwoven that advanced study in one often necessitates considerable comprehension of another. For example, advanced study in modern biology surely necessitates a working knowledge of both inorganic and organic chemistry as a basis for the study of biochemistry. Secondly, inasmuch as half the secondary schools of the country enroll fewer than four hundred pupils, science teachers are normally required to teach two or three different science courses. Despite the special interests of the teacher, he should have some background on which to approach the diversity of classes. We are not arguing here whether these conditions *should* exist or not; they *do* exist and are likely to continue for some years.

If there is general agreement on these recommendations, then why do we continue to have grossly underprepared teachers in our schools with others still being employed each year? The answer, like so many in education, has several components. First, the number of new science teachers each year whose training approximates the recommendations is far short of the need for new teachers. Even reasonably precise figures are difficult to obtain; however, the National Education Association publishes each year figures on the number of individuals able to be certified in each general subject area by the state within which they attended college.[10] The most recent figures for 1961 report 8249 such individuals available as a new supply of science teachers. Yet year after year hardly more than half of these appear the next September as new teachers. Thus the supply is short of the annual need, which is not clearly known, but is estimated between eight and ten thousand per year for the upper four grades of the secondary school without consideration of those, probably a comparable number, needed for grades seven and eight.

Second, the certification laws of the several states have required only a bare minimum of preparation in the subjects to be taught.[11] Thus, numerous individuals have been certified as teachers although their knowledge of the subject was woefully inadequate. Nationally, the trend now is to assign the responsibility for certifying teachers to accredited colleges whose programs will, hopefully, be more demanding.

Third, short supply and rising demands have put many school administrators in a most unenviable position—few competent new teachers of science are available. Often the only alternative to canceling a science course has been the assignment to it of a teacher not prepared in science or not even really interested in science. The frequency of such assignments, and the unenviable life of such a teacher, was explored several years ago by Victor and Watson.[12]

Fourth, many individuals who become science teachers made

10. *Teacher Supply and Demand in Public Schools*, 1961. Research Report R-9, 1961, National Education Association Research Division, April 1961.
11. Mrs. R. C. Woellner, and M. A. Wood, *Requirements for Certification* (Chicago: University of Chicago Press. Published annually).
Also D. S. Sarner, and J. R. Frymier, "Certification Requirements in Mathematics and Science," *School Science and Mathematics*, LIX (1959), 456.
12. "The Converted Science Teacher," New England School Development Council, Cambridge, Mass., 1959.

this career decision when they were well along in their collegiate studies. Often no realistic or sympathetic advice was available to them from the collegiate faculty. Consequently, they completed a too-narrow departmental major and subsequently found themselves with diversified responsibilities for which they were unprepared.

Constructive action to remedy the continuing employment of ill-prepared new science teachers requires the co-operative effort of many people. In the colleges deliberate efforts must be made to identify and encourage potential teachers. Realistic programs of study should be created for them and should include in the under-graduate years the breadth of introductory courses needed by a teacher. College professors, science educators, school administrators, and employed teachers must work co-operatively to strengthen and make realistic the certification standards of the several states and the programs of colleges. In 1960 New York State made a marked increase in the subject requirements for certification in all subjects. In science the requirements were doubled from the old standards, and the new requirements approximate those recommended by the AAAS Co-operative Committee.

While efforts must be made to discourage school administrators and school boards from appointing or using unqualified teachers, some motivation greater than good intentions may be necessary. The public, now generally concerned about quality instruction in our schools, would be alerted if some significant penalty were made for the use of a grossly unqualified teacher in a science classroom. The withholding of sizable amounts of state aid would dramatize to the taxpayers the difficulties of finding sufficient numbers of competent science teachers for our schools. Iowa and Illinois [13] seem to have such restrictions in their state laws, but the extent to which they are applied is not apparent.

Finally, we must conclude that some "watch-dog" activity is necessary to insure that the requirements are actually met. Presumably this should be a responsibility of the professional or-ganizations of science teachers, with the co-operation and support of the several organizations of collegiate scientists. Only by some

13. "Working Papers for the San Diego Conference on the Education of Teachers: Certification," *Journal of Teacher Education*, June 1960, pp. 212, 214.

such pattern of co-operation between colleges, schools, and state departments of education can the reasonable and desirable introductory preparation of competent new science teachers be assured.

Professional Preparation: the Course in Curriculum and Methods

At least four distinct kinds or dimensions of responsibility seem inherent in teaching. Certainly knowledge of the subject field is critical, for this is the stuff from which the instruction will be fashioned. But just an acquaintanceship with the content is not adequate. The teacher must understand the structure, arguments, and limitations of the subject to the point that he can see in it the potentialities for effective instruction. This is probably the basis for the common statement "You never understand a subject until you have taught it." Even if the teacher is presented with a tight syllabus of material to consider, he always has freedom to decide what particular ideas deserve emphasis and under what allocation of time.

A second responsibility involves choosing those characteristics of the whole field of science which should be and can be illustrated through the choice of particular topics. Science deals with man's attempt to find order or invariance in the many phenomena of the world. How is this done? What precautions must be taken against gross error? Not only must we be concerned with what we know, but also with how we know it, and how well we know it. If science instruction is to have meaning to the great majority of the pupils who will become the laymen of the future, this problem of the nature of scientific knowledge must be faced squarely. Every topic and every laboratory experience contain latent possibilities for examining "What we know and how well we know it."

Teaching science, like the teaching of any subject, is not just a philosophical analysis or argument. The basic purpose is to produce desired changes in the behavior of the learner. Therefore, who the learner is in terms of motivation, aspirations, age, sex, and innate academic ability makes a great difference in deciding how instruction should be planned, developed, and evaluated.

Finally, analysis regarding the subject material, the general nature of scientific knowledge, and the nature of the learner must come together in a dynamic interaction under the guiding hand of the teacher in that brief but critical interval known as "the lesson." How that time is used by both teacher and pupils determines whether or not all the analysis and planning will come to fruition.

The future teacher, from being the consumer of instruction to becoming the social agent responsible for guiding the learning of youngsters, must make a great shift in role and orientation. As a student the future teacher has been the recipient of instruction, knowledge, and attitudes selected and organized by his instructors. Intent upon learning what was desired and performing satisfactorily such tasks as laboratory work or examinations, he has rarely been conscious of the criteria on which the instruction was designed and ordered. But as a teacher he abruptly becomes responsible for choosing content and emphasis, for selecting techniques and timing, for evaluating the pupils' progress and modifying or pacing the teaching procedures. The only opportunity for the future teacher to explore these operations objectively within the context of the particular subject occurs in the course on curriculum and methods; therefore, it has a singularly significant place in the development of a beginning teacher.

Methods courses in science, like those in other fields of study, are pointed toward the close interaction of information and pupils. Planning, realistically done, is the central operation. Constantly interworking in the classroom are these components: the teacher's objectives, the pupils' purposes, the consideration of evidence, use of materials—both equipment and references, and continuous evaluation. These factors raise the basic questions: what do we (teachers, pupils) wish to accomplish, how may we accomplish it, and how well are we accomplishing it?

Answers to the question why, and for what purposes, are we studying this material, comprise what we call teachers' objectives. In every field of study, and especially in science, the material that might be considered is vast. Selection is always necessary, even in college courses. On what basis then is the selection made?

Many screens can operate in this sifting process. First, because the pupils are doing the learning, the material should be interesting to them. This does not mean that it must be trivial or easy; in fact, nothing could be more disastrous. Children immediately recognize that which is too simple, already known, or unimportant to them. Boredom and then disciplinary troubles follow. By "interesting" we mean topics or problems which are significant to the pupils. Such problems involve more than they know and evoke questions they would like to answer and can expect to answer. We cannot assume that every pupil has an active interest in every topic, but such interest can be awakened by a skillful, observant teacher.

Content within the sciences may be selected on the basis of one or more of many criteria. It may provide a deepening or a broadening conception of the internal structure of arguments and evidence which comprise the particular science. It may be a vehicle for causing the pupil to focus attention upon certain types of analytical processes. It may illustrate the complex processes by which new knowledge is accommodated into new technological devices. It may include information which "every citizen should know." Often it serves several of these purposes simultaneously.

Another screen of great importance is the knowledge of the teacher about the topic. Unless he is informed, how can he plan significant instruction? How can he know what he and the pupils might achieve from the study of recent scientific advances? This implies that the teacher should continue his learning so that his knowledge is not static or obsolete. Surely he must continuously read and study in anticipation of incorporating new knowledge into his teaching. In the methods course we have an obligation to help the future teacher know how to keep up-to-date while on the job. Still other screens operate to reduce the "possible" to the "practical." The interests and special facilities of the community influence the choice of what to consider, and to what extent. An agricultural region certainly offers different possibilities from an urban region. The materials of instruction on hand, plus those that may be improvised, restrict the firsthand evidence which may be utilized. For example, to study nuclear reactions without a Geiger counter, an electroscope, or radioactive materials, or comparable equipment, is sterile. At best the instruction is a discussion based on reading and films without any firsthand evidence. It may result only in an impressive vocabulary and empty verbalisms. The time and effort expended could have been used more profitably for developing some other topic.

But after consideration of the possible and the practical, there are still likely to be more topics than can be considered in a year or even in twelve years. The selection of the "desirable" may turn in part on community characteristics, but it must involve still one other criterion: what aspects of scientific work can be best stressed or illustrated through the study? This brings us to a central concern of the methods course.

What about science is important to stress? This is a central question to which there are many answers among which each school or teacher must choose. Before coming to grips with this issue, however, we must remind the future teachers that they will be teaching all the children—not just those few who will become the scientists of the future. What about science is important for all the girls, as well as all the boys, for the "science-shy" as well as the "science-prone?" What about science is important for the vast number of laymen of the future who will complete their formal education in the secondary school? Haunting us always is the knowledge that for many pupils this is their last course in science. Their knowledge and especially their attitudes throughout a long life may be shaped and oriented while in this class.

Students in the methods course, influenced by collegiate study in formalized courses often intended for future specialists, have difficulty in seeing how to reshape and reorganize their knowledge to interest all (or almost all) the secondary school pupils. This reorganization is an important operation which must run consistently throughout the methods course, and be made more significant during the practice teaching.

Evidently there are some writers and some teachers who consider science as a body of organized knowledge to be learned, that is, remembered, by the pupils. This is a simple answer acceptable to those who are willing to "teach the book." Yet it is a static answer which presents science as a "finished" field of study. The resulting instruction is often as dull and uncreative as memorizing the periodic table. In such courses science appears to consist of "answers" to questions which were never asked, at least not asked in the classroom.

In contrast there is a growing realization that science is both dynamic and accumulative. Science is an active verb; as Bridgman called it, "sciencing." Following this line, we are plunged into the complex process by which scientists gather, judge, and organize data; how they create and select large ideas, or concepts, as adequate and consistent explanations for the available data, and then hopefully test the usefulness of these ideas by predicting from them further results to be confirmed or not by specific, new observations. Here the emphasis is put on science as a means of question answering, of struggling to create embracing, stable explanations that bring order among the multitudinous phenomena of the world.

Unfortunately, most prospective teachers are unaware of science as a "process of knowing." This conclusion, based upon considerable experience both with teacher-candidates and with experienced teachers, is confirmed by a recent paper of Frances Behnke.[14] Based on 621 replies from a nation-wide sampling of science teachers and 70 from practicing scientists, she found the greatest difference in opinions between the groups on items dealing with the nature of science. For example, over 50 per cent of the teachers indicated a belief that the conclusions of scientists were *not* tentative. In conclusion, she observed that "the modern science teacher needs to know much more than his predecessor, but he must have more than knowledge of the science content. Knowing a great deal *about* science is no guarantee that he will know *what science is about*." Even when a course on the history and philosophy of science is included in the student's program, the curriculum and methods course might well include a paper on "Basic Aspects of Science" developed from the writings of many eminent scientists.

Now we see the necessity of two types of objectives for the teacher—the *results* of scientific inquiry (a working knowledge of large concepts and principles), and a sympathetic comprehension of the *process* of scientific inquiry. In the latter category we look

14. "Reactions of Scientists and Science Teachers to Statements Bearing on Certain Aspects of Science and Science Teaching," *School Science and Mathematics,* LXI (1960), 193.

for opportunities to exhibit or experience such factors as these: the way new instruments are contrived and their importance in opening up new lines of evidence, the importance of systematic exploration in a new field of study, the role of accidental discovery, the move from qualitative description toward quantitative mathematical models, the importance of brain-work (hunches, ideation, conceptualization), the feedback of new results on prior explanations, the importance of communication between scientists in many countries, the confirmation of important new results, the necessary "skepticism" of a scientist as well as his faith in an organizable universe. Such a consideration of "what we are trying to do," the teacher's objectives, is one important component of a methods course.

Since the teacher's prime responsibility is to develop many desirable forms of learning within each pupil, the future teacher must be centrally concerned with the conditions under which children learn what we select to teach them. Therefore, in addition to some examination of the nature of science, these future teachers must consider at least some simple aspects of applied psychology. This point was made starkly by B. Rosen of Belgium in a recent conference on the teaching of physics: "The problem is: How can a teacher make comprehensible and clear to pupils of twelve to eighteen something that he himself has learned at a much older age. . . ." [15]

Not all the children facing a teacher are highly inclined toward the study of science, or even toward any form of academic work. Yet they are normal human beings who can be curious about almost anything. If their curiosity is aroused and the classroom atmosphere is encouraging, they will strive to answer their own questions—sometimes quite sophisticated questions. Each component of the instruction must therefore be introduced by some "interest-getter." As this must be significant to the pupil, the teacher must watch children and search for interesting leads useful in the classroom. With leads from the pupils a number of subquestions can be stated for study, sometimes in parallel groups with reports to the total class, and sometimes in an accepted sequence. Ultimately the en-

15. *International Education in Physics* (Boston: MIT Technology Press, 1960).

tire block of study must be summarized and appraised to see how well the initial questions have been answered.

Some readers may, at this point, be muttering about "pandering to the pupils." They fail to recognize that the most effective collegiate instruction follows much the same pattern. Even though the collegiate students are more mature, are selected from those who have completed the earlier schools, and generally have chosen for personal reasons to be enrolled in the course, still collegiate instructors pose questions, and try to give excitement and pertinency to their instruction. The basic proposition is clear: people learn more, and more quickly, when they see the purpose of the learning. Since the learning of adults must be self-directed, we can show them in school how to learn by practicing effective ways; these differ somewhat with the rules of evidence, permitted operations, criteria of acceptability, and the bases of judgment in each field of study. Also, teachers must assist pupils in developing the ability to appraise the effectiveness of their learning and to acquire sophistication in being self-critical.

Most beginning teachers have great difficulty in seeing both the desirability of "packaging" their instruction around questions of interest to their pupils, and of being able to find various possible centers of interest. Therefore, the methods course must include a continuous search for interesting questions which will focus the attention of the pupils and provoke significant learning. To imply that such a course could possibly produce completely competent teachers would be absurd. At best we can hope only to produce "apt apprentices" who are sensitive to the wide diversity of their responsibilities and capable of learning further from experience. But not all their learning is restricted to this single course. Visits to schools are important in the awakening process. There children of different ages and academic promise must be watched closely. Mature and competent teachers can be observed in action. Different types of communities should be appraised in terms of their concern for and support of particular types of learning. So reading, talking, planning, and visiting alert the future teacher to the nature of his work.

But such a remote appraisal would still be inadequate; the

future teacher must have personal experience under wise, sympathetic, and critical guidance. Therefore, practice teaching is a major component of the training program. It is the "real thing" for which we have been attempting to prepare the future teacher. How the student is handled during this critical field-testing is of great importance. Merely to put him in front of a class on a "sink or swim" basis is irresponsible. How will his mistakes and omissions in planning, class management, and evaluation be corrected unless a sensitive observer is present to see the difficulties and analyze their cause? How the supervising teacher reacts is also important. He must be friend, solace, guide and yet a demanding critic as well. Since ultimately the teacher-to-be must recognize and analyze his own difficulties, and modify his own behavior, we encourage the critic teachers to help the beginner perform these functions. Merely to tell the beginner what is wrong and what would have been better does not build self-appraisal and self-correcting abilities. Therefore, especially mature and sensitive critic teachers must be sought. As they are partners in the planned development of the student teacher, mutual respect and close working relations with the instructor of the methods course are essential.

While there are many ways by which courses could be structured to provide the widely diverse skills and knowledge of a future science teacher, one example may provide a basis for argument and discussion. Inevitably the writer must report on the course which he knows best, his own. It has evolved through several phases and will probably continue to change in the future. The "methods course in science" is offered to graduate students in two sections, one during the summer with special facilities for observation and practice teaching. The other, enrolling about fifteen to twenty students, offered in the fall term and followed by practice teaching, is described here. Classes meet for two-hour sessions twice a week for a total of about sixty class hours. In other institutions with three-unit and two-unit courses the amount of contact is less, but even sixty hours is hardly sufficient for the task to be done. The text by Brandwein, Watson, and Blackwood is used, but it is not followed in detail or even used in chapter sequence. Specific references and assignments are made to similar texts, as well as other types of publications.

The students have majored in one science and often have a high commitment to that field of specialization. Basic in the course is the intent to recognize and to make planned use of general skills in the teaching of science—or any of the specialized sciences. To utilize the special knowledges of some, and encourage a broadening of knowledge of others, the contexts of some assignments are chosen from sciences such as geology and astronomy in which the students have little knowledge. Also, students compile a self-appraisal list of "what I don't know," and suggested reading lists are provided to help them fill gaps in their scientific knowledge. Student membership in one or more national organizations concerned with science and its teaching is encouraged.

At present the course outline is this:

Lesson planning	about 12 sessions
Demonstrations by the students	about 3 sessions
Unit planning	about 3 sessions
Curriculum in science (history of, biology, chemistry, physics, general science, elementary school science)	about 6 sessions
Special pupil activities (projects, science fairs, etc.)	about 2 sessions
Evaluation (teacher-made and standaradized tests)	about 4 sessions

This schedule is not rigid, but serves to indicate the approximate emphasis of the course. Sessions on the manual skills of operating numerous audio-visual aids and visits to schools require additional out-of-class time.

A card-file of reference and sources of materials useful to the teacher is required of each student and is returned after appraisal. Two major papers are also required. One deals with the purposes of science instruction and classroom procedures for attaining these ends. The second is a resource unit for about a month of instruction; insofar as practical, these units are related to the teaching which the students will perform in the second term.

The course opens with the assignment of the preparation of a lesson plan for an eighth-grade class. Some typical science topic is assigned as the context. Students are required to record separately the questions which occur to them as they attempt to plan this lesson. This evokes from them an awareness of the kinds of skills and knowledge which a teacher needs. Thus the whole complex of aims, pupil characteristics, planning, class operation, materials, demonstrations and laboratory work, as well as continuous evaluation, comes up for systematic consideration. Different phases are considered in subsequent sessions, and more lesson plans for particular purposes or groups of pupils are prepared and appraised. Visits to schools also aid in clarifying the important aspects for which a teacher must plan.

Experience in the handling of simple materials, often with improvisation, is provided through demonstrations by class members. Group criticism follows. Often mature and competent students will panic when obliged to present a simple demonstration before sympathetic colleagues. But the only way to get over this nervousness is to practice. In preparation for the development of a unit, some attention is then given to purpose and format. Sources of evidence (films, equipment, special reading sources, and field trips) must be specified here and selected through personal appraisal.

How the present curricular patterns and courses in science have developed through past years, and various proposals for their modification, are considered. The various possible sequences of science courses is also discussed. Possible bases and procedures for curricular changes are considered briefly because within a few years these teachers will be involved with such revisions.

Although continuous evaluation through the observations of pupils is stressed throughout the course, and some attention to assessment of pupil achievement is included in other courses, nevertheless special attention to teacher-made tests in science is necessary. Too often teacher-made tests are inconsistent with the major objectives sought by the teacher. The elements of competence in test-making can be taught. Also, the variety of standardized tests as well as their interpretation and use need to be explored, albeit briefly.

No short description of a course can delineate all the components or emphases which develop. But at least one major criticism may be aimed at this outline. Relatively little attention is given to developing manipulative skills, for example, glass-blowing, slide-making, blood-typing. This is deliberate. Presumably, as a science major in college the student has learned how to use scientific equipment. This is, alas, often an illusion but such skills can readily be learned. Numerous books and journals describe many procedures which the teacher can practice in private. In addition, such skills are readily learned from other mature teachers who will be pleased to show the beginner what he needs to know. But more basic is the use of class time for developing attributes which are less available through reading or contact with other teachers. We delegate to the critic teacher many aspects of classroom management and record-keeping which can be learned best during practice teaching. But an understanding of the nature of science and its importance in schooling, as well as a deep concern for the dignity and potential of each pupil, involve attitudes and competencies which only develop slowly under constant attention. Without these to set the framework for a lifetime of creative teaching and self-evaluation, the other skills and knowledge may lack significant focus. We look upon the "methods course" as the introduction to a lifetime career. Therefore, while we must develop in the student enough skills and self-confidence to "go on," we wish to create a perspective for him to "grow on."

Current Textbooks on the Teaching of Science in the Secondary School

Brandwein, P., Watson, F. G., and Blackwood, P., *Teaching High School Science: A Book of Methods*. New York: Harcourt, Brace and World, 1958.

Burnett, R. W., *Teaching Science in the Secondary School*. New York: Rinehart, 1957.

Heiss, E. D., Obourn, E. C., and Hoffman, C. W., *Modern Science Teaching*. New York: Macmillan, 1950.

Hoff, A., *Secondary Science Teaching*, rev. ed. New York: Blakiston Division of McGraw-Hill, 1950.

Richardson, J., *Science Teaching in Secondary Schools*. Englewood Cliffs, N.J.: Prentice-Hall, 1957.

Thurber, W. A., and Collette, A. T., *Teaching Science in Today's Secondary Schools*. Boston: Allyn and Bacon, 1959.

Washton, N. S., *Science Teaching in the Secondary School*. New York: Harpers, 1961.

Wells, H., *Secondary Science Education*. New York: McGraw-Hill Co., 1952.

Other Useful Books

Joseph, A., Brandwein, P., Morholt, E., et al., *A Sourcebook for the Physical Sciences*. New York: Harcourt, Brace and World, 1961.

Laybourn, K., and Bailey, C. H., *Teaching Science to the Ordinary Pupil*. New York: Philosophical Library, 1957.

Miller, D. F., and Blaydes, G. W., *Methods and Materials for Teaching Biological Sciences*, new ed. New York: McGraw-Hill, 1962.

Morholt, E., Brandwein, P., and Joseph, A., *A Sourcebook for the Biological Sciences*. New York: Harcourt, Brace and World, 1958.

Richardson, J., and Cahoon, G. P., *Methods and Materials for Teaching General and Physical Science*. New York: McGraw-Hill, 1951.

Science Masters Series (numerous titles on experiments), London: John Murray, Albermarle St., W.I.

CHAPTER X

W. WARWICK SAWYER:

The Teaching of Mathematics

Mathematical Education

American teachers of mathematics are in much the same position as an army attacked by superior numbers from all directions. This is not to say that they should be resigned to defeat. On many occasions outnumbered armies have secured brilliant victories by vigorous and unconventional action. The reason for emphasizing the adverse factors are, first, to make clear that the situation is quite out of the ordinary, that it will not yield to routine procedures, and second, to establish some system of priorities—of all the tasks which confront us, how shall we select the essential ones on which we should concentrate our limited resources? For the greatest mistake an outnumbered army can make is to spread itself too thin, to attempt to hold all positions and to end by holding none.

The criticism most frequently heard in the past few years has been the lack of "modern mathematics"—the curriculum does not reflect the mathematical research of the present century. This last statement is true enough, but it is rather like telling a man who has forgotten to put his trousers on that his tie is not straight. Imagine a visitor from the past, a mathematician educated in the 1880's. He knows nothing of the content or the spirit of modern mathematics. Will he therefore be satisfied with what he finds in the schools? Not in the least. He has been trained to solve problems; he has all the standard methods and theorems at his finger tips;

he is ingenious in coping with the unexpected; his whole attitude is one of attack. But he finds hardly anyone in the schools who can solve the problems in the bible of the 1880's, Hall and Knight's *Higher Algebra*. Instead, algebra is taught as a series of isolated, museum exhibits: a student can obtain a high grade by doing ten routine applications; he is then free to forget it. Ingenuity, original discovery, the readiness to attack the subject for oneself—these are rare indeed. The curriculum is quite as defective in ancient mathematics as it is in modern.

These weaknesses are accentuated by the package system. Traditionally, the subjects are separated in time: instead of teaching algebra, geometry, and trigonometry concurrently, the student encounters these subjects in separate years. At the end, he does not know any of them. He graduates on the basis of grades earned in subjects he has already forgotten. When students preparing to become teachers are told that a competent teacher has the whole of high school mathematics in his mind, they usually regard this as an extremely novel idea. If an incoming student is asked to write briefly the main theorems he remembers from Euclidean geometry, a very meager harvest commonly results.

The curiously static teaching of algebra is also reinforced by the separation of mathematics from physics. Where these two subjects are taught together, each helps the other. In dealing with a problem in mechanics, the student has to formulate it algebraically, with symbols for the unknown forces, and then solve the resulting system of equations. The mathematical formulation makes physics more systematic. The physical problems illustrate the mathematical concepts and show mathematics in action, instead of as a museum piece.

To anyone familiar with education in Europe, the most startling feature of traditional American education is the intellectual vacuum in grades four through eight. These are the most wonderful years in the life of a child. The storms of infancy are behind; adolescence is yet to come. Children are eager to learn, ready to play with ideas, fascinated by the patterns of the universe. As intellectual nourishment for these beautiful years, the traditional curriculum provides commercial arithmetic, moving at a snail's pace, completely devoid of beauty or surprise, and culminating in the three cases of percentage. In the same years, on the other side of the Atlantic, an able student acquires a more thorough knowledge of algebra, geometry, and trigonometry than most high school students obtain here. Unless one believes—which nobody does—that American children are biologically inferior to European children, and are intellectually retarded by four years, it is clear that we tragically underestimate our students. Particularly the abler students, with an excess of unused and undirected mental energy, are liable to become bored, idle, troublesome, or delinquent. But even the weaker students have a right to something more stimulating than percentages, and (later on) that desert of boredom, "general mathematics."

Grades four through eight have a double significance. They represent the strategic point at which a given effort will produce the maximum response. Much teaching at college level is merely a waste of time, a belated attempt to change attitudes already firmly established and to convey knowledge that should have been acquired years before. The same can be true of high school teaching. There are some high schools where an atmosphere of intellectual inquiry prevails and useful work can be done. But there are many at which the students are already "too old at fourteen." There are many pressures on the students; they are too busy; their attitudes are formed. Grades four through eight may thus be a period of make-or-break, the last opportunity of influencing the student effectively.[1]

This phase of education is thus of central importance for anyone concerned with the future supply of mathematicians, scientists, engineers, teachers and so forth. But this aspect—the public aspect, which regards the student as someone who may be needed by others in the future—this is only one half of the story.

Even if there were no shortage of mathematicians, if industry had reached the final goal of automation and supplied all our wants without effort on our part, one would still wish to see a change in

1. A high school teacher conducted a poll of her students. She asked them, "Do you like or dislike mathematics? Which teacher caused you to like or dislike the subject?" *The replies did not mention the name of any teacher in high school.* Whether the student had come to love mathematics or to hate it, this feeling had already been established in elementary schools.

grades four through eight. For the intellectual awakening of these years is a thing good in itself. You cannot help feeling this as you observe the interest and the eagerness that young students display when some topic intrigues them. This is what a good society would wish its children to experience; this is what parents should hope to provide for their children. It seems, incidentally, not easy to provide: education swings uneasily between the anti-intellectuals, who seem to feel that the less you know the better, and the academic pedants, whose philosophy appears as a mixture of sadism and masochism—"It doesn't matter what the students are doing, so long as they don't like it."

The provision of intellectual stimulation in the elementary grades is a central task but it is also an extremely difficult one. The whole weight of tradition is against it. The purpose of arithmetic lessons a century or so ago was to produce clerks who could keep accounts accurately. The mood of the early twentieth century led to a relaxation of actual arithmetical achievement, and the arithmetic texts became essentially without purpose. They had inherited the one aim of accuracy, and this they failed to achieve. I do not know any arithmetic text, used here in the period 1920–1950, which seems to have the object of stimulating interest and intellectual curiosity. Indeed, arithmetic lessons have proved a most effective way of destroying children's power of independent thought. A very young child looks at things and seeks to understand them. After a few years of school he no longer does this. Instead, he tries to remember a rule; he usually remembers a rule that does not apply, and makes a statement that is sheer nonsense. Vision is destroyed in the elementary school, and the process of destruction often continues in high school and in college.

The increased demand of industry for mathematicians and scientists is a factor, partly adverse and partly favorable. It is adverse insofar as industry tends to absorb those who might make a contribution to teaching. It is favorable insofar as industry's demand for skilled employees constitutes a powerful force, making the improvement of education an urgent question of practical politics. The strength of this force can hardly be overestimated. For the role of mathematics in society has completely changed since 1945. Prior to that time, a mathematician was in almost the same position as a classical scholar; he had the choice of doing research and discovering more mathematics, or of teaching other people mathematics; he lived in a closed circle. Insurance absorbed some mathematicians, and industry a few—much fewer than most people realized. An extremely competent report[2] to Congress in 1941 estimated that industry in the United States could absorb *ten* mathematicians a year. A country as large as the United States does not have to organize to produce ten mathematicians a year. They happen spontaneously. Before 1945, in almost every country, the supply of mathematicians exceeded the demand. This was shown by the fact that students with good mathematical degrees went into occupations where mathematics was not used at all. There was an element of realism behind the neglect of mathematics in American schools. No one, here or elsewhere, foresaw the change that was coming.

After 1945, the demand for mathematicians far exceeded the total available. Statistics have been thrown around, estimating how many tens of thousands of mathematicians industry could absorb in the coming years. Even so, the figures correspond to a very small proportion of the population. To the best of my knowledge, no one has suggested that a quarter of a million mathematicians, or any number near to that, will be needed in the present century. It could therefore be argued very reasonably that the education of future mathematicians is a highly specialized problem, that provision should be made for these exceptional individuals, the general scheme of education remaining as it is. But this overlooks another aspect of the revolution. Electronic computers and automation do not merely create a demand for skilled workers; they also make obsolete unskilled and semiskilled workers. The industrial revolution in fact is moving toward its logical conclusion, in which every mechanical task, whether physical or mental, will be performed by a machine. Surveys of employment already show the first signs of this process, a shortage of highly skilled workers alongside a surplus of the unskilled and untrained. As far ahead as we can see we can expect this situation to continue and to become intensified.

2. By Dr. Thornton Fry. Reprinted in *American Mathematical Monthly*, XLVIII, No. 6 (June–July 1941), Part II Supplement.

This development cannot fail to influence education. A person whose services are in strong demand is secure and influential; a person on the edge of unemployment is insecure and his opinions are little regarded. In the society that is now passing, a certain shrewdness and common sense were often enough to take a man into the ranks of the secure and influential. It seems likely that much more will be required in the society of tomorrow; that shrewdness without a considerable background of knowledge will be insufficient. The first to appreciate this change will undoubtedly be professional people and executives. Suburban schools will begin, as they are already doing, to provide a richer curriculum in the elementary grades, and to attract competent teachers by giving higher salaries, by relieving teachers of all unnecessary clerical duties, and by providing scope for experiment and individual initiative. Other areas will then be faced with the choice of making similar changes or accepting the exclusion of their children from the key positions in society. One section of the nation that is clearly unwilling any longer to accept an inferior position is the negro community. The demand of negroes for the best possible education will be intensified, and the present waste of negro ability will, in all probability, be brought to an end.

One aspect of technology is its perpetual and ever-accelerated change. A few years ago there was a bottleneck caused by the shortage of computer programmers. This led to devices by which the machine did much of the work of programming itself; the detailed drudgery was transferred from the human being to the machine. Thus a new industry demanded a new skill, and within five years the industry had so transformed itself that this new skill was no longer needed. This development is typical of this age. Change is constant and rapid. Students in schools today are preparing themselves to perform unknown tasks in industries not yet invented. This implies the emergence of a new branch of the teaching profession, inside industry, with the task of perpetually retraining engineers and technicians. This new branch of the profession makes exacting requirements—the ability to learn new ideas quickly, to disentangle the essentials from the complicating nonessentials, and to put these ideas into a form which can be readily grasped by those who are not specialists in that particular field. Similar qualities are needed for institutions that will surely become a permanent feature of the landscape—summer schools and academic year institutes, designed to keep teachers aware of new developments in knowledge, both pure and applied.

In a primitive tribe, boys and girls commit to memory the precepts of the elders. In this way they absorb the traditional wisdom and also the traditional mistakes of their society. Education in a modern society differs remarkably little from education in the tribe. It too passes on wisdom and folly, and this must be so, for we have no way of identifying the unconscious errors in our own reasoning; we have no rule for distinguishing farsighted generosity from idealistic illusion, or justifiable caution from mean and self-destroying suspicion; we have no way of telling how much of our science is in fact tribal superstition, and how much of our superstition may be science. At times, when we consider the record and prospects of mankind, we may wish that the slate of memory could be wiped clean, that the continuity of history could be broken, and that a generation could grow up, uninfluenced by parents or teachers, and able to look at life with the eyes of the newborn and see it as it is. This experiment will certainly not be tried, and if it were tried, the result might be a world even worse than the one we have now. Children are born capable of adapting to almost any order of society. The one thing they cannot endure is anarchy. Thinking has to be within some framework, within some tradition. Each generation, of necessity, faces a painful search to separate the truth from the falsehood in the tradition received and a struggle to decide which parts of that tradition shall be passed on to the next generation. In an age of stability the search and the struggle are limited in scope; in an age of change, they dominate the scene.

We are living in an age of exceptionally rapid and continued change, an age which calls above all for independence and openness of mind, for resourcefulness and initiative, for flexibility. It might seem that our prospects are almost hopeless, for the tradition in the American teaching of mathematics and science lacks precisely those qualities; it is dominated by rote learning and the quiz, by the memorizing of words and isolated facts, rather than an understanding of general laws and the reasons for the facts. Yet this reflects a paradox in American culture, for the temper of American thinking is rational and analytic. Where a European will ask, "What is the history of this thing? How has it been done in the past? How does that limit our action in the future?" an American will say, "Never mind the past. How should this thing be done? What is the logical way of doing it?" It is indeed strange that minds accustomed to this heroic courage in thinking about the infinitely complex problems of human society should recoil in terror when asked to give a logical account of some simple theme in arithmetic, such as the procedure for multiplying twenty-seven by thirty-eight. But it is so. The overwhelming majority admit, without shame, that they are afraid to think about arithmetic, and prefer to rely on the rules handed down by the elders of the tribe. The salvation of mathematics and science in American schools lies in breaking the barrier between these subjects and the general culture, in allowing them to become subjects for discussion and thought, in the same way that matters of current interest are topics for discussion and thought.

We certainly do not lack for tasks. More mathematics needs to be taught, as a subject unified in itself and related to other sciences, in a more lively and enterprising manner, to students at a younger age, by scholarly teachers who are themselves continually extending their own knowledge. We have a big advance to make, and we begin farther back than many other nations. This is the challenge. It is a considerable but not a superhuman task.

The Criteria for Decisions

In view of the variety of the problems confronting us, it is not surprising that a variety of solutions are proposed. These solutions correspond, as a rule, to the activity of the proposer. One professor may be dealing with Ph.D. students who hope to do research work in pure mathematics; another professor may be teaching freshmen engineers. It is inevitable that the ideas of each will be influenced by his circumstances: each will tend to imagine mathematics in terms of the themes he teaches; each will make proposals designed to make his work more effective. And each may easily forget that the other exists at all. The divergence of viewpoints just instanced is merely one example out of many; mathematicians differ in innumerable ways. To the teacher, looking at the disputes, it seems that mathematicians are completely unable to make up their collective mind. The teacher, with a very limited mathematical training, has to decide which mathematician to believe. The school principal is often in an even worse position, with no mathematical training at all. The professor of mathematics in a teachers' college stands at the junction of the two worlds, between the embattled specialists and the bewildered teachers. By what criteria can he make his choice?

To a certain extent the choice makes itself, as soon as one recognizes the existence of diversity. It is clearly not the business of an educational system to identify itself with any one kind of specialist and to despise all the others. Society both will and should continue to produce pure and applied mathematicians, mathematical physicists, scientists who are not mathematicians but who use some branch of mathematics in a routine manner, engineers, teachers, and many others. All of these stand in different relationships to mathematics; all of them see different aspects of the subject. Clearly, schools should be sufficiently flexible to value and to encourage all these varieties of mathematicians and users of mathematics.

It cannot be too strongly emphasized that these different varieties *are* different. The layman usually thinks of mathematics as a subject serving practical ends, and he tends to assume that research mathematicians share this viewpoint. If a pure mathematician speaks of some topic as important, the layman interprets this as meaning that the topic has applications of practical utility. Nothing could be farther from the truth. A pure mathematician works on problems which he considers interesting or beautiful. The mathematics of engineering he frequently finds dull, and tends to despise. One might think that the tremendous development of technology in the United States would have affected mathematicians here, and that American mathematicians would be more interested in practical applications than mathematicians are elsewhere. The reverse is true. In the words of an authoritative report: [3]

"As American mathematics grew up during the first quarter of

3. F. J. Weyl. *A Survey of Training and Research in Applied Mathematics in the United States.* Society for Industrial and Applied Mathematics. 1956.

this century to join the older European schools in the front line of mathematical advance, it did so primarily in the purest, most abstract branches of mathematics. . . . With the exception of a few pioneers, mathematicians in the United States did not actively participate in the corresponding development of applied mathematics until the outbreak of World War II."

One should not consider a pure mathematician as being in the least like an engineer. He resembles rather, say, a chess player. You do not expect any economic benefit or scientific advance to come from reading a book on chess. But you may expect to find intriguing and beautiful positions and examples of ingenuity and resourcefulness. The analogy between chess and mathematics is not perfect; indeed, there is nothing that can serve as a complete and satisfactory analogy for mathematics. For each chess problem is more or less self-contained; it does not lead anywhere. On the other hand, every mathematical result is a part of one vast structure. The close of one investigation is the beginning of another. There is no knowing what direction the exploration may take, nor whether some new result may show a connection between parts of mathematics that seemed entirely separate. The pure mathematician engages in this exploration for its own sake, and is rewarded by the richness and intricacy of the patterns he uncovers. The applied mathematician engages in the exploration in the hope that it will lead to other territories outside mathematics. Somewhere, he hopes, mathematics borders on science and technology. But the shape of mathematics is still vague and incomplete; we do not always know where the desired borders are, nor even for certain that they exist at all.

According to the poet Keats, it is inevitable that first in beauty should be first in might. If so, those parts of mathematics valued by pure mathematicians for their beauty should be the same as those valued by applied mathematicians for their power. In the long run, this may be true; in the short run it does not seem to work out at all. Most applied mathematicians must have had the experience of hearing of some new branch of pure mathematics that sounded promising and exciting, but which, after being laboriously mastered, made no contribution at all to the problem in hand.

One might illustrate this by that part of modern algebra which lies close to Galois theory. This theory is built around the idea of symmetry, and it allows one to prove, for example, that the equation of the fifth degree cannot be solved by the methods of elementary algebra, and that there is no general procedure for trisecting an angle with the means permitted by Euclid. This theory affects in quite different ways the mathematician, the teacher, and the engineer. All mathematicians would agree that it is a singularly beautiful and satisfying theory. A teacher has a direct concern in it because it lies near to familiar subjects; a student in a geometry class may claim to have trisected the angle; a student in an algebra class, who has been shown how to solve quadratics, may well ask whether similar devices will work with equations of the third, fourth, fifth, and higher degrees. A teacher should know enough to deal with discussions arising in this way. An engineer, to the best of my knowledge, never meets a problem for which Galois theory is helpful in any way. If an engineer meets an equation of the fifth degree, he will solve it numerically; if he needs to trisect an angle, he will certainly not restrict himself to Euclid's compass and ungraduated straightedge. In some very indirect and general way, the study of Galois theory might influence an engineer's philosophy and assist him in the solution of some particular problem. But this would be a rare event, affecting an exceptional engineer. Put crudely, Galois theory is a central topic for some mathematicians, a topic of interest for teachers, and a waste of time for engineers.

Too often, all these distinctions are slurred over in some slogan such as "modern mathematics." We must be up-to-date. Galois theory is a worthy representative of modern mathematics, a profound and beautiful subject. But one can imagine the growing bewilderment of an engineer who happened to wander into a course on Galois theory, as he tried to see how this type of mathematics could be applied to engineering problems.

It is not only engineers who can become bewildered. A young professor of mathematics at a teachers' college attended a course on modern algebra. He came back somewhat puzzled and reported that the course had not contained any applications. He did not mean simply engineering or scientific applications. The course had contained no applications at all. The lecturer, presumably, had explained what groups, rings, and fields were, and had proved some properties of these. And that was all. But the young professor knew that, if he returned to his college and began to teach modern algebra, the first questions his students asked would be, "What can we do with this? What is it *for?*" He had no idea what it was for. He only knew that people were saying we ought to be modern and this, apparently, was modern.

Much mystification has been caused by the manner in which the campaign for "modern mathematics" has been handled. Recent work in mathematics, of course, has yielded beautiful and valuable results, but one cannot arrange the branches of mathematics in their order of importance simply by giving the dates of discovery. It is necessary to be highly specific; to show for what purpose any branch of mathematics can be used, and by whom.

Mystification is the great enemy of mathematical thinking. Mathematics, above all other subjects, is that in which you expect to produce reasons for whatever you do. The way to avoid mystification is to be extremely explicit.

Mathematics is not an aimless subject. New branches arise, in a way that can be traced, from particular problems in the older branches of mathematics or in the world outside mathematics. Usually one can foresee that these new branches will serve certain purposes and lead in a particular direction. Sometimes, of course, a discovery serves quite unexpected purposes, not dreamed of by the discoverer.

We may then state a principle—almost a platitude, one would have thought, but certainly a principle often ignored in practice: *the work should make sense to the student.* The student should experience the subject, not as a mass of foreign information pressed upon him, but as a natural growth of his own consciousness. He should have some idea, at the outset, of the problem that is being attacked, and why we consider it worth attacking. He should know from which parts of mathematics it arises and to which parts it leads. He should know the purpose of the work, because purposes vary. For example, in some courses we expect to arrive at new results; in others, we know all the results before we start and are trying simply to provide a sounder logical basis for these. As soon as possible after meeting any new concept, the student should meet a worthwhile application of this concept. Then he sees how the work has increased his mathematical power. It is most unsatisfactory if, instead of this evidence of his own experience, he is given some vague, authoritarian justification—"this is the modern way," "this is how great mathematicians do it." The student, in short, should have some indication of where the work he is doing fits into the scheme of mathematics and, indeed, of human knowledge as a whole.

The traditional curriculum had at least this virtue, that its purposes were evident. The purposes were sometimes humble, but at least they were not mysterious. A text on physics, or engineering, or astronomy or surveying or plumbing or sheet-metal work, opened at random, would provide examples of algebra, geometry, trigonometry, and perhaps of calculus. The purpose of modern mathematics, on the other hand, is often obscure to the student. There is an obvious reason why this tends to be so. Twentieth-century mathematics was built on the foundation of nineteenth-century mathematics. But the student is often unfamiliar with nineteenth-century mathematics. Some of it he may have learned and forgotten; some he never knew at all. Thus he cannot possibly see the motivation for more recent work. It is particularly noticeable how calculus plays the role of a connecting link between the older and the newer mathematics. Cantor's work on sets and transfinite numbers grew out of his study of Fourier series. Lebesgue's use of sets was intimately connected with the theory of integration. Hilbert space and Banach space began with the theory of integral equations. Fréchet's work on metric spaces grew from a variety of topics in analysis. Topology was stimulated by the theory of the Riemann surface and of integration over complex numbers. If a student is not aware of these and other connections, he is bound to be mystified. He finds mathematicians treating with great reverence topics that to him must seem trivial and pointless. Topology will appear to him as a matter of Möbius strips, the Königsberg bridges, and the four-color conjecture, entertaining perhaps but of doubtful significance. It is the good student who will be puzzled, the student of integrity, who expects mathematics to make sense. The poor student will be quite happy to jump on the bandwagon, and take the new material on trust. All his life he has taken things on trust, not submitting statements to the court of his inner judgment, but repeating the phrases of the lecturer and the text. This, he believes, is the way to win friends and influence professors. But mathematics cannot be learned so. All the nonsense of the type $(x + y)^2 = x^2 + y^2$ is written because the student writes irresponsibly. He does not feel that he is committing himself to the truth of a statement, with a duty to ascertain the meaning of this statement, and see whether he really believes it. He is merely trying to write something like something he heard some time, and the result is usually as incorrect as the purpose. Indeed, the greatest difficulty in teaching college students is that they are usually so anxious to please and so unwilling to think.

A key principle, then, in any course of mathematics is that *it must encourage and establish the student's habit of examining evidence for himself.*

A future teacher must not only think for himself; he must be prepared to encourage others to do the same. His classroom must not simply be a place where students are told things, but a place where students engage in discussion. Now this is a very severe stipulation, for no one can foresee where discussion may lead. Many teachers, in fact, try to avoid discussion, for fear they may get out of their depth. But free discussion is the essential part of a mathematical lesson. In order to face discussion, *a teacher must know with extreme thoroughness the actual subject being taught and also have a good knowledge of other topics that arise naturally from this subject.* The reason for this, our third principle, is not that the subject necessarily contains vital information. Our concern here is less with *what* is taught than with *how* it is handled. Whatever material we teach, we may wish twenty years hence that we had taught something else. But if we have used this material to form correct habits, if the students are ready to think for themselves, to make conjectures, to debate the evidence for and against these conjectures, to attack nonroutine problems—then they are well armored to face the unknown future.

This emphasis on student thinking, student discovery, student discussion, on the way in which the subject is approached, of course does not mean that the choice of content is unimportant. A student's thinking is inevitably influenced by what he knows, as well as by how he has learned it. We should try to see that material is carefully selected. Nevertheless, the emphasis on *how* over *what* remains: if a student has not learned to think about mathematics, he knows nothing of mathematics. Rote-learned information, whether ancient or modern, is not mathematics, and will in any case be remembered only inaccurately for a short time and soon forgotten altogether.

Thinking is an activity, and one that cannot be produced by compulsion. A teacher, therefore, must seek for subject matter and for methods of teaching that will create in the students a desire to learn. A teacher's selection of material differs both from a mathematician's and an engineer's. The engineer selects material that can be *used;* the mathematician tends to select material that can be *systematically developed.* The teacher's first concern, however, is to *stimulate.* A teacher should choose material that makes children want to think. This thinking should not be a form of self-torture. It should be the natural outgrowth of a child's interest and curiosity. The most depressing thing in our educational system is not the student who decides to terminate his education. It is rather the student who slaves away for the sake of grades, without ever realizing that it would be possible to study a subject for its inherent interest.

The present ferment in education offers some hope of achieving a united society, instead of one divided into two separate camps: eggheads and blockheads. At present, intellectual endeavor is like a play acted in an empty theater or a game with no spectators. The spectators do contribute something to a game. If they are not themselves experts, they at least understand what the experts are trying to do, because they have played the game themselves. It would give tremendous impetus to all kinds of creative work if it were done as part of a general culture, instead of an exclusive, minority undertaking. Such an objective is not visionary; there have, in the past, been societies which attained it. We shall not achieve it, however, by impressing on the public that mathematics and science are important for industry or strategy or what not. Rather we shall achieve it if children themselves take part in mathematical and scientific activities which they enjoy.

Now young children do enjoy mental activity. They enjoy thinking and discovering. But, as has been noted earlier, this enjoyment decreases with the years, and is in fact systematically, though no doubt unconsciously, destroyed by our institutions. Once destroyed, it is almost impossible to restore. If, then, any change is to come, it must come through those who are in contact with young children. Now there are very many teachers of the young. It might be possible to identify high school students who gave promise of becoming brilliant research workers in mathematics or science, and to provide special treatment for them. It would be extremely difficult to identify students who are likely to become teachers of grades four through eight. Very well, it might be argued, wait until teachers' college and deal with the problem there. But teachers' college is already too late. A student who has learned mathematics by rote through twelve grades is not likely to blossom out as a creative thinker in college. This is the essential problem of educational change, the vicious circle we always meet. The reform of the schools can only occur within the schools. Not the least significant aspect of the high school curriculum is the part it plays in determining the outlook of future teachers in elementary schools, for it is they who hold the key position in determining the nature of our future society. A high school teacher has, in fact, great responsibilities in connection with elementary education. He has to co-operate in the transfer to elementary school of parts of the traditional high school curriculum. More important, he has to see that this transfer changes and revitalizes these topics. A mechanical, rote-learning approach to algebra, for example, will prove even more fatal in grade five than it used to be in grade nine. He has to assist those who are already teaching in elementary and junior high schools in his neighborhood. And above all, he has a duty to his present students who may become teachers in the future. As he does not know exactly which students these are, he has an obligation to see that *all his students are able to think and enjoy thinking.*

At this point a certain element of conflict enters. The thinking of mathematicians tends to be logical and abstract. The thinking of the population in general tends to be intuitive and concrete. Only a few seem able to think in the way demanded by a graduate school of mathematics. Almost everyone is able to think, more or less effectively, in the way demanded by everyday life.

Two points of view are therefore current today. Some take as their goal that children should learn to think like research mathematicians as quickly as possible. Advanced mathematics is abstract and general. Therefore elementary instruction should be abstract and general. Others take the opposite view. Let the classroom be full of apparatus which the children can see and touch. Then they will certainly learn to think and some of them, later on, may learn to think more abstractly.

These diverging views directly affect practice. For example, an equation has traditionally been illustrated by means of a balance. An enthusiast for apparatus might well have an actual balance in the classroom and use it to demonstrate the steps of solving an equation. To a purist, this is most distressing. A balance is a *thing*. Mathematics is not about things. It is only obscured by physical illustrations. The proper method (he would say) is to bring in the axiom

$$\text{“If } a = b, \text{ then for all } c, a + c = b + c\text{”}$$

and let the students appeal to this axiom every time they add the same quantity to each side of an equation.

There can be no doubt how the methods would compare for teaching effectiveness. The balance, seen and touched, would leave a definite image in the students' memories. It may seem strange to mathematicians, who are accustomed to looking at statements very carefully and remembering exactly what they say, but the fact is that on the next day many students would not be able to reproduce the axiom correctly. Some might have forgotten that an axiom had been mentioned at all. And those who did remember the axiom might very well fail to appreciate its meaning.

My own belief is that there is no conflict between the illustration of the balance and reliance on the axiom. Indeed, probably the most effective way to teach the axiom would be to do a physical demonstration with the balance, and *let the students carry out the process of abstraction and generalization.* The teacher could say, "I have added three pounds to each side and it still balances. Could I have added any number of pounds? How shall we express, in the language of algebra, the conclusion this demonstration suggests to us?" The concrete experience thus becomes a means of recalling the abstract statement.

This belief, that concrete material can help, rather than hinder, the formation of abstract ideas, is held by a number of mathematicians. Professor Marguerite Lehr, in her introduction to Catherine Stern's admirable book, *Children Discover Arithmetic,* says that Stern's treatment of arithmetic has something of the spirit of modern higher algebra. Now modern higher algebra is a highly abstract subject, and Catherine Stern's method is inseparably bound up with the use of measuring rods.

J. E. Littlewood writes in his *A Mathematician's Miscellany,*[4] "A heavy warning used to be given that pictures are not rigorous; this has never had its bluff called and has permanently frightened its victims into playing for safety. Some pictures of course are not rigorous, but I should say most are (and I use them whenever possible myself) . . . pictorial arguments . . . can be quite legitimate . . . For myself I *think* like this whenever the subject matter permits."

S. Ulam, writing about the truly exceptional mathematician, John von Neumann, expressed surprise that von Neumann was apparently able to think without pictorial aids. "It seems curious to me that in the many mathematical conversations on topics belonging to set theory and allied fields, van Neumann even seemed to think formally. Most mathematicians, when discussing problems in these fields, seemingly have an intuitive framework based on geometrical or almost tactile pictures of abstract sets, transformations, etc. Von Neumann gave the impression of operating sequentially by purely formal deductions."[5]

At a conference of mathematicians concerned with summer school

4. (London: Methuen, 1953), pp. 35–36.
5. *Bulletin of the American Mathematical Society,* LXIV, No. 3, Part 2 (May, 1958), 12.

institutes, reference was made to a habit that many professors have. The professor finds himself in difficulty in presenting a chain of formal deductions. He makes a little drawing on the blackboard, erases it, and then continues with the formal presentation. But often he makes no reference to the drawing and the help it gives him. The drawing is, so to speak, the professor's own private affair. Only the finished argument, the formal proof, is for publication.

It is a great pity that mathematicians make this particular distinction between public and private life. The whole process of mathematical creation, beginning with "geometrical or almost tactile pictures" and then analyzing these pictures and extracting the essential ideas in a form suitable for abstract development—this whole process is much easier to understand than the final result taken in isolation. A von Neumann or an Emmy Noether may not find it necessary to work in this way, but if most professional mathematicians, as adults, find it necessary to use physical models as an aid to mathematical imagination, then surely children, who are just beginning to build up their system of thinking, are entitled to do the same. Many teachers as college students have suffered in courses that were too abstractly presented. Such a course does not teach a student to think like a mathematician. As a rule it teaches him not to think at all.

We may state our conclusion as a principle. *The most important task of mathematics teaching in elementary and high school is to strengthen intuition. The teacher should feel perfectly free to use drawings, apparatus, and other physical aids to the imagination. The student should be prepared for more formal treatment at a later stage, by having his attention drawn to paradoxes and fallacies in which intuition, pushed too far, leads to contradictions and incorrect results.*

Mathematical Content

If a student in his senior year at high school decides to become a mathematics teacher, to what topics should he be exposed in four or five years at college? What course will best prepare him for his future work?

It is clear that there can be no hard and fast answer to this question. Very much depends on the quality of the student. Is he a first-rate mathematician who has responded to the changing atmosphere of the times and has decided to teach in high school instead of in graduate school? Or is he a student who has drifted into teaching because he has no qualifications for anything else? Clearly very different courses will be appropriate. College should provide the flexibility we hope to see in high school. There should be every opportunity for students to work independently and for able students to forge ahead on their own.

As a rule, the first course taken by students in college should be one of rehabilitation. Its purpose is to free the student of any static, rote-learning habits he may have acquired in high school. The academic content of this course is not important. Any material can be included that is simple enough for students to experiment with, and at the same time complex enough to stimulate curiosity and interest. The essential thing is that the work should proceed by student discovery, that each student shall succeed in solving the problems presented to him so that he gains in confidence and begins to think of himself as an originator and discoverer. The importance of such training has been well explained and demonstrated by Polya. It represents a vital and irreplaceable ingredient in the course. If the student fails to become an independent thinker, he fails in everything. The rest of the work becomes a fake. The student pretends to do mathematics, and hopes the pretense will deceive his professors. It will be quite impossible for such a student to stimulate genuine thinking in children.

Since this initial course is so vital, it should be taught by the best teachers the college has. It is the hardest course of all to teach, since it aims not merely to impart information, but, in a sense, to change the character of the student by awakening powers and energies that have hitherto been dormant. The teacher should have the utmost freedom to vary the content of the course, to individualize instruction, and to adapt his material to the needs and interests of each student.

Earlier, we accepted the principle that a high school teacher must know, thoroughly and expertly, the material he is actually teaching. If, for example, a child in a geometry class produces an alleged trisection of the angle, the teacher should be able, by means of trigonometry and co-ordinate geometry, to calculate by how many parts in a million the construction is in error—and generally be able to decide for himself, by more powerful methods, the truth or falsity of any conjecture produced by a geometry student. This means that the teacher must be able to handle algebra and trigonometry very competently, not merely in the modern sense of knowing axioms, but in the old-fashioned sense of being able to perform calculations. Such facility is only acquired by continual practice. It would probably be psychologically wrong to begin a college course with a review and a reteaching of the traditional high school syllabus. The student is probably hoping for the stimulus of novel material. But every opportunity should be taken to launch the student on investigations that will require the sustained use of elementary algebra or trigonometry. Facility in these subjects is made more than ever necessary by the trend to include co-ordinate geometry in the high school curriculum. Without a good command of algebra it is impossible for a student to work effectively on problems of co-ordinate geometry.

It was mentioned earlier that subjects tend to become fragmented. To avoid this, the topics of the college curriculum should be interwoven. As each new subject is brought in, it should be applied to earlier subjects. Calculus naturally involves elementary algebra and co-ordinate geometry. Through Taylor series one is naturally led to the connection between the trigonometric and the exponential functions. Expressing sine and cosine as algebraic functions of $e^{i\theta}$ reduces all trigonometric identities to algebraic identities. It would be natural to illustrate this by exercises which students work. The use of i naturally raises the questions of the logic involved in the use of complex numbers, and allows one to compare four or five different ways in which their use may be justified—as geometric operations, as matrices, as polynomials modulo $x^2 + 1$, or as an abstract algebra. The use of infinite series leads naturally to problems of convergence and to the theory of functions of a complex variable. Since i can be regarded as a matrix, the use of $e^{i\theta}$ naturally raises the question of exponentials of matrices and of infinite series of matrices. One can show that the methods used to prove the convergence of an absolutely convergent series of complex terms can be generalized to metric spaces, and applied to series of matrices.

The vocabulary of calculus should be established early—differentiation and partial differentiation, integration, differential and integral equations. With the rise of electronic computers the solution of particular differential equations decreases in importance, but a student should be able to visualize the meaning of a differential equation and the way in which a differential or integral equation can be used to define a function. Students should know enough about Fourier series to appreciate their historical significance and to realize how unexpectedly such a series can behave.[6] The student will then be able to see that some of the situations considered in real variable theory are by no means as arbitrary and artificial as at first sight they may seem to be.

Calculus opens the road to all kinds of mathematics. The numerical solution of differential equations leads to the theory of finite differences, a subject that can add considerable interest to the study of elementary algebra, and one that has risen in importance with the spread of electronic computing. From Fourier series one could motivate an introduction to Hilbert space and perhaps Lebesgue integration. Much, of course, would depend on the interests of the professor and the ability of the students. One could also turn back toward trigonometry and re-examine this subject, pointing out to students that $\cos \theta$ and $\sin \theta$ are merely co-ordinates of a point on the unit circle. The real problem is to calculate θ which, being the length of an arc, raises a problem of integration. Again, many problems in differential equations can be put naturally in matrix form. Some of these, such as vibration problems in dynamics, show the importance of reducing a matrix to canonical form. The rather old-fashioned symbolic method of solving linear differential equations with constant coefficients provides a natural example of a ring involving an entity, D, which is not a number. One can hark back to trigonometry yet again in connection with matrices. The matrix

6. Chapter IV of Piaggio, *Differential Equations*, in the space of three or four pages says enough about Fourier series to act as an eye opener.

representation of the orthogonal group in two dimensions gives a simple way of deriving the formulas of trigonometry—one which, indeed, could be used in high school. From the orthogonal group in two or three dimensions, the student might also obtain a first insight into the subject of topological groups.

The curriculum here suggested is vague in outline. To some extent, vagueness is proper to the subject. No one can know the whole of mathematics. Different students will naturally attempt to master different sectors, corresponding to their individual tastes and temperaments. But some of the vagueness in this chapter is due to its being a kind of interim report. I am still at work investigating such questions as: "What parts of modern mathematics are both intelligible and useful to a high school teacher?" "What parts of mathematics are likely to become of scientific or technological importance in the next half century?" [7] Teachers and teacher-training institutions have the responsibility for answering such questions. Our viewpoint will of necessity be different from that of most research mathematicians, for they are mostly concerned with the furthering of pure mathematical discovery, while we are concerned with that and also with the education of the future scientist, engineer, and citizen. It is our task to search through the literature of mathematics, of science, of technology, and to select those topics which will stimulate our students and provide them with principles around which future knowledge can be organized.

We would like teachers to know as much as possible. An intuitive treatment of a subject can be taught rapidly; a formal, axiomatic treatment requires a considerable length of time. Which is preferable, to teach many ideas in a "sloppy" manner or a few ideas in full-dress development? The correct policy seems to be the following:

All ideas should be presented first in an intuitive manner. Some of the ideas should then be analyzed, in discussion between the students and the professor, until they have been clarified and brought to a rigorous form. This should be done sufficiently often

---

7. Some discussion of the latter question will be found in my paper, "The Reconstruction of Mathematical Education," *Journal of Engineering Education*, LI (November, 1960), 98–113.

for the students to recognize the process by which loose ideas are tidied up and made rigorous. The students should then be able to appreciate the possibility of axiomatizing those parts of the subject that have been presented only in intuitive outline.

It would be a mistake to cut down the curriculum to what can be treated with complete rigor. At all costs, a student should leave the course full of ideas. It is regrettable if a high school teacher commits an error of logic. But it is a mortal sin to teach mathematics in a way that obscures the generating ideas.

Naturally, the most thorough treatment should be given to those subjects which now are, or are soon likely to be, in the high school curriculum—co-ordinate geometry, matrices, vector spaces, calculus. We can anticipate (very conservatively) the time when intuitive calculus will figure in the junior year, with a more rigorous treatment of calculus in the senior year of high school. High school teachers will need to know epsilontage, and above all, how to make epsilontage intelligible. This can be achieved by a careful study of the process by which a proof in analysis is constructed. This process usually begins with a picture, and ends by translating the pictorial argument into formal deduction. Incidentally, it usually calls for fairly expert manipulation of elementary algebra.

In addition to the thorough treatment of these subjects, there will also be some sampling of topics in mathematics. Here there is no pretense of conquering a territory; merely a solid bridgehead is established. Some small part of the subject is explored thoroughly enough for the student to work problems and exercises—otherwise the student will remember nothing. As mentioned earlier, the student must see how this subject arose, and to what it leads. In this way, the student at least comes to know the general nature of certain branches of mathematics, and sees some of the interconnections between these branches. The connections with high school subjects are particularly important. Two or three years after leaving college a student forgets whatever he has not used. If he is to retain any recollection of more advanced mathematics, the links with elementary work must be securely forged in his mind so that, as he prepares his lessons or answers questions in class, his college work will pass through his mind in perpetual review.

In considering any program for the training or retraining of teachers, one cannot escape a certain sense of frustration. However well and however fast we improve teaching, we cannot keep pace with the demands of the situation. In classrooms throughout the country, hundreds of thousands of students will continue to have their intellect blunted and their enthusiasm destroyed. The ablest students do not constitute the most serious problem; if administration has the vision to let such students read ahead on their own, they will educate themselves and each other. The hardest problem lies in the remainder of the students, from those just below brilliance to those just above mental defect. These need teachers. Nearly all of them will respond to lively teaching and to some explanation of their difficulties. If we could keep them mentally alive, we should be able to draw on them for a future generation of teachers. Our most important problem is to find some way of doing this.

NOTES ON CONTRIBUTORS

Notes on Contributors

THEODORE ANDERSSON received his undergraduate and graduate degrees at Yale, where he also began his teaching. He has taught at the American University and Wells College, and has served as Director of the Master of Arts in Teaching Program at Yale. On several occasions he has participated in international conferences under Unesco auspices and has given leadership to the foreign language program of the Modern Language Association. Among his publications is *The Teaching of Foreign Languages in the Elementary School*. He is Professor and Chairman of the Department of Romance Languages at the University of Texas.

REGINALD ARCHAMBAULT majored in philosophy at Brown. He was in the first graduating class of Wesleyan's M.A.T. Program, then went to the Harvard School of Education for a doctorate. He returned to Wesleyan to teach Philosophy of Education and to assist in the administration of the M.A.T. Program. In 1960–1961, during a sabbatical leave, he studied the relationship between philosophy and the study of education in England. He is now Chairman of the Department of Education at Grinnell College.

GEORGE GOETHALS majored in English at Harvard College and went on to complete graduate degrees in the School of Education. For four years he was on the faculty of psychology at Sarah Lawrence and also acted as director of teacher training. He then returned to Harvard, where he is Senior Tutor in the Department of Social Relations. He is co-author with Wesley Allinsmith of *The Role of the Schools in Mental Health*.

JURGEN HERBST was educated at the Universities of Göttingen, Nebraska, Minnesota, and Harvard, where he received his doctorate in American civilization. For two years he served as educational advisor to the United States Information Agency in Germany. He is presently completing a book on the influence of German scholarship on the social sciences in American universities. Since 1958 he has been Assistant Professor of History and Education at Wesleyan.

GERALDINE MURPHY received her Ph.D. from Radcliffe. She has taught English in high school, and is currently Associate Professor of Education and English at Wesleyan, where she teaches English and the teaching of English. As a research fellow at Harvard in 1961–1962, she completed a book, *The Teaching of Literature*, scheduled for publication in 1963.

WARWICK SAWYER took his degree in mathematics at St. John's College, Cambridge, and has taught in England, Ghana, and New Zealand. He came to the United States in 1957, spent a year at the University of Illinois, and was then appointed Professor of Mathematics at Wesleyan. He has lectured at teachers' conferences, served as a consultant for mathematics texts, and conducted experiments in the teaching of algebra in grade five. Among his books are *Mathematician's Delight* and *Prelude to Mathematics*.

ERNEST STABLER began his teaching career in the elementary schools of Stratford, Ontario. Following graduation from Queen's, he completed an M.A. in English at McGill and a doctorate in education at Harvard. For ten years he was on the staff of Sir George Williams University in Montreal, and since 1952 he has been Chairman of the Master of Arts in Teaching Program at Wesleyan. In 1959–1960, under a grant from the Ford Foundation, he investigated teacher training and secondary education in England, France, Germany, and Denmark.

FLETCHER WATSON completed his undergraduate training at Pomona and his graduate work, in astronomy, at Harvard. He began teaching at the Harvard College Observatory and served in the U.S.

Naval Reserve in World War II. Since 1946 he has been on the faculty of the School of Education at Harvard, with responsibility for the education of science teachers. Among his publications are *Between the Planets, General Education in Science,* and *Teaching High School Science.*